POST-CORONA CAPITALISM

The Alternatives Ahead

Andreas Nölke

BRISTOL
UNIVERSITY
PRESS

First published in Great Britain in 2022 by

Bristol University Press
University of Bristol
1–9 Old Park Hill
Bristol
BS2 8BB
UK
t: +44 (0)117 954 5940
e: bup-info@bristol.ac.uk

Details of international sales and distribution partners are available at bristoluniversitypress.co.uk

British Library Cataloguing in Publication Data
A catalogue record for this book is available from the British Library

ISBN 978-1-5292-1942-5 hardcover
ISBN 978-1-5292-1943-2 paperback
ISBN 978-1-5292-1945-6 ePDF
ISBN 978-1-5292-1944-9 ePub

Cover design: Gareth Davies, Qube Design
Front cover image: Shutterstock/Iryna Imago
Bristol University Press uses environmentally responsible print partners.
Printed and bound in Great Britain by CMP, Poole

For Andrea, Anouk and Antonia

Contents

List of Abbreviations

BEPS	Base Erosion and Profit Shifting
BMF	Bundesministerium der Finanzen
BRICS	Brazil, Russia, India, China and South Africa
CDC	Centers for Disease Control
CEO	Chief Executive Officer
CEPI	Coalition for Epidemic Preparedness Innovations
CETA	Comprehensive Economic and Trade Agreement
CFIUS	Committee on Foreign Investment in the United States
CME	Coordinated Market Economy
DME	Dependent Market Economy
ECB	European Central Bank
ESG	Environment, Social, Governance
ESM	European Stability Mechanism
EURODAD	European Network on Debt and Development
FAO	Food and Agriculture Organization of the United Nations
FDI	Foreign Direct Investment
FIND	Foundation for Innovative New Diagnostics
GATT	General Agreement on Tariffs and Trade
GAVI	Global Alliance for Vaccines and Immunization
GDP	Gross Domestic Product
GFC	Global Financial Crisis
GVC	Global Value Chain
HERA	Health Emergency Response and Preparedness Authority
HME	Hierarchical Market Economy
ICC	International Chamber of Commerce
ICSID	International Centre for Settlement of Investment Disputes
ICU	Intensive Care Unit
IMF	International Monetary Fund
IPE	International Political Economy
IPR	Intellectual Property Rights

ISDS	Investor–State Dispute Settlement
LDCs	Least Developed Countries
LIO	Liberal International Order
LMEs	Liberal Market Economies
MERS	Middle East Respiratory Syndrome
MMT	Modern Monetary Theory
NAFTA	North American Free Trade Agreement
NGO	Non-Governmental Organization
NHS	National Health Service
ODA	Official Development Assistance
OECD	Organization for Economic Cooperation and Development
PE	Private Equity
PEPP	Pandemic Emergency Purchase Programme
PHEIC	Public Health Emergency of International Concern
PPE	Personal Protective Equipment
R&D	Research and Development
SAP	Structural Adjustment Programmes
SOE	State-Owned Enterprise
SME	State-permeated Market Economy
SSA	Social Structures of Accumulation
SURE	Support to mitigate Unemployment Risks in an Emergency
TALF	Term Asset-Backed Securities Loans Facility
TRIPS	Trade-Related Intellectual Property Rights
TTIP	Trans-Atlantic Trade and Investment Partnership
UBI	Universal Basic Income
UK	United Kingdom
UNCITRAL	United Nations Commission on International Trade Law
UNCTAD	United Nations Conference on Trade and Dealing
UNIDO	United Nations Industrial Development Organization
USMCA	United States–Mexico–Canada Agreement
VET	Vocational Education and Training
WB	World Bank
WFH	Working From Home
WFP	World Food Programme
WHO	World Health Organization
WTO	World Trade Organization

Acknowledgements

This book would not have been possible without the contributions of my friend Arie Krampf (Tel Aviv). Arie and I developed the conception of the book together and we co-authored the original publication proposal. Moreover, Arie has written early drafts of several chapters in the book, as well as outlines of many more chapters. Unfortunately, he was charged with conflicting commitments later on. Correspondingly, we decided that I should complete the book on my own. I am very grateful that Arie has allowed me to use his intellectual input to the book in an extremely generous way.

Another big thank you goes to Anna-Katharina Thum, Brigitte Holden and Robin Jaspert who were very helpful in providing the research assistance for this book. The book is predominantly based on some 300 academic studies on the coronavirus pandemic that have been published in late 2020 and early 2021 and it would have been impossible to write it without the excellent – and often challenging – assistance in gathering these publications. Related thanks also go to the team of the 'Universitätsbibliothek Johann Christian Senckenberg' that has enabled our access to the large number of journals covered for the book – and of course to the many colleagues in the Social Sciences that have tackled the coronavirus implications early on.

Given that the book project was quite daring, I'm also grateful to the people that have provided advice, encouragement and inspiration during the process, including Alban Werner, Benjamin Braun, Christian May, Daniel Mertens, Fritz Scharpf, Hubert Zimmermann, Ian Bruff, Kai Koddenbrock, Laura Horn, Martin Höpner, Michael Schedelik, Patrick Kaczmarczyk and the students of my seminar on 'Post-Corona Kapitalismus' at Goethe University during the spring term of 2021.

For the same reasons, I'm deeply indebted to Emma Cook and Paul Stevens at Bristol University Press who were receptive to this highly unusual project and supported the development of this book in the most efficient manner. Bristol University Press also arranged for four anonymous reviews that were not only very encouraging, but also very helpful for clarifying my arguments.

Of course, the biggest thank you of all goes to my family – Andrea, Anouk and Antonia – who not only supported me during the writing of this book in manifold ways, but also had to suffer from my frequent absent-mindedness throughout the process. Thank you for your patience!

Preface

Given the complexity of the coronavirus crisis, many members of the lay public, but also many Social Science students feel overwhelmed by the various topics and the policy initiatives responding to the health crisis and the later recession. This limits citizens' ability to exercise their democratic rights in steering the future course of events. The book aims at narrowing the uncertainty regarding the future of the economic system, thereby contributing to a more informed decision-making process on the side of governments and of public discourse on the side of citizens.

In order to pursue this target, this book analyses modern capitalism by dividing it into several policy areas and spheres of action. These include the relationship between economy and society as well as the environments, domestic and international economic institutions, geo-economic shifts and core ideological controversies. For each of these features, the book examines the core alternatives, based on established debates in Political Economy scholarship, and reviews the early evidence at hand.

By breaking down the monumental developments within capitalism into manageable chunks, I try to assist readers in making up their mind about current political alternatives. The book is not necessarily meant to be read from front to back. Its main purpose is to serve as a post-coronavirus digest and as a guide towards literature with more in-depth discussions. Readers might want to focus on the topics they are most interested in. The book includes many cross references between chapters, but discussions do not build upon previous chapters.

Given that the book addresses readers with very diverse previous knowledge in the field of Political Economy, it explains theoretical concepts in a very accessible language, without assuming large amounts of previous knowledge. Based on this very basic approach, the book should also be useful as reading for introductory modules in (Comparative or International) Political Economy, particularly by highlighting how useful classical controversies in Political Economy are for understanding issues raised by the coronavirus pandemic. In order to assist students in connecting the dots, the book links discussions on the pandemic with widely used textbooks and readings of Political Economy. It should also assist in stimulating discussions among students, based on its systematic focus on alternatives that was inspired by a previous textbook (Zimmermann and Dür, 2021).

At the same time, the book should be accessible for educators, journalists, politicians and a general audience without any background in the discipline and only basic knowledge of Economics and Political Science. The main purpose here is to assist in an informed participation in political debates. For colleagues specialized in Political Economy, the main value will be the overview on research related to the pandemic and its consequences during 2020 and 2021, based on a very comprehensive bibliography.

While the book eschews purely social phenomena caused by the crisis (such as individual health protection behaviour), as well as short-term domestic political developments (such as changes in the popularity of individual parties and politicians in specific countries), it still will serve as a one stop-guide to the more general consequences of the coronavirus crisis in contemporary capitalism. The years after a big economic and social crisis are decisive for the long-term development of our economies and it is important that all political alternatives are on the table.

Introduction: Confronting a Multidimensional Crisis of Capitalism

Every few decades, the international economic system suffers an economic crisis, which changes its institutional path, in a way that dramatically affects the day-to-day operation of the system and the institutions it is embedded in. In such cases, we say that capitalism has been transformed and that we entered a new era in global capitalism. Among such events, we can name the Long Depression (1873–77), the Great Recession (1930s), the inflation shock (1970s) and the Global Financial Crisis (2007–09). Deep economic crises do not change capitalism by themselves; they rather provide a fertile ground for subsequent struggles about the economic order. They also are not isolated events, but rather parts of long-term processes that have started some time before – and will continue thereafter.

None of the crises listed in the previous paragraph revolutionized the economic system, but all of these crises transformed it: they accelerated processes that would have probably taken place irrespective of these events, they led to the dissolution of old institutions and created opportunities to the creation of new ones. The coronavirus crisis, like the transformative events named mentioned earlier, is likely to affect the nature of global capitalism. The pandemic marks the most severe global economic disruption since the Second World War. It has not only led to the most severe recession since the 1930s, but also to deep societal and political changes triggered by this recession.

When events of this scale happen, uncertainty regarding the future is very high, and societies try to collect any shred of knowledge in order to make sense of these monumental changes. The purpose of this book is to offer a broad but concise analysis of the political and economic dimensions of the coronavirus crisis –domestically and internationally – based on up-to-date knowledge about the operation, institutions and ideologies of contemporary capitalism and with a view on the potential alternatives that are still possible.

Even if it is unclear when the coronavirus crisis will be over, negotiations about the post-coronavirus order have already begun. A crisis of this scale will serve as a magnifier for tensions that have been around for many years, but at the same time, it will open options that seem impossible in normal times. In negotiations about the future order, certain interests will be favoured and others marginalized. Today, political decisions will be taken that will be impossible to revise later – or at least only at very high costs.

The question regarding the 'correct' way of framing the crisis is at the core of this book. Currently, the coronavirus crisis serves as a mega Rorschach test. Each social group sees something else in it. Libertarians see in it evidence for the capacity of free markets to perform despite government interference. Socialists and social democrats see in it proof for the need of state intervention and perhaps an opportunity to revive the welfare state. For nationalists and populists the crisis is one more justification for rolling back globalization. And for globalists, the crisis demonstrates the need for international coordination and for international organizations. In this book, it is assumed that all of these potential solutions are still on the table. They will be a matter of political struggles in the years to come. This book goes against those that favour a certain option and claim that 'there is no alternative/ TINA' (Margaret Thatcher). Instead of TINA it puts forward TAMARA; that is, 'there are many alternatives ready and available'. The focus of the book thus is on the political choices that are ahead during the next years.

Approach: a combination of Political Economy concepts with early coronavirus crisis evidence

Although the coronavirus crisis has the potential to lead to tremendous economic, political and social changes, it will not turn the world completely upside down. It will build on pre-crisis dynamics and structures. Most of the options that are currently being discussed build upon prevailing conflicts, cleavages, interests and institutions. Correspondingly, our task is to build upon existing knowledge about the operation and dynamic of the economic regime and make conjectures about alternative options for responses to the coronavirus crisis shock. Therefore, we do not need to reinvent the wheel, but rather combine recent developments with well-established concepts.

In order to make sense of current changes, the book maps the positions, justifications and ideologies in classical debates in Political Economy. It seeks to answer the question: what do these debates tell us about options for the post-coronavirus era? Political Economy as an academic discipline is uniquely qualified to provide some guidance with regard to the broader implications of the coronavirus crisis, given that the crisis equally affects politics and the economy. Employing Political Economy theories, we are able to disentangle the complex interaction between economics, politics and societal developments, both on the domestic and the international levels. The coronavirus pandemic causes not only an economic crisis, but also a crisis of the institutions that serve as an infrastructure for contemporary capitalism. Therefore, political-economic theories are essential to provide critical insights that purely economic theories or purely political theories miss. Due to its usual openness to interdisciplinary cooperation – being itself an 'inter-discipline' – Political Economy scholarship easily can integrate insights from neighbouring disciplines, from Climate Studies to Sociology. Finally, in spite of the modern tendency towards increased sub-disciplinary specialization, this book is based on the concept of unity of Political Economy. While modern scholarship either takes place in Comparative Political Economy or in International Political Economy, this book highlights the importance to integrate the diverging strands of Political Economy scholarship.

Due to the ongoing pandemic, the empirical observations contained in this book necessarily are preliminary. Correspondingly, the predictions on the future of post-corona capitalism have to be seen as merely educated guesses. These guesses rely on the basic assumption of 'path-dependency', which is that developments after the coronavirus crisis will generally follow the patterns observed during the crisis and the years leading to the latter. As far as predictions are involved, the book thus follows the perspective of historical institutionalism and assumes an important role for existing institutions and policy legacies (Pierson, 2000). However, this perspective still allows for path-departing change, which takes place during rare cases of critical junctures (Capoccia and Kelemen, 2007) and often is based on major political struggles. The coronavirus pandemic may range among these situations. Correspondingly, it will require a fine balancing act between assessments of continuity and change (Campbell-Verduyn et al, 2021).

Purpose: a focus on political alternatives

The core feature of the book, however, is not on predictions, but its focus on alternative options. Discussions about future developments during the coronavirus crisis usually tend to be limited to the members of the same policy community, with increasingly narrow views: 'Momentous events such as the current crisis engender their own "confirmation bias": we are likely to see in the COVID-19 debacle an affirmation of our own worldview. And we may perceive incipient signs of a future economic and political order we have long wished for' (Rodrik, 2020).

In order to overcome the confirmation bias, the book refrains from making strong normative claims regarding the 'best' way to go from here in the first sections of each chapter. Instead, it presents alternative paths, leaving it to the reader to make his or her own judgement, based on his or her socio-economic world views. The purpose of the book is to politicize post-crisis debates. The crisis is a major opportunity for social reform, but we should also not close our eyes to the option that it can lead to political degeneration, as during the 1930s. Given this crucial situation, the book enables the reader to think for himself and herself, instead of simply accepting the wisdom of their peer group, media or the government. For this purpose, they need to understand the alternatives at hand, in order to make a fact-based judgement and to develop their own position.

Readers also should be enabled to see what kind of general (Political Economy) theories lie behind arguments and policy proposals forwarded in public debate. Concepts derived from Comparative Political Economy play a particular important role here, because they demonstrate that institutions that may look without alternative in one country are completely different (and successful) in another. But also International Political Economy can inform our thinking with regard to potential policy alternatives, given that international coordination often is hampered by different policy preferences held by different governments.

The focus on alternatives and diversity also pertains to geographical regions: while the focus of the book is on the situation in the Global North (due to the availability of more academic studies on the effects of the pandemic in the latter), it also looks at the situation in the Global South – although this general North–South juxtaposition necessarily has to remain very crude. Given the global approach of the book, it does not discuss specific policy features relevant in individual countries, but rather the broad political alternatives that are available throughout a number of countries.

Time horizon

The focus of the book is on the political alternatives that are available in the immediate post-crisis environment, say in the next five to ten years. It is about politically feasible alternatives in the short to medium term. Correspondingly, the book does not contain speculation about long-term developments stretching into the 22nd century. The focus on the book is on post-coronavirus capitalism, not on alternatives to capitalism. While the author does not want to exclude that alternatives to capitalism are feasible (and desirable) in the long run, he does not expect the coronavirus crisis to end capitalism as such.

While the book draws on studies of empirical developments during the pandemic, the development of the health crisis, the related recession and the immediate management of the two are not the topic of the book. The focus, instead, is on the political challenges we are confronted with *after* the immediate health and economic crisis is over, say from 2022 onwards. Thus, the book does not discuss alternatives on how countries have dealt with the coronavirus, but rather what the experience with the virus tells us about the question whether, for example, our health systems should be privately or publicly funded in the future.

Chapter content

Each chapter in the book has a broadly similar structure. It starts with an issue that has become prominent during the coronavirus crisis and highlights the alternatives at hand. Next, it links these observations to classical debates on capitalism in (Comparative or International) Political Economy, such as the juxtaposition of public and private health systems or debates between liberal and protectionist positions on global trade. The chapters explain these debates and the alternative policy options that are available in very accessible language. The third step in each chapter consists of confronting these debates with the very early evidence during the coronavirus crisis (up to the summer of 2021). A fourth and final step formulates conclusions, with regard to the empirical developments so far (first paragraph) and with regard to desirable political options (second paragraph). Thus, the concluding paragraph of each chapter contains a normative suggestion – again with the purpose to provoke the reader towards independent thinking, after the rather balanced discussion of the previous sections.

Readers should note that the empirical evidence only covers the early phases of the coronavirus pandemic. For this evidence, the book relies on some 300 academic studies that have been published between the beginning of 2020 and the summer of 2021. Later empirical developments – and later academic studies – may well reverse some of the findings. The various investigations documented in this book hopefully inspire students to further this research agenda. In any case, the main purpose of the book is not to give a detailed picture of the empirical changes inflicted by the coronavirus pandemic, but to highlight the alternative political options that are available to shape post-coronavirus capitalism. And the arguments in favour or against these alternatives will remain relevant, even if the one or the other empirical observation becomes outdated at some point in time.

Book structure

The book covers all major infrastructures of contemporary capitalism affected by the coronavirus crisis, from its societal embedding over domestic and international institutions to the basic nature of the state. The analysis of the book assumes that what we generally call the 'coronavirus crisis' consists of four types of crises: a *health crisis*, an *economic crisis*, a *social crisis* and a *political crisis*. Each of those crises consists of unintentional or uncontrolled elements – such as the pandemic itself – and of the authorities' responses to the crises. The coronavirus crisis, therefore, consists of a sequence of events, response, unintended consequences and further responses. These sequences transmit the crisis from one policy area to another. It is our aim to reach an understanding of these sequences, in order to depict their impact on contemporary capitalism (see Table 1.1).

Based on these considerations, the book contains seven sections:

1. Capitalism and society
2. Domestic institutions of capitalism on the demand side
3. Domestic institutions of capitalism on the supply side
4. The international institutions of capitalism
5. Anthropocene capitalism (that is, environmental issues)
6. Geopolitical shifts in global capitalism
7. Ideologies in contemporary capitalism

The coronavirus crisis first affected the health system, before reaching other sectors of social reproduction, gender relations and the situation of immigrants, as well as of less privileged groups of society. Correspondingly, the book starts with a section on capitalism and society. The lockdown of economic activities during the second phase of the crisis required massive public action in order to keep a minimum level of demand, leading to questions about the limits of monetary policy, a maximum volume of debt and the contours of investment programmes after the lockdown has been

Table 1.1: The coronavirus crisis as four types of crises

	Health crisis	Economic crisis		Social crisis	Political crisis
		Domestic	International		
Bottom-up aspect ('uncontrollable events')	The pandemic	Consequences of immediate responses to the crisis	Reaction of global markets	Social implication of the economic crisis	Public ideological changes
Top-down aspect ('response')	Immediate response of authorities (closure and distancing)	Measures taken to address the economic crisis	Response of international organizations or dominant states in the international system	Measures taken to address the social dimension of the crisis	Response of party politics

lifted. The book discusses these issues in the second section, on domestic institutions of capitalism on the demand side. In the long run, the effect of the crisis on supply-side institutions becomes more prominent. Issues covered in the third section, for example, relate to the conditions imposed on companies supported by state rescue programmes, the stability of financial sectors in times of widespread credit default or the question whether we need to counter increasing economic concentration by a more aggressive competition policy.

However, not only the domestic institutions of capitalism will be affected by the coronavirus crisis and the subsequent recession. One can also expect substantial changes with regard to the international institutions of capitalism – the topic of the fourth section. Topics include, for example, not only the management of the strongly rising levels of foreign debt in the Global South, but also the fate of the institutions of global economic governance. The coronavirus crisis does not terminate the other major contemporary crisis; namely, climate change. Correspondingly, the focus of the fifth section is not only on options for a Green New Deal or even degrowth, but also new challenges for food-importing countries.

The crisis does not only offer common challenges to all economies, but also affects global economic regions in a differential manner. In section six, the focus is not only on the implications for the three major economic powerhouses, the EU, US and China, but also the situation in conflict-ridden regions. Finally, the coronavirus crisis will also tilt the balance in some of the great ideological divides that are typical for contemporary capitalism. These include the contests between democracy and authoritarianism, between populism and technocracy or between communitarianism and cosmopolitanism. The book discusses these issues in the seventh section.

Core message

The book consciously departs from existing discussions on the coronavirus crisis by discussing the issues ahead in 31 interlinked chapters, each dealing with a specific aspect of the crisis. By mobilizing existing knowledge on these different aspects, it provides a somewhat more solid diagnosis of the crisis than those books that try to summarize the crisis under one overarching theoretical interpretation. At the same time, this approach leads to a more coherent and systematic result than asking individual authors to deal with one aspect of the crisis they are specialized in and compiling the latter in an edited volume.

While it is difficult to summarize the results of discussions on 31 topics in one simple core message, one overarching theme becomes clear, as highlighted in the concluding chapter: there is a high likelihood that the pandemic strengthens authoritarian tendencies in contemporary capitalism. In order to prevent this unwelcome development, we need to make sure that the fate of post-coronavirus capitalism is based on broad social debates. This book contributes to the feasibility of the latter, by highlighting the alternative options at hand.

PART I

Capitalism and Society

Traditionally, the impact of capitalism upon society has been a core prerogative of Sociology. Over the last decades, however, we have seen the emergence of a research (and teaching) programme on 'Everyday International Political Economy' (Hobson and Seabrooke, 2009; Andersson, 2020: 15–40) highlighting that decisions and developments in the global political economy have important repercussions on daily life – and that everyday behaviour of non-elite actors can have important consequences for the global political economy, if aggregated.

Crucially, social factors such as gender, race and class – woven together in the concept of 'intersectionality' that indicates that some people combine several dimensions of discrimination (Crenshaw, 1991) – are important variables for post-coronavirus capitalism. However, the most immediate implications of the coronavirus pandemic on individuals were mediated by the health system (Chapter 2) and the welfare state (Chapter 3), at least in the Global North. In day-to-day life, a core question was the sharing of reproductive work within families (Chapter 4) and we need to ask how gender differences in sharing this load affects the gender pay gap (Chapter 5). Many important tasks – in the health system and in reproductive work – are performed by migrant workers and we need to establish whether the crisis has ameliorated or deepened previous divides along race lines, among others (Chapter 6). Finally, divides along gender and race lines are only a small part of the inequalities within our societies and we need to measure the effect of the pandemic on income and wealth differences (Chapter 7).

2

Health Systems: Private or Public?

The immediate impact of the coronavirus crisis on individual well-being depends on the ability of the health system to deal with the pandemic. Countries differed widely with regard to the qualification of their health system. From a Political Economy perspective, a core question is whether a national health system should be predominantly private or public. Moreover, the coronavirus crisis caught health infrastructure of some countries unprepared, after several decades of lowering investment in health systems. Why was this the case and what can be done about it? Finally, some countries have autonomous and powerful central health agencies, whereas others incorporate questions of public health into government ministries. Which strategy was more successful?

Health systems in Political Economy

Health systems can be predominantly organized in a private or in a public way. A good example for the latter would be Scandinavian health systems, but also the core of the National Health Service (NHS) in the United Kingdom that defies the usual classification of the UK as a welfare state with a high degree of commodification. The principle of commodification generally assumes that the individual has to cater for protection mostly himself or herself and that health protection should be based on the market logic (Andersson, 2020: 30; see also Chapter 3). The most well-known case for a predominantly private health system is the United States where health provision even has become an important focus for financial market speculation during the last decade (see Chapter 13).

However, health systems are not necessarily 'born' private or public; their character can change over time. A widely discussed issue in Political Economy scholarship is the privatization of public services, including health systems. Privatization has been a core element of the rise of (neo)liberal capitalism since the 1980s (Menz, 2017: 244–52; Eagleton-Pierce, 2019; see Chapter 31). Privatization of healthcare can incorporate several elements, notably including the selling off of public healthcare facilities to investors and the increasing financing of health provisions via private insurances and fees. However, even without straightforward privatization we have seen a tendency towards the incorporation of market mechanisms in healthcare; for example, by introducing competition between (public) healthcare providers (Eckhardt and Lee, 2019: 668–9).

The privatization of health provisions is not a prerogative of the Global North, but can be found in the Global South as well. A particularly prominent case is Chile where the military dictator Augusto Pinochet removed the obligatory National Health Service and introduced private health insurance institutions that currently cater for about 20 per cent of higher-income Chileans (Rotarou and Sakellariou, 2017). Arguably, the privatization (or at least commercialization) of health-care systems can be seen as an important intermediate step to its financialization; that is, the expansion of private financial capital in the health-care sector. Today, this not only takes place in the US, but is also promoted by multilateral organizations in order to realize the Sustainable Development Goal 3 that focuses on universal health coverage (Hunter and Murray, 2019).

Proponents of health system privatization highlight the importance of individual incentives for health prevention. Moreover, they argue that private health systems – with different levels of health provision depending on financial contributions – are necessary in order to make research and development for new drugs profitable (see Chapter 21). They also assume that public health bureaucracies are inefficient and lead to a waste of resources, in comparison with private systems based on competition. Opponents of health system privatization, in contrast, highlight that private health systems lead to massive – and sometimes even deadly – disparities. They also argue that there are limited opportunities for individual prevention in case of hereditary diseases. Similarly, with communicable diseases, there are limits for individual protection, if prevention is not comprehensive (as in case of the coronavirus). Finally, they point towards the strong societal interest in case of health, given that only healthy citizens are socially and economically productive.

Systematic studies on the effects of healthcare privatization on communicable diseases are very rare. The only exception is a study of 99 countries in the Global South, which demonstrates that private health expenditures do not significantly impact tuberculosis rates, whereas public health expenditures reduce these rates (Austin et al, 2016). Tuberculosis has some important parallels with the coronavirus, since it is very easily transmittable. Moreover, the results of the regression analysis are corroborated by more qualitative studies. The latter indicate that private clinics in the Global South are more accessible in comparison with public providers, but lack the resources and levels of care to treat a complex infection such as tuberculosis (Austin et al, 2016: 452–3).

However, the ability of health systems to tackle health challenges such as infectious diseases not only relies on their predominantly private or public character, but also their level of funding. Political Economy scholarship has highlighted two particularly important limitations with regard to the funding of social policies. On the one side, it has studied the origins and effects of so-called 'austerity policies' that have been enforced in many countries during the last decade; for example, in Southern Europe after the Eurozone pandemic (see Chapter 9). On the other side, Political Economy points towards the fundamentally different levels of public health spending in the Global North and the Global South. Again, this has been in part a consequence of externally enforced austerity policies, particularly due to the so-called 'structural adjustment programmes' prescribed by the International Monetary Fund (IMF) and the World Bank (WB) during the 1980s and 1990s (Eckhardt and Lee, 2019: 669).

Finally, both private and public health systems need some kind of authority that provides overall guidance; for example, with regard to the severity of a health challenge and to the necessary precautions. There are three alternative options on how to organize this authority. On the one side, these authorities can follow the US model of the 'Centers for Disease Control and Prevention/ CDC'; that is, 'a high-level central agency with extensive scientific capacities that can organize surveillance, conduct research and laboratory analyses, formulate guidance, advise government, and communicate its recommendation to the rest of government (for implementation) and the public' (Greer et al, 2021a: 25). Alternatively, the functions of public health guidance can be part of ministries of health, without an independent public health agency, or the latter is independent and research-oriented, but limited to an advisory role (as in the case of Germany). The CDC option was particularly prominent in the decades before the coronavirus pandemic, since it fitted well with the paradigmatic shift from 'government' to 'governance' in the context of discussions about the 'regulatory state'. In the context of the movement to (neo)liberal capitalism, the latter was supposed to replace the hierarchical 'command-and-control' state (Jones and Hameiri, 2021: 3).

Private and public health systems during the coronavirus pandemic

The privatization of health systems often is motivated by attempts to boost short-term efficiency, but it seems to have a very negative impact on the ability of countries to fight pandemics. A systematic study of 147 countries during the first wave of the pandemic with regard to the balance between public and private expenditures demonstrates that a 10 per cent increase in private health expenditures correlates to a 4.3 per cent increase of COVID-19 cases and a 4.9 per cent of COVID-19 mortality, if we control for variables such as per capita income and health inequality (Assa, 2020). Behind these statistics, we can identify a number of specific mechanisms that inhibited a suitable response to the pandemic in the Global South where private health-care provision often plays a particularly prominent role. This has led to tragic outcomes, given that private hospitals provide nearly 80 per cent of national capacity in some of these countries: 'Simply put, when capacities and beds were needed in the viral crisis there was no real alternative to private providers precisely when their business and service models were in crisis' (Williams, 2020: 182).

More specifically, the acute liquidity crisis that forced many small- or medium-scale private hospitals to close or furlough staff during the crisis had a number of reasons. Governments ordered the temporary shutdown of elective services when the pandemic emerged. Patients have postponed treatments because of fear of infections or have been unable to access hospitals due to lockdowns. The economic crisis did not allow to pay insurance contributions or out of pocket. At the same time, costs escalate because of the need for intensified infection control and quickly rising prices for personal protection equipment. The liquidity crisis of private health providers, in turn, had a number of problematical repercussions on patients. In many cases, patients that could not afford co-payments (or high upfront payments) or that might cause high costs (with unclear settlement) have not been accepted. In many countries across Asia, Africa and Latin America, private hospitals were hiding beds from governments and patients, with patients dying after failed admissions in several hospitals. For those that have been admitted, private hospitals often charged oversized payments, in order to recoup some of the losses mentioned earlier (Williams, 2020: 183).

The negative relationship between health privatization and the ability to deal with the coronavirus crisis is not limited to the case of the Global South. Also in countries of the Global North, privatization of healthcare led to dire consequences during the pandemic. In the US, this does not only refer to the problems caused by the increasing degree of financialization of the health system (see Chapter 13). For example, the job-based insurance system failed when the coronavirus recession caused mass unemployment; about 3.5 million Americans became uninsured. This has led to a higher degree of infections and coronavirus-related deaths in those US states that did not expand Medicaid in order to compensate for uninsurance (Wiley, 2021: 38). And even for those that were insured, typical features of private health insurances such as cost-sharing limited an effective response to the pandemic, for example, with regard to testing and vaccination. Finally, the privatized system also led to highly problematical decisions about the distribution of essential resources such as ventilators which did not go to those states, regions and hospitals with the most urgent need, but to those with the best commercial conditions and connections (Wiley, 2021: 39–42).

In the UK, the outsourcing of medical supplies procurement to private companies led to disastrous consequences: 'The contractors were mostly middle-men, not manufacturers. To maximize their profits, they prominently sourced supplies overseas, often on a "just-in-time" basis, leaving them extremely vulnerable to global supply chains disruptions. All of these just-in-time providers failed to supply required items on time' (Jones and Hameiri, 2021: 15–15). These shortcomings are not only bureaucratic failures, but they also had deadly consequences during the pandemic. This has become particularly obvious in the case of the outsourcing of Britain's Pandemic Influenza Preparedness Stockpile to a private company that failed to dispatch its stockpiles when the pandemic broke out. Correspondingly, the NHS had to ration personal protection equipment, forcing health- and social-care workers to improvise with items such as snorkels and trash bags. This has increased occupational exposure and contributed to 8,152 cases of infection and 126 deaths among these workers in 2020 (Jones and Hameiri, 2021: 16).

Interestingly, health systems that have remained public, but had introduced market mechanisms in order to increase efficiency during the last decades, such as the one in China, suffered from some similar problems as private systems during the pandemic. A high degree of service fragmentation led to overcrowding of some hospitals and, correspondingly, to high infection rates. However, public ownership allowed for a fast reorganization of services, based on the clear hierarchy of city administrations (Liu et al, 2021).

Health spending and coronavirus impact

The ability of national health systems to provide society with a protection against the pandemic not only depends on whether the system is publicly or privately organized, but also the volume of health spending. The two factors are not independent: in the Global South, the neoliberal conditionality imposed by the IMF and the WB not only led to a reduction of public spending in favour of private spending, but also to a reduction of overall health spending (Austin et al, 2016: 452–3). In the Global North, the Southern European economies have been hit particularly strongly because of the spending cuts in the public health system because of austerity policies after the Eurozone crisis (see Chapter 9). In Italy and Spain, the number of doctors and of hospital beds per inhabitant dropped significantly in the years before the outbreak of the pandemic (Navarro, 2020: 274). In Italy, the insufficient number of intensive care units (ICUs) was a clear outcome of the economization of the health-care sector, driven by austerity policies (Giraud et al, 2021: 105). In a global comparison, a well-funded public health-care system clearly assists the effectiveness of lockdown measures in combatting the pandemic. It not only decreases the share of severe cases, but also increases the survival risk in case of the latter. Whereas rich economies in the Global

North differ with regard to the priority given to health expenditures, many countries in the Global South suffered badly from the underfunding of the public sector (Hansen et al, 2021: 24–5). The problem is particularly pronounced in countries where a substantial size of the population is rural and poor such as India, given the lack of reliability of the private health sector during the pandemic (Gauttam et al, 2021).

The volume of health spending, however, is only a small part of the relevant spending. A comparative study of health politics during the first phase of the pandemic demonstrates the crucial importance of social and fiscal policies for any emergency intervention (Greer et al, 2021b: 616–18). The effectiveness of the most important interventions against the pandemic – such as business closures to reduce the initial wave of infections – crucially depends on whether people can afford this type of policy. The most effective interventions – as in Denmark or Germany – used social and fiscal policies to cushion the impact of interventions and related demand shocks: 'They effectively put their economies into medically induced comas, using short-time work, unemployment benefits, and other replacement schemes to pay people to stay at home. … They also reduced political pressure to reopen because they ensured that business could close, ensuring their own safety, without suffering' (Greer et al, 2021b: 616; see also Chapter 3 and Chapter 9). However, due to fiscal constraints, this option was not available for the southern Eurozone members – and for the economies of the Global South.

The role of autonomous science-focused health agencies during the pandemic

A comprehensive survey on the model of powerful autonomous agencies staffed with public health professionals during the pandemic comes to a surprisingly clear result: it did not work (Greer et al, 2021a: 25–6). In nearly all cases where they existed, the agencies were stripped of their power soon after the dimensions of the pandemic became clear. In 'model countries' for this type of agency – such as the US with its CDC – this was particularly shocking. Given public discontent about the handling of the pandemic, in nearly all countries political leaders sidelined autonomous science-focused health agencies and took pandemic-related decision-making in their own hands. In countries where agencies were designed to be only advisory from the start (for example, Canada and Germany), however, the cooperation with governments worked frictionless.

Only in two cases autonomous science-focused health agencies clearly were in the lead, in Sweden and South Korea. The results were extremely dissimilar. Sweden pursued an extremely liberal – and deadly – infection model that even toyed with the idea to stop the spread of the pandemic via 'herd immunity' (that is, tolerate high numbers of infections based on the assumptions that overcoming the diseases provides immunity and that a further spread of the infection is impossible when a large number of people have been infected). South Korea was particularly effective in eliminating the threat of the pandemic, based on a science-focused leadership. Still, even in these cases it was a conscious political decision of the government to step back and let the agency do the work (Greer et al, 2021a: 25–6).

An opportunity to refocus national health systems on democratic public good provision

The fate of different national health systems has demonstrated that public health systems generally fare better than private systems with the fight against pandemics, if we control for expenditure levels. Moreover, well-funded public health (and social policy) systems also provided a better protection during the pandemic than health systems with massive funding constraints; for example, due to austerity policies. Correspondingly, there is a certain likelihood that the tendency towards privatization of health systems that had begun during the 1980s will be reversed and hopefully many public health systems will be better funded in the future. Finally, the experience with autonomous science-focused health agencies during the pandemic clearly indicates the primacy of politics in a situation of national emergency.

Given that the character of health as a public good has become abundantly clear during the pandemic, there are strong arguments for increasing levels of public health spending. This should also be noted by the international bureaucracies of the European Commission and the IMF that sometimes prescribe funding cuts for health systems in the context of public sector austerity policies. Questions of health often are a matter of live and death. Correspondingly, they should neither be left to market forces, nor to austerity considerations. Finally, it also indispensable that the ultimate responsibility rests with political leaders, not with health professionals. Putting the latter into the role of decision-makers themselves does not only risk tarnishing their essential resource of scientific authority, but also blurring the lines of political accountability. Clear responsibilities are very important in a pandemic situation. Given that most governments will assume the decision-making role in this situation anyway, it seems to be better to set up a highly competent science-based public health agency, but also clarify that its role is only advisory.

3

Welfare State: Restoration or Universal Basic Income?

The burden of the coronavirus crisis did not distribute evenly: the pandemic harmed some groups more than others (see Chapter 7). How did the welfare state cater for the most severely affected victims of the crisis? Did some welfare states fare better than others? At the same time, the widespread loss of work during the pandemic has led to renewed calls for a replacement of the traditional welfare state by a universal basic income, as a simple and safe form of social security. Will this become the social cushion in post-corona capitalism or will we restore the welfare state?

Welfare states in Comparative Political Economy

The study of the welfare state ranges among the most widely established topics in Comparative Political Economy (Clift, 2014: 257–8; Menz, 2017: 217–40; Vermeiren, 2021: 90–117). The simply typology of three basic ideal types of welfare capitalism in the Global North as developed by Esping-Andersen is still a useful point of departure, even if individual countries often do not fit neatly into one type. According to his typology, the three types of welfare state differ considerably in their degree of decommodification; that is, the extent to which people are able to 'maintain a livelihood without the reliance on the market' (1990: 21–2). They also differ in their degree of social stratification; that is, whether income inequality is high or low.

The highest degree of decommodification is to be found in the Scandinavian Social Democratic ideal type. If people become unemployed in the latter tax-based system, the state offers not only an adequate level of compensation, but also generous training and skill development, in order to be reintegrated in the labour market fairly quickly. A high level of decommodification – also supported by strong protection against dismissal – goes hand in hand with a low level of income stratification, given that it provides labour with a good bargaining position versus capital. Much employment is provided by the public sector; for example, in the education and health systems, historically important labour markets for women (Menz, 2017: 208).

The Continental European Conservative (or Bismarck) ideal type provides a medium level of decommodification and leads to a much higher level of social stratification. At its centre is not the universal coverage by the welfare state, but a social insurance system. Labour pays into the system, in order to be protected against the unpredictable risks of illness, unemployment or old age, based on proportional benefits that replace income from work. Given that the welfare state is closely linked to employment and that male employment historically was far more frequent than female employment, it carries a patriarchal character, centred around the male breadwinner and his family (Menz, 2017: 209–10).

The Liberal Anglo-American ideal type, finally, offers the lowest level of decommodification and is supposed to go hand in hand with a high level of social stratification. In this model, the individual has to cater for protection against risks mostly himself or herself. The tax-based provision of social security is kept at the absolute minimum, both with regard to the level of support and to its focus on the particularly poor, to be identified via means-testing (Menz, 2017: 210–11).

While each typology necessarily simplifies reality, Esping-Andersen's work arguably does not pay sufficient attention to a number of structural changes that has affected all welfare states since the 1980s. These changes include the rise of neoliberal ideology (as, for example, propagated by the IMF, the Organization for Economic Cooperation and Development (OECD) and the European Commission); a rising number of divorces (a particular challenge for the Bismarckian male breadwinner model); an increasing life expectancy combined with declining fertility (a particular problem for all pension systems); major economic crises such as the Great Recession and the Eurozone crisis (the latter leading to substantial problems for Southern European welfare states); labour market changes such as increasing part-time employment and (pseudo) self-employment (reducing payments into social security systems); a weakening of labour unions (as important supporters of generous welfare funding); and external constraints on welfare state funding stemming from the liberalization of financial markets, increasing foreign direct investment and cross-border work migration. In response to these changes, the strong growth of welfare state provisions that characterized the first three decades after World War II has stopped. Moreover, many countries – not only those following the Anglo-American model – have introduced 'active labour market policies' that require a high degree of individual initiative. Not only labour markets but also the welfare state witness an increasing degree of dualization between insiders and outsiders, with an increasing share of the latter becoming working poor (Menz, 2017: 212–40; Vermeiren, 2021: 96–117). Another major shortcoming of the Esping-Andersen typology, finally, is its Euro-centrism. Countries of the Global South mostly have a much lower level of welfare state expenditures, often further reduced by the structural adjustment programmes of the 1980s (see Chapter 23) and no welfare state provisions at all for those working in the informal sector.

Universal basic income as alternative to classical welfare state models

Decreasing welfare state payment levels and increasing eligibility thresholds – particularly for unemployment insurance – have made the idea of a 'universal basic income' (UBI) more attractive. UBI consists of periodic payments made by the state to all citizens – employed or unemployed – without means-testing and without requirements on the side of the recipient (for example, to seek a job or undergo a qualification). UBI is one of several alternative types of transfer payments that have been considered in recent years to complement or to replace unemployment insurance. Other alternatives are negative income tax and non-universal – selective – basic income payments (Johnson and Roberto, 2020). The common denominator to those new types of transfer payments is that they weaken the link between labour and compensation as well as between the productivity of the citizens and his or her share in aggregate income.

UBI raises lively debates, which cut across the traditional ideological camps of left and right. Whereas there is a sound social-democratic rationale for a UBI, in particular for reaching the very poor that are not well integrated into the conventional welfare state, many social democrats are concerned that UBI would deepen social cleavages between so-called productive and non-productive citizens. They are also afraid that UBI would lead to a massive loss of qualifications (and long-term earning), because of the decreased incentives for further education and training. Moreover, they are worried that the need to mobilize sufficient financial resources for UBI would lead to the destruction of the other parts of the welfare state, in particular in the fairly well-funded Nordic and Continental European models. On the other hand, UBI is considered by right-wing think tanks less paternalistic and intrusive, more efficient (due to the termination of many welfare administrations) and less disincentivizing for working as some traditional insurance-based unemployment benefits. Young outsiders to the labour markets particularly cherish the non-intrusive character of UBI that goes along without cumbersome means-testing and stressful active labour market policies. Proponents of UBI, from both the left and right, perceive it as an unavoidable welfare tool, designed to address a world in which human labour will be replaced by technology and automation. According to this view, as lifetime will be replaced by a precarious job market consisting of freelancers, part-time workers and micro-workers, UBI seems to fit this new world of labour better than the traditional welfare state measures.

The reactions of different types of welfare states during the coronavirus period

During the early phases of the coronavirus crisis, we can observe a striking degree of path dependency with regard to the reactions of the welfare states in the Global North. Countries roughly following the Bismarckian model such as Belgium and Germany have used their traditional social insurance system in order to protect labour from the socio-economic effects of the pandemic; for example, based on the well-known short-time work scheme (*Kurzarbeit*) in Germany. At the same time, crisis-related measures have further deepened the dualization of the welfare state in Germany that had started in the years before. Family-related spending for those in well-paid work – for example, paid parental leave – was extended, whereas spending for those at the bottom of the labour market – for example, in atypical employment that does not include unemployment insurance – was minimal, although the latter group was most severely affected by the reduced economic activity during confinement (Cantillon et al, 2021). The four Scandinavian countries also stuck to their Social Democratic model during the crisis, at least during its early phases. The state continued to provide generous and universal benefits for those affected by the pandemic and the related recession, while continuing to ensure sufficient demand for labour (Greve et al, 2021). Finally, the welfare state of the UK remained less than generous also during the pandemic, particularly for those that have to rely on the basic Universal Credit scheme. The introduction of the Coronavirus Job Retention Scheme ('furlough') was a novel response which became (politically) necessary, because funding for middle-income workers by the usual system would have been inadequate – and in this way represent a case of path dependency (Hick and Murphy, 2021: 322).

A feminist perspective comparing a Scandinavian, Continental and Anglo-American welfare state highlights another type of path dependency: whereas both the Scandinavian (Denmark) and the Continental (Germany) welfare state provided generous subsidies – and the Anglo-American very limited, particularly for the most vulnerable groups – the first two differed considerably with regard to gender inequality, based on the 'cultural infrastructures' that are necessary for policies to work, with Germany moving back to the established male breadwinner model (Bariola and Collins, 2021; see also Chapter 4).

However, there may be yet another form of path dependency with regard to the reaction of the welfare states in the Global North when faced with a major economic crisis. Studies of the reaction of the latter during the 2008/2009 Global Financial Crisis show rather similar patterns, independent from the type of welfare state (Béland et al, 2021). All countries first stabilized their banking systems (less relevant in case of the coronavirus pandemic), followed by a phase of Keynesian demand management and labour market protection (including a temporary expansion of social programmes) and, finally, a third phase of austerity and work-related policies (Vis et al, 2011).

The likely turn from 'emergency Keynesianism '(Hall, 2013; Bremer and McDaniel, 2020) – also making use of the very strong automatic stabilizers contained in comprehensive welfare states – towards retrenchment and pressure to work in a third phase after the coronavirus recession may give the idea of universal basic income additional popularity. The latter will particularly appeal to the long-term unemployed and atypically employed victims of the recent dualization of welfare states – not only in Germany – and probably less to the beneficiaries of this dualization; namely, the middle classes that have benefitted from the expansion of the welfare states to 'new social risks' – for example, by the introduction of paid family leave. A comprehensive survey of welfare state measures across the OECD notes that innovative social measures introduced during the coronavirus crisis – generous wage subsidy schemes and support for mortgage-holders – mainly cater for the working middle classes (Moreira and Hick, 2021). Correspondingly, the latter will hardly be inclined to join the broad chorus for UCI.

The situation may be different in many countries of the Global South (Blofield and Hoffmann, 2020; Gerard et al, 2020). Here, the repercussions of the coronavirus crisis were much more severe. At the same time, welfare state measures were much more limited, given the high degree of informality; that is, people either working in unregistered business or in formal business, but without registration for taxation and welfare systems, and the limited resources for welfare funding. Instead, the focus was on (cash) social assistance programmes, given that many countries in the Global South have registries for the latter that cover a broad share of the population, including the informal sector. Putting these programmes on a more permanent basis may be an attractive option for improving welfare.

The coronavirus crisis and universal basic income

During the coronavirus pandemic, discussions about UBI have become more prominent. This is because economic relief programmes in many countries implicitly took on UBI characteristics. The US, for example, repeatedly has sent out economic stimulus checks to all households, unless the latter had a particularly high income. The South Korean government equally has given financial support to all citizens (Chung, 2020). UBI proponents have taken this opportunity to renew their proposals, given that the crisis arguably has demonstrated the usefulness of a support measure that is simple and easy to administer, given that traditional social security systems sometimes were too selective and cumbersome for providing comprehensive and quick relief during the crisis (Johnson and Roberto, 2020; Nettle et al, 2021).

According to recent survey studies, support for UBI during the coronavirus crisis differed considerably between countries. UBI seems to be more popular in countries with an Anglo-American welfare state (Nettle et al, 2021) and in emerging economies such as Korea (Chung, 2020), both welfare states with rather limited levels of social support. No comparable discussions are reported from countries with a Scandinavian-type welfare state. And even in countries with welfare states close to the Bismarck ideal type such as Austria, UBI proposals did not receive a measurable boost (Nemeth, 2020).

The need for differentiated approaches towards welfare state reform

Generally, welfare state reactions to the coronavirus pandemic show a high degree of path dependency, in spite of the magnitude of the crisis. Bismarck-style welfare states continue their path of dualization between even more comprehensive coverage for the middle classes and marginalization of those with atypical work. Scandinavian countries continued their generous welfare provision. The introduction of the novel furlough scheme in the UK seems to be the exception proving the rule, but this hardly will become permanent. Also in terms of gender equality, welfare states kept their direction, with progressive (Scandinavia) and regressive (Continental Europe) traits. Finally, we may be witnessing a new round of welfare state austerity, if the experience of the Global Financial Crisis further indicates the direction of events. Austerity may somewhat increase the attractiveness of UBI schemes, but here we need to distinguish between different types of welfare states. The coronavirus crisis erupted after four decades during which welfare systems in most Northern countries became somewhat less decommodifying. Whereas governments did not fundamentally reduce social spending during these four decades, labour activation policies exposed workers to precariousness, instability and social risks. Correspondingly, UBI concepts have gained some ground in public discussions. The coronavirus pandemic seemed to further this trend, given that economic stimulation programmes in some countries had UBI-like traits. Still, it is highly unlikely that the pandemic will lead to a general turn towards UBI. The introduction of a UBI may look attractive for countries of the Global South without comprehensive welfare states and for those countries of the Global North with rather minimalist welfare states. For countries close to the Scandinavian welfare state ideal type and those close to the Continental type – with comparatively high levels of funding – the introduction of a UBI is less attractive, at least from the perspective of most beneficiaries of welfare funding.

4

Reproductive Work: Positive Re-evaluation or the Same Old Neglect?

The coronavirus crisis has led to an increased – although so far mostly symbolic – appreciation of (paid and unpaid) reproductive work traditionally dominated by women, such as care work (for the sick, but also for the very young and very old), education (home schooling) or food preparation. As people increasingly moved to work from home, the modern separation between the economy and the household has collapsed and therefore large parts of society have realized that this work is not only badly paid, but also often quite challenging or even outright dangerous. Correspondingly, we are hearing many calls for a positive re-evaluation of reproductive work after the crisis, even by mainstream politicians. Is this only temporary or does it lead to a permanent change with regard to the type of work?

Political economy and reproductive work

Political economy work on gender relations can assist us in answering this question. First, it points towards the fact that women do most of reproductive work in the household. Women spend upon average about 201 days of unpaid care work during a year, while men spend 64 days (Lokot and Bhatia, 2020: 1). Reproductive work often is 'invisible' in official economic data. Still it is as vital as the formal economy and indispensable for the survival of our societies. Moreover, the unequal distribution of reproductive work is not only a problem for equitable gender relations, but also has massive repercussions in terms of lost wages, social security benefits and career opportunities for those that perform the lion's share of this work. The pandemic has highlighted the importance of this work very clearly. Does it also lead to a more fair distribution?

Second, political economy work on gender relations highlights the deep institutional hurdles that have to be overcome in order to ensure a higher appreciation of reproductive work outside families (for example, in hospitals). Again, this work is mainly borne by women that constitute about 70 per cent of workers in health and social care globally (Lokot and Bhatia, 2020: 1). This work usually does not pay well and very often suffers from unattractive work conditions. In part, this stems from highly problematic social attributions that, for example, argue that this work does not require particularly high skills. From a Political Economy perspective, however, low payment and bad working conditions are closely related to the weakness of unions in these sectors. Workers in these occupations – education, health and social working – traditionally have a relatively weak degree of inclusion in wage-bargaining systems. Part-time work – in order to combine the latter with childcare – makes organizing difficult. Moreover, outside options for these workers are few and their bargaining position therefore is weak. The pandemic improves their bargaining position, but does it also lead to better working conditions?

Finally, in the economies of the Global North these sectors often rely on female migrant work (transnational care chains), which makes organizing work even more challenging. There is a very high number of women from the Global South and Eastern European transition economies that are being 'exported' to the rich economies of North America, Western Europe or the Gulf region in order to provide services such as childcare, housework or care for the elderly. For countries such as the Philippines or Sri Lanka, the remittances by these women are a major economic factor (O'Brien and Williams, 2020: 213–14). The core question is whether the importance of this work during the pandemic leads to a higher degree of protection of these domestic workers; for example, via social security schemes, written contracts, minimum wages or decent living conditions (Lokot and Bhatia, 2020: 3).

Dual-earner couple's reproductive work sharing and the coronavirus pandemic

The empirics of the early phase of the coronavirus crisis highlight that the inequality with regard to reproductive work in families has increased even further, given the gender differences with regard to juggling the particular challenges of home office and reproductive work. During the coronavirus crisis, the closure of schools and childcare facilities has strongly increased the need for childcare. The challenge for families – and single parents – was even further intensified by the fact that grandparents often were unable to stand in, because of the higher mortality rate for the elderly (Alon et al, 2020). Generally, mothers spent more additional time with childcare and home schooling than fathers. In Germany, the share of households where mothers take over childcare (nearly) completely even doubled, from 8 to 16 per cent (Jessen et al, 2021). The gender gap in hours of household reproductive work even further increased in many poorer societies such as Kenya and the Philippines (Lokot and Bhatia, 2020: 2).

Undoubtedly, the intensification of the asymmetric handling of reproductive work also has repercussions on material conditions. In the short run, it has increased the gender pay gap and reduced the labour participation rate among women (see Chapter 5). In Germany, 27 per cent of mothers in households with at least one child have reduced their paid labour during the first wave of the pandemic, but only 16 per cent of fathers (Kohlrausch and Zucco, 2020). In the long run, however, the coronavirus crisis may potentially help to reduce the phenomenon of asymmetric distribution of reproductive work (Alon et al, 2020). First, the coronavirus crisis has intensified the trend in remote working – working from home. Remote working enables people in tele-commutable industries to be more flexible with their working hours. In principle, it opens an easier path for men in these industries to work from home and to take on a larger share of reproductive work, particularly if combined with preferences for an equal sharing of these tasks. Studies on the effects of the introduction of remote work in Germany during the early phase of the coronavirus crisis indeed demonstrate an increasing amount of time fathers spend on reproductive work – with mothers, however, increasing their workload even more (Samtleben et al, 2020). Next, many employers have realized the importance of the childcare needs of their staff. Often, these employers have introduced more flexible work schedules, in order to cater for these needs. This also offers the potential for many fathers to increase their share of childcare.

Both changes, however, will not matter much without changing social norms. There are some early indications for the latter. During the coronavirus crisis at least, not only mothers, but also many fathers have taken on a larger responsibility for childcare than before. This is also because many women were occupying essential jobs – as doctors and nurses, but also in grocery stores and pharmacies – thereby forcing their partners to deviate from established patterns. Empirical studies on dual-earner parent couples in Australia indicate that the gender gap in care hours even narrowed because the relative increase of childcare was higher for fathers than for mothers, although the absolute increase of unpaid hours worked by mothers still was higher (Craig, 2020; Craig and Churchill, 2021). Similar results were measured in the UK, including a higher absolute load of increased childcare by women, but also that in a substantial number of households men even took on the role as primary childcare providers (Hupkau and Petrongolo, 2020). Surveys on the effects of the early phase of the coronavirus pandemic in Germany indicate that particularly some men with low and medium levels of education changed their behaviour with regard to reproductive work considerably (Kreyenfeld and Zinn, 2021). While this is also due to the fact that these fathers often were affected by unemployment or in short-term work (and mothers generally took on the lion's share of additional reproductive work in Germany), it still offers the option for long-term behavioural changes.

The coronavirus pandemic and collective action in paid reproductive work

Reproductive work outside the household in sectors such as healthcare was particularly dangerous during the pandemic, putting many women at great risk. This courage of 'essential workers' was widely praised, but usually without lasting (material) consequences. The coronavirus crisis would have offered an excellent opportunity for demanding better payment in reproductive work sectors such as health, given that the vital importance of these sectors became abundantly clear. Women make up about 70 per cent of the global workforce in the health sector (Smith et al, 2021: 5). However, the professional ethics in the sector did not allow for industrial action during a pandemic and most employers did not match symbolic appreciation with a material one. Correspondingly, it does not seem likely that the pandemic will lead to a better payment of salaried reproductive work.

Transnational care chains and the coronavirus pandemic

Reliance on transnational care chains posed particular problems during the coronavirus crisis. First, sudden border closures frequently have interrupted these chains, therefore leading to major difficulties both on the side of the supply and the demand for care work (see Chapter 6). Moreover, the pandemic has made life miserable for those transnational care workers that stayed in their country of occupation. They not only missed contact with their families, but also were confronted with a lot of pressure because families back home expect remittances rather to increase than to decrease, because of the difficult economic and social situation in the country of origin. However, in most cases it was very difficult – or even impossible – to increase employment in order to match these demands. Even worse, female domestic workers often faced dangerous situations by being forced to continue their services in spite of coronavirus infections on the side of their employers. Other female domestic workers were abandoned without payment by their employers (and faced the risk of deportation), given that the economic situation of the latter worsened during the recession (Lokot and Bahtia, 2020: 3). All in all, the more positive re-evaluation of reproductive work did not lead to an improvement of the situation for workers in transnational care chains, but rather aggravated the situation of the latter.

Seizing the moment: towards a lasting re-evaluation of reproductive work

In spite of the rhetorical re-evaluation of many forms of reproductive work during the coronavirus crisis, however, positive outcomes for the people performing this work are rare. Collective action with regard to paid reproductive work hardly took place. Partially, the situation has even been aggravated, particularly for the people working in transnational care chains. Inequality with regard to the distribution of reproductive work within families increased even further. However, increased opportunities for remote working and changing social norms have some potential for a more fair distribution in the long run.

Based on the experience of the pandemic, governments should put policies in place that prevent negative outcomes during future crises, such as improving the legal status of migrant care workers and generally increasing the coverage of collective agreements in sectors with salaried reproductive work. With regard to the distribution of unpaid reproductive work within families – and the particular challenge for single parents – measures could include increased government subsidies for parents that stay at home in order to provide childcare during a closure of schools and day-care institutions (Alon et al, 2020: 24). Still, there is hope that social norms have changed during the crisis and more fathers than before will take on a fair role in childcare. Earlier experiences with externally induced temporary changes in gender roles – the strong increase of women participation in paid labour due to the absence of men during the Second World War – indicated that these changes can have a durable character. Lasting effects with regard to a positive re-evaluation of paid reproductive work, finally, will only be possible if unions seize the opportunity and negotiate for substantial improvements during the health crisis. After the end of the health crisis, the old mechanisms for discounting this work may well bite back, if this opportunity is wasted.

5

Gendered Occupations: Equality or Back to Traditional Patterns?

The effects of the coronavirus crisis on gender relations are not only limited to reproductive work but also affect other fields of capitalism, in particular via gendered occupations. Not only due to their central role in the care sector, women were at the centre of the response to the pandemic, but also because of their frequent employment in badly paid service sectors. The health crisis was followed by a major recession with increasing unemployment and the implementation of major economic stabilization programmes, particularly in the economies of the Global North. Does the subsequent recession-related unemployment and the distribution of benefits of economic stabilization programmes lead to more or less gender equality with regard to economic opportunities?

Political Economy and gendered occupations

Gender-related inequalities – based on 'socially learned behaviours that distinguish masculinity and femininity' (Peterson and Runyan, 1993: 5, cited after O'Brien and Williams, 2020: 198) – are widespread and range from education attainments over political empowerments to health and survival; the focus here is on questions of economic opportunities. The phenomenon of gendered occupation is well documented in the Political Economy literature: women's ratio in reproductive work occupations (see Chapter 4) or low-level service work are disproportionally higher than their ratio in society, while their ratio in digital occupations – which are more lucrative and high-paid – is lower. Moreover, the employment relations for women often are temporary and less secure than for men, thereby affecting women more strongly during periods of increasing unemployment. Due to these features, we are observing a massive gender pay gap even in normal times (O'Brien and Williams, 2020: 203–5).

The situation is even worse in extraordinary times such as a major recession. Usually, women suffer more from increasing recession-related unemployment than men. Moreover, the structural adjustment programmes (SAPs) that are being set up in order to stabilize economies after a balance-of-payments crisis – predominantly in the Global South – often carry negative repercussions with regard to gendered occupations. SAPs not only rely on unpaid work by women – they have to take over reproductive work previously provided by the state or have to give up their paid work in order to care for their families – but also they often suffer from reductions in health and education spending going hand in hand with these programmes (O'Brien and Williams, 2020: 211). Will the pandemic – and the later recession – lead to an increase or a decrease in the gender pay gap? And will the economic stabilization programmes after the pandemic better take into account the situation of women, if compared with traditional structural adjustment programmes?

The coronavirus crisis and the gender pay gap

How will the coronavirus crisis affect gendered occupations? In the short run and medium run, there is no doubt that the crisis increases gendered inequality in the labour force. In the short run, due to crisis-related closures of childcare and schools, the demand for reproductive work within families increased, and more women than men have supplied for this demand (see Chapter 4). Research about individual concerns during the first four weeks of the lockdown in Germany demonstrates that the pandemic boosts gender-related differences with regard to thinking about work: while fathers were more worried about paid work, mothers were more worried about childcare (Czymara et al, 2021). Correspondingly, mothers often decided against paid employment. The gender time gap in Germany has grown during the pandemic: while working mothers on average worked ten hours less than working fathers in paid employment before the crisis, this has grown to 12 hours in spring 2020 and still 11 hours in November 2020 (Zucco and Lott, 2021). Early empirical studies on the effect of the coronavirus crisis on the gender gap in work hours in the US also show a negative effect, with mothers of young children reporting a four to five times higher reduction of work hours than fathers (Collins et al, 2021).

Women's participation in the labour market is not only at least temporarily reduced during the crisis, thereby negatively affecting their short-term income, but also their long-term career patterns, given the high returns to experience in the labour market. This phenomenon will further increase the gender pay gap. The latter refers to the phenomenon that women very often earn less than their male counterparts working on the same level of formal qualification. Correspondingly, women already were economically more vulnerable at the onset of the crisis – a process that has been intensified by the crisis. While the increased gender pay gap already becomes apparent by the different participation in reproductive work in two-parent families (see Chapter 4), the particularly vulnerable single parents (mostly mothers), are even worse off. Given closed schools, they often had to stop working altogether, at least temporarily (Smith et al, 2020: 8). In some sectors, finally, the boosting effects of the crisis on the gender pay gap will only become obvious in the very long run. For example, in the UK women's academic output was reduced during the crisis – due to strong involvement with reproductive work – which will negatively affect their careers in the future (Smith et al, 2021: 8).

Gendered occupations, the coronavirus crisis and shut down-related unemployment

The socio-economic vulnerability caused by an intensification of the gender pay gap was further increased by the pandemic, because women were overrepresented in the sectors – very often in the wider field of services requiring personal interactions – affected by shutdowns (Smith et al, 2021: 7). This is in clear contrast to 'regular' recessions – in a usual economic crisis – where men are more affected by recession-related unemployment (Alon et al, 2020). In this crisis, sectors with a high participation of women, such as restaurants and hospitality, were more strongly affected by unemployment than sectors with a high participation by men, such as construction and industry:

> Historically, most economic recessions are seen as 'he-cessions' followed by 'she-recoveries' where female-dominated industries form the backbone of the economic recovery. The opposite is true for COVID-19, which has been colloquially termed a 'she-recession', as female-dominated service sector jobs were the first to disappear, while male-dominated sectors such as construction have remained viable, and thus men's wallets have been less affected. (Fisher and Ryan, 2021, 239)

A study on sector shutdowns in the UK during the early phase of the coronavirus pandemic demonstrates that women are one third times more likely to work in a sector that was affected by a shutdown (Joyce and Xu, 2020). They work over-proportionally often in sectors such as retail and hospitality. Similarly, sectors dominated by men – such as logistics and some industries – in China were allowed to return to work earlier than sectors dominated by women. In Canada, re-employment after the first wave of shutdowns in spring 2020 increased twice as fast among men than women (Smith et al, 2021: 7–8). Even worse, official unemployment figures do not necessarily give full justice to the fate of women, because many simply dropped out of the labour market altogether, particularly in sectors such as care (Klatzer and Rinaldi, 2020: 6).

In the medium run, some female-dominated occupations will suffer a higher unemployment rate than the average because they will have difficulties to recover from the pandemic shock, while some male-dominated occupations – particularly, jobs in technology-intensive industries – will be the least affected by unemployment. These trends deepen the existing phenomenon of the gender pay gap and may even overcompensate any advances for a reduction of this phenomenon during the last decades. The background of this expectations is a large literature that has documented substantial lifetime losses in earnings that go hand in hand with job losses (or a delayed entry into the labour market), particularly if related to a recession, due to the close link between job experience and earnings (Alon et al, 2020).

The situation is even much worse for women in the Global South. The vast majority of their employment is in the informal sector – roughly 70 per cent according to the United Nations (2020a: 4) – and this means that they neither benefit from protection against dismissal, nor from paid sick leave. Experience with previous pandemics in the Global South, such as Ebola, demonstrates that typical prevention measures such as market closures affect women far over-proportionally. Correspondingly, gender differences with regard to economic effects of the pandemic are a global phenomenon. A first comprehensive study – drawing on data from China, Italy, Japan, South Korea, the UK and the US – calculates that 'women are 24 per cent more likely to permanently lose their job compared to men' because of the pandemic (Dang and Nguyen, 2021).

Gendered effects of fiscal rescue packages and structural adjustment programmes

Matters for women in the Global South will be made worse in the medium term because of the economic effects of attempts for fiscal recovery and balance-of-payments stabilization. It is yet too early to measure the gendered impact of structural adjustment programmes that undoubtedly will be implemented in the next years, given the strong increase of public debt (see Chapter 23). Still, there is a very high likelihood that these programmes will affect women in over-proportional ways, given the female-dominated sectors such as health often fall victim to the highest reductions in public spending.

In the early phase of the coronavirus pandemic – and in particular in the Global North – the fiscal rescue packages that have been put in place in order to reduce the economic impact of the crisis show a similar picture as is expected for the later adjustment programmes. For example, new mothers in Canada were excluded from emergency relief programmes in spite of corona-related unemployment, since they did not work the necessary number of hours in the previous year because of parental leave (Smith et al, 2021: 7). Similarly, an analysis of short-term work schemes in four European economies demonstrates various gender-insensitive features, such as the exclusion of domestic workers from these schemes or the non-exemption of family leave from replacement income calculation, which severely affects women on maternity leave (Cook and Grimshaw, 2021). Moreover, countries differ strongly with regard to the degree by which government support programmes were able to protect vulnerable groups such as women. Whereas the long tradition of gender mainstreaming policies in Denmark has led to quite successful effects in this regard, support programmes in the US were designed in a way that have resulted to a major set-back with regard to female labour market participation (Spendzharova, 2021). The problem is even much worse in those economies of the Global South that have been able to put fiscal response packages in place. Due to their informal employment and the corresponding lack of inclusion in social security systems, women mostly have been left out of cash transfers and related measures.

Finally, even mid-term stabilization programmes such as the EU Recovery and Resilience Facility – the core of the Next Generation EU Programme – probably will have negative impacts on gender inequalities (Klatzer and Rinaldi, 2020). They focus on sectors with high degrees of male employment, such as digital technologies, energy and transport infrastructures, agriculture and construction. Sectors with a high importance for female employment such as care, in contrast, play a rather minor role. Correspondingly, it is highly likely that they will further increase gender inequalities.

Changing course: the need for gender-sensitive economic recovery programmes

Early studies about the effects of the coronavirus pandemic on gendered professions indicated that the latter deepens existing inequalities and may even lead to a loss of any advances that we may have made during the last decades with regards overcoming the gender pay gap. The unequal distribution of unpaid household labour (see Chapter 4) and the corresponding withdrawal of some women from paid work will deepen the gender pay gap. Moreover, the strong representation of women in service sectors with a particular strain during the coronavirus crisis, such as retail and hospitality, also work in this direction.

While some of these negative developments are difficult to correct by public policies, others can easily be remedied by governments and parliaments. Future rescue packages, but particularly structural adjustment programmes, should be designed in a way that not only avoid disadvantages for women, but also compensate the latter for the disadvantages suffered during the crisis. The usual focus on physical infrastructures in fiscal recovery programmes needs to be complemented by measures on social infrastructures in fields such as childcare, healthcare and education (Isele and Dubois, 2020). Investments in care have much higher employment effects than investments in construction (Klatzer and Rinaldi, 2020: 7), thereby even further strengthening the case for a prominent inclusion in these packages.

6

Migration: Closed Borders or Open Doors?

The coronavirus crisis deepens the dilemma economies face with regard to immigration. On the one hand, the crisis created an immediate communitarian impetus (see Chapter 32), characterized by prioritization of domestic social ties and community-based solidarity. This trend undermines the public legitimacy to accept foreigners. On the other hand, the coronavirus crisis deepens health and economic divides between the Global North and the Global South. Therefore, migration pressures will increase. Next to these fundamental questions about the long-term trajectory of migration, the coronavirus crisis also raises immediate questions for migrant workers and their relatives; for example, with regard the closing of borders, accommodation conditions and remittances. Does the crisis lead to a recognition of the crucial work provided by migrant workers or does it negatively affect the situation of the latter?

Migration and International Political Economy

Questions of migration do not belong to the classical issues in Comparative or Political Economy, but have found quite some attention in recent scholarship. On the one side, political economists have become involved in the very controversial debates on migration and the rise of exclusionary populism in the EU and the US. On the other side, political economists working on the Global South have developed a keen interest in the living conditions of migrant workers and the remittances they are sending back to their families.

During the last years, the rise of exclusionary populist parties in many European countries, but also in the US (Republican Party during the Trump administration) has led to a very controversial discussion of cross-border migration. Scholarship on exclusionary populism distinguishes between two basic motivations for anti-immigration sentiments. The cultural perspective highlights the importance of status anxiety for exclusionary populism, whereas the economic perspective explains these sentiments by concerns regarding the individual economic situation (Gidron and Hall, 2017), with migrants as potential competitors for jobs, social benefits or affordable accommodation. Scholarship in International Political Economy primarily focuses on the latter perspective and studies not only the economic impact of cross-border migration on the receiving societies, but also the push and pull factors motivating cross-border migration (Clarkson, 2019). Political Economy scholars also have become involved in the normative debates on immigration in Northern societies (Streeck, 2018). For example, they have pointed towards the negative labour market effects of cross-border inward migration of low- and medium-skilled workers for domestic workers with similar qualifications in Northern societies (Nölke, 2019a).

In discussions on the Global South, International Political Economy scholarship mainly is interested in the effects of migration, the related establishment of diasporas and the remittances these diasporas are sending back to their families on processes of development. Diasporas, for example, can contribute to development via the skills of diaspora members or their influence on social norms in their societies of origin. Remittances are valued as substantial economic transfers, with a much higher volume and stability than the transfers via Official Development Assistance (ODA) and other external resource flows (Busumtwi-Sam, 2019). However, a strong reliance on remittances can also make economies too dependent on a particular source of capital, deviate attention away from domestic employment creation and can lead to a currency appreciation that make exports uncompetitive (Withers et al, 2021: 7–9, 12).

Public debates during the coronavirus crisis and their implications for migration

Particularly during the early phase of the coronavirus pandemic, countries have reacted unilaterally by closing their borders, even if this went against international obligation and long-standing practices. Large parts of the population saw the virus as something that was transmitted across borders. Indeed, the International Organization for Migration of the United Nations concedes: 'Intense population movements, in particular of tourists and business workers, have been a key driver of the global spread of the outbreak' (Guagdagno, 2020: 2). Communitarian impulses and the related border closures, however, did not only have immediate negative impacts on migrant workers (to be discussed later), but also tilted domestic public debates against a positive stance on this type of labour migration.

Before the coronavirus crisis, many Northern societies witnessed controversial discussions on how to treat inward labour migration of low- and medium-skilled workers. Arguments of Christian mercy, universal human rights and industry demand for labour, on the one side, stood against concerns about the high costs incurred (particular if compared with other humanitarian options for helping migrants), the challenges for the welfare state and affordable accommodation and the risk of increased segregation between groups within the domestic population. Political Economy perspectives highlight the distributive concerns behind these debates. While additional migration may have broadly positive connotations from a macro-economic perspective – for example, by way of additional demand by migrants, or by public investments to cater for their needs – it does not necessarily have positive effects on all social groups within the receiving society. Domestic social groups with qualification levels similar to those of the new entrants are more likely to suffer from increased competition (Streeck, 2018; Nölke, 2019a).

While there was the potential for a public debate that focuses on the importance of the challenging and often outright dangerous work provided by migrants in the economies of the Global North during the pandemic – or on the severe situation of this socio-economic group – this opportunity has not been used. Policymakers also did not make use of the pandemic to devise more rational policies with regard to future immigration policies (Fernández-Reino et al, 2020). Many debates at least implicitly focused on the health hazards for the domestic population going hand in hand with intense population movements, such as caused by cross-border labour migration. The massive recession affecting many economies due to the pandemic further deepened the negative assessment of migrants, up to outright xenophobia (Esses and Hamilton, 2021).

The immediate impact of the crisis on migrants

The coronavirus crisis has affected migrants in an immediate way. Borders were closed for most traffic early during the crisis, thereby forcing many migrants to stay where they were. Arrivals at EU external borders in 2020, for example, were markedly lower than in 2019 (Dimitriadi, 2020: 3). Border (and office) closures also created massive problems for migrant workers with regard to visa application and renewal, leading to frequent visa overstaying and loss of official status (Guadagno, 2020: 10–11). Moreover, border closures often have forced migrants to stay in overcrowded accommodation with considerable health hazards.

In many countries, migrant workers have been suffering particularly strongly from coronavirus infections. This was often due to poor accommodation conditions, as in the case of migrant workers in Singapore dormitories (Guadagno, 2020: 3). Similarly, migrants in Greek hotspots suffered severely from bad sanitary conditions (Dimitriadi, 2020: 5). Particularly during the early phase of the pandemic, hubs of international activity such as the

Lombardy region in Italy, New York and Madrid were particularly affected by coronavirus infections – and also housed an over-proportional share of migrants (Guadagno, 2020: 3).

Factors leading to a particularly strong socio-economic effect of the pandemic on migrants inter alia include the limited awareness of recommended health measures (also due to linguistic barriers), the reliance on public transportation, the lack of entitlement to healthcare, the loss of precarious jobs (migrants very often work in the latter) and the exclusion from specific coronavirus income support schemes and welfare systems more generally (Guadagno, 2020: 4–8). While some of these factors also affect other marginalized citizens – such as, for example, homeless people or gig workers – migrants often combine several of these factors.

Moreover, the crisis very often has led to racist discrimination of (formerly) migrant workers; for example, with regard to Asian minorities (due to association with China as the likely origin of the virus), but also to Black, Indigenous and people of colour more generally (Smith et al, 2021: 10). Using migrants as scapegoats is a typical behaviour during major emergencies (Guadagno, 2020: 11–12). This behaviour is particularly absurd if we take into account that migrant workers perform large shares of the very challenging social and dangerous reproductive work (see Chapter 4) that has become much more visible during the crisis.

However, there are also some cases where the crisis has improved the situations of migrants, at least partially. Portugal, for example, has given citizenship rights to all migrants and asylum seekers with applications underway, in order to safeguard their access to health provisions during the crisis. Italy has regularized the status for all migrant workers in agriculture and domestic care that were able to prove through official documents that they have worked in these sectors (Dimitriadi, 2020: 4). In general, however, the recession rather has led to restrictive migration policies. This has also negatively affected remittances to the home economies of migrants.

The effects of the crisis on remittances

The coronavirus pandemic has increased the pressure on migrant workers to send back remittances to their home societies. Many of the main countries of origin for migrant workers have suffered more during the crisis and the subsequent recession than the countries where migrant workers are employed. Correspondingly, there is a strong expectation on the latter to increase the volume of remittances back home. This expectation, however, does not fit with the economic reality of most migrant workers during the pandemic. As mentioned earlier, migrant workers have not only suffered over-proportionally from the health effects of the pandemic, but also from racist discrimination and lockdown-related unemployment. Some of them were unable to reach their prospective workplaces due to border closures, which is a particular severe problem if they and their families have taken on debt in order to pay for recruitment and travel (Guadagno, 2020: 9).

The economic impact of a reduction of remittances on the receiving economies potentially is severe. In 2019, remittances with a volume of US$554 billion for the first time have overtaken foreign direct investments as the most important resource flow to low- and medium-income countries; official development assistance not even provides a third of these resources (World Bank, 2020: 7). According to the same WB calculations, remittances might be reduced by up to 20 per cent in 2020/21 (although this later has been reduced to a 14 per cent drop, see Tsingou, 2021). At the same time, the economic importance of the remaining flows even increases, because the reduction in foreign direct investments is even steeper (35 per cent), not to mention the highly speculative private portfolio flows (80 per cent).

The reduction of remittances is particularly severe for South Asian economies, with the particular case of Nepal where remittances make up for 27.3 per cent of GDP (Withers et al, 2021: 1). Given these macroeconomic dimensions, the reduction of remittances not only seriously affected the economic situation of millions of low-income families, but also has led to a massive shortage of foreign currencies and increasing unemployment in many economies. However, receiving economies are not without means, as demonstrated by the government of Bangladesh that has provided an incentive scheme on cash remittances, thereby being able to even increase the volume of officially recorded remittances in 2020 (Chowdhury and Chakraborty, 2021). Generally, remittances have remained resilient, in particular if compared with initial expectations and with the technical restrictions of cross-border payment systems that still are limited in terms of speed and reliability (Tsingou, 2021).

Towards a more stable context for migrant workers and their relatives

The coronavirus crisis has demonstrated the fragility of the social and economic position of many migrant workers very clearly. They have become under pressure from several sides, from public debates to daily living conditions. At the same time, the crisis has highlighted that many of these workers perform essential services and that their often-difficult living conditions can contribute to prolong a health crisis. Finally, many countries of origin had to realize that remittances by migrant workers cannot always be considered a safe source of permanent access to foreign currencies.

The current situation is not only cruel to many migrant workers, but also unsatisfactory to both sending and receiving societies. In order to ameliorate this fate, we need open and pragmatic discussions about labour immigration in Northern societies, with a focus on low- and medium-skill migration, given that immigration of the highly qualified usually is much less controversial in these societies (but usually not desirable from the perspective of sending societies). All too often, this discussion is avoided – migration of low- and medium-skilled workers then either is idealized by highlighting the miserable situation of refugees, or migration is demonized by xenophobic and racist agitation. Hopefully, a pragmatic debate will lead to a more rational treatment of low- and medium-skilled migration. If the usefulness of a limited amount of the latter is broadly accepted within Northern societies, we are in a much better situation to effectively tackle the daily concerns of these migrants, from safe working conditions and accommodation to social security access. At the same time, a more orderly and rational approach towards migration may also contribute to reducing the too strong reliance of some Southern economies upon remittances. Internationally, the 'Global Compact for Safe, Orderly, and Regular Migration' adopted by the UN in 2018 provides a suitable framework for the cooperation between countries of origin and destination, and hopefully will prevent unilateral action in the future (Newland, 2020).

7

Inequality: Increase or Reduction?

At the onset of the crisis, the coronavirus was considered by some to be the 'great leveler' (Scheidel, 2017). In contrast to the economic and social challenges of the Global Financial Crisis, the virus poses a risk to everybody. Moreover, major crises such as wars and pandemics often have reduced inequality, if combined with high mortality rates that lead to a scarcity of workers, thereby improving their bargaining position (Scheidel, 2017, 2020; Sayed and Peng, 2021: 54). Finally, rebuilding efforts after major wars also reduced inequalities via massive government interventions into the private sector, based on tax increases (Scheidel, 2020: 293). However, soon concerns about corona-related inequality loomed large in the general public. The rich were able to sit out the lockdown in their villas much easier than the poor in their small apartments were, and the previous were able to work from home, whereas the latter had to risk infections in their dangerous jobs. Still, these are only two among the many dimensions of inequality. Concepts from Political Economy allow us to bring some order in the various effects of the pandemic and to study whether the crisis leads to an increase of inequality or offers opportunities for a reduction of the latter.

Political Economy and inequality

Questions of inequality are a core concern of substantial parts of Political Economy scholarship. Traditionally, 'Critical' (or 'Marxist' or 'Structuralist') approaches to International Political Economy (IPE) share a strong interest in questions of inequality, particularly on the exploitation of the labourers by the bourgeoisie, with the latter as the owners of the means of production. While traditional Marxist thought focused on individual economies, later revisions in theories of imperialism, dependency and World System Theory additionally highlight the exploitation of the periphery of the world economy – simplified: the Global South – via the core of the world economy (Balaam and Dillman, 2014: 78–100; O'Brien and Williams, 2016: 16–19). Correspondingly, questions of inter-country inequality always are very prominent in IPE scholarship on North–South relations (Phillips, 2020; Wade, 2020). More recently, new aspects of inequality have found a prominent role in IPE scholarship; namely, gender and race inequalities. Intersectional approaches in Political Economy highlight that how the combination of class relations with colonial legacies and traditional patterns of social reproduction lead to particularly severe inequalities (Andersson, 2020; LeBaron et al, 2021).

In mainstream Comparative Political Economy, questions of inequality were less prominent during the last decades due to the dominance of the rather functionalist 'Varieties of Capitalism' approach (see Part III), although some important origins of this research programme lie in the study of 'industrial districts' and the related spatial inequalities (Crouch et al, 2009) and inequality with regard to access to skill formation is a core concern of the field (Busemeyer, 2012). During the last years, however, the turn towards the 'Growth Model' perspective has given new prominence to questions of inequality (see Part II); it has even become the focus of a major new textbook (Vermeiren, 2021). Macroeconomic (fiscal or monetary) policies that focus on unemployment or inflation are central to the Growth Model perspective and have very important redistributive consequences. Particularly, the welfare state plays an important role. Moreover, the Growth Model perspective also focuses on inter-sectoral inequalities; for example, on redistributive conflicts between the domestic consumption and the manufacturing export sectors (Nölke, 2021).

Increasing household income inequality during the coronavirus pandemic

The question whether the pandemic increased or decreased inequality has motivated a lot of research in the Social Sciences. Answers to this question differ, depending on the specific aspects and determinants of inequality. The analytical instruments mentioned earlier help us in disentangling these various factors. The focus of Political Economy analyses is on income and wealth inequalities – less on health inequalities, which also played an important role in the context of the pandemic, with many studies demonstrating racial disparities in US infections and mortality. This is particularly to the disadvantage of Black people (for example, Laster Pirtle, 2020; Wrigley-Field, 2020; Abedi et al, 2021; Zelner et al, 2021). Similar results are reported for Brazil (Nassif Pires et al, 2021) and South Africa (Nwosu and Oyenubi, 2021: 9). Of course, health inequalities deepen income inequalities in turn (to be discussed later).

Due to the early point in time, it is not yet possible to provide a sound assessment on the repercussions of the crisis on functional income distribution; that is, between capital and labour. Still, we can at least distinguish between the effects on monthly (labour) income (this section) and on accumulated wealth (next section). Within income inequality, we should separate between the impact of the crisis on primary distribution (household incomes before taxes and transfers) and secondary distribution (after deduction of taxes and the inclusion of transfer payments); tertiary distribution (benefits from public expenditure via government services provided for free or below market prices) is only important for certain countries.

Generally, the most important causal mechanism how major crises such as pandemics and wars decreased inequality in previous times (luckily) did not work: the casualties were far too low to rise workers' scarcity and, therefore, their bargaining position. To the contrary, rising unemployment even weakens the latter without massive state intervention (Scheidel, 2020: 294). Correspondingly, the impact of the coronavirus pandemic on income inequality generally is similar to those of other recessions during the last decades: whereas income inequality roughly stays the same during phases of economic growth, it increases during phases of GDP falls (Darvas, 2021: 6–9). In addition, specific features of the coronavirus pandemic increase its tendency to deepen inequality; in particular, the differential impact of shutdowns and of teleworking for different groups of society (Darvas, 2021: 10–12).

Large-scale quantitative studies on the impact of the coronavirus pandemic on income inequality come to clear conclusions: the crisis substantially increases inequality with regard to primary incomes, but compensation by the state is able to compensate this increase, as long as the extraordinary fiscal measures last. The Bank of Italy, for example, finds that the crisis would have substantially increased labour income inequality without the highly effective compensation by the welfare state (Carta and De Philippis, 2021). The causal mechanisms on how the pandemic increased income inequality are similar across countries. First, low-income workers often work in (services) sectors such as entertainment, gastronomy, hairdressers and travel with rather comprehensive lockdown measures and therefore more often lost income by furlough or complete job loss (Carta and De Philippis, 2021: 17; Möhring et al, 2021: 26). In the UK, 'low earners are seven time as likely as high earners to have worked in a sector that is now shut down' (Joyce and Xu, 2020: 2). Second, low-income workers could hardly compensate lockdowns by working from home, in contrast to highly educated professionals in the services sector (Carta and De Philippis, 2021: 17; Möhring et al, 2021: 26). The option of working from home – fairly easy for people working in professional services; very difficult in auxiliary and mechanical occupations – provided a good protection against unemployment (Adams-Prassl, 2020: 10). Generally, low levels of formal education were far more conducive to economic hardships than high ones (Darvas, 2021: 1–2; Perry et al, 2021: 2). On average, working from home privileges older, high-educated, high-paid and male employees (Bonacini et al, 2021). The rise of working from home also deepens regional inequalities, since already poorer regions have fewer jobs where working from home is feasible, at least in Germany (Irlacher and Koch, 2020). Moreover, those wealthy (US) regions where high-speed internet is available were able to support social distancing in a more effective way (Chiou and Tucker, 2020). Third, young workers earn less than older workers and often only have temporary contracts. Due to the latter, they were more affected by unemployment (Carta and De Philippis, 2021: 17). Generally, unemployment predominantly was a problem for workers on temporary contracts, non-salaried and with varying working hours (Adams-Prassl et al, 2020: 11). Moreover, lockdowns affected young workers more than old workers. In the UK, 'employees aged under 25 were about two and a half times as likely to work in a sector that is now shut down as other employees' (Joyce and Xu, 2020: 2). The particularly negative impact of shutdowns on young groups of society is even more problematic if one considers that the young also suffered more in terms of social relations and that the shutdown primarily benefitted the old, due to their higher health hazards. In the Global South, the self-employed in the informal sector had a particularly high probability to lose their livelihoods (Bottan et al, 2020: 4–5).

As for the compensating role of the welfare state (secondary distribution), it is striking that the extraordinary measures introduced during the coronavirus pandemic even in usually less generous welfare states (see Chapter 3) were able to compensate for increasing primary inequality sometimes very well. In France, Germany, Italy and Spain, income-support policies to compensate for COVID-related losses temporarily even reduced overall household inequality, because they had a particular focus on those at the bottom of the income distribution (Clark et al, 2021: 19). In Italy, for example, a lump sum bonus of €600 given to all self-employed individuals during the months of March, April and May 2020 was particularly effective in reducing inequality (Carta and De Philippis, 2021: 17). In Germany, short-time work protected the income of workers (of all kinds of qualification) in the manufacturing sector in particular (Möhring et al, 2021: 26). Also in the Global South, some emergency programmes introduced during the pandemic were even able to reduce overall income inequality (and absolute poverty) while they lasted; for example, the Brazilian 'Auxililio Emergencial' (Emergency Aid) cash transfer programme (Menezes-Filho et al, 2021; Nassif Pires et al, 2021: 52–3) and the 'Ingreso Familiar de Emergencia' (Emergency Family Income) in Argentina. However, these programmes only address the poorest, not those in the middle of the distribution (Lustig et al, 2020) and not each country in the Global South was able to afford one.

Next to the inequalities with regard to household incomes during the crisis years, we need to look at the long-term inequalities that will be caused by the pandemic. A core issue is education. Many students have lost important learning time. Among the young, disparities will increase between those that can easily participate in digital learning and those that lack the necessary resources. Studies indicate that school closures during the COVID-19 pandemic increase social inequality in educational opportunities (Dietrich et al, 2021).

Further inequalities within the distinctions observed mentioned earlier can be found along gender and racial lines. Women lost more income than men because they have taken on a larger share of unpaid reproductive work, to the detriment of paid work (Oreffice and Quintana-Domeque, 2020: 16–17; see also Chapter 4). Females were also more often affected by shutdowns than male workers; in particular, because of their high share of low-wage service employment (Joyce and Xu, 2020: 2; Möhring et al, 2021: 27–8; see also Chapter 5). Women became unemployed more often than men, particularly because of their atypical work arrangements; for example, part-time work (Kristal and Yaish, 2020; Reichelt et al, 2021: S240). Black adults in the US did not only suffer more from more infections and casualties than Whites, but also from food insecurity and unemployment (Perry et al, 2021: 2). Similarly, migrants often were strongly affected by the crisis (see Chapter 6). In the EU, for example, workers from ethnic minorities and migrant workers were over-represented in economic sectors with many face-to-face contacts, often without suitable personal protective equipment. Moreover, they also suffered from weak employment statues based on precarious contracts and inadequate paid sick leave (Purkayastha et al, 2021).

The crisis and wealth inequality

Whereas income inequality was at the focus of economic assistance packages during the beginning of the crisis, effects on wealth inequality become more important in the long run. The main issue here are the effects of the very unconventional measures by the central banks (see Chapter 8). During the last years, we have seen an intense debate whether these measures – already implemented after the Global Financial Crisis and intensified during the coronavirus pandemic – have an effect on inequality. The issue cannot be easily resolved, because many different causal channels are at stake (Colciago et al, 2019: 1203). If we focus on the most obvious effects during the coronavirus pandemic, arguably unconventional monetary policy has increased house prices as well as equity and bond prices. The effects on wealth equality tend to cancel out in economies with a high share of residential property owners: whereas increased equity prices benefit rich households, middle and lower households benefit from increasing property prices and lower interest rates and liabilities (Colciago et al, 2019: 1221). However, in countries with low property ownership and an important role of conventional savings for middle and lower households – such as Germany and Austria – the crisis should clearly increase wealth inequality, due to lower interest on savings and few gains via equity or property. Correspondingly, the unconventional monetary policy is very controversial in these societies.

However, there is another mechanism how the crisis interacts with wealth – or lack of the latter: high debt burdens – mainly because of residential mortgages – force low-income individuals to work during the pandemic, leading to additional COVID-19 cases. This effect is pronounced in US counties with residential mortgage recourse; that is, where not only the home that was used as a collateral but also other assets of the borrower can be confiscated by the lender, if the foreclose sale does not lead to sufficient revenues to pay back the loan. It also affects Black/African American and Hispanic/Latino borrowers in particular (Davydiuk and Gupta, 2021). However, at least during the early phase of the crisis the disparities were not as grave as during the Great Recession, which 'truly devastated the median black and Latino household wealth' (Mizota, 2020: 13).

The crisis and between-country inequality

Finally, next to inequality within societies, the coronavirus crisis will also have massive repercussions on international inequality (that is, inequality between countries as measured by differences in per capita income). Studies usually either focus on a comparison between countries in the Global North or between the Global North and the Global South. Within the Global North, many studies point towards the intensification of between-country inequality between Northern and Southern European countries. This is based on the much deeper 2020 recessions in Italy and Spain (and, to a more limited degree, France), if compared with Germany (see also Chapter 9). This will reverse the process of slowly decreasing European income inequality that had begun after the end of the Eurozone crisis in 2013 (Darvas, 2021: 18–19).

In the first phase of the pandemic (until October 2020), the poor countries of the Global South have been hit less hard than the rich countries of the Global North in terms of GDP contraction. The main reason for this development was the lower per capita mortality during the first phase of the pandemic. Per capital mortality correlated strongly with per capita income; that is, a loss of life and money went hand in hand. Some large emerging economies, such as Brazil, India, Mexico and South Africa, however, have been severely affected in terms of mortality (and income) already during this phase, in contrast to China (Deaton, 2021). While it is too early to estimate the effects of the coronavirus recession on international inequality in any comprehensive way, there are profound reasons to assume that the coronavirus recession increases global income inequality. As of early 2021, these effects are moderated by the positive development of China and are limited if compared with the decrease of global income inequality since the 1980s, thanks to the rise of China and India (Darvas, 2021: 14–16). Given that their population numbers are limited, the difficult situation in some particularly poor economies (see Chapter 23) will not affect this overall picture. Finally, global (between-country) inequality should not be confused with global poverty. It is almost certain that global poverty – following the WB usually measured by the number of people living with less than US$1.9 per day – has increased since the outbreak of the pandemic (Deaton, 2021: 16).

Fuel to the fire of inequality – but also a unique opportunity for its reduction

So far, the pandemic and the related recession have strongly increased socio-economic inequalities of all kinds. This is in stark contrast to previous global pandemics where a high mortality rate among workers have led to higher wages via labour scarcity; during the coronavirus pandemic, in contrast, fatalities were mainly concentrated in older age groups (Sayed and Peng, 2021). Income inequalities were increased via lockdown measures for low-income workers, whereas highly educated professionals were able to work from home. The young, women and ethnic minorities were particularly disadvantaged. Wealth inequality has increased even more than income inequality. Inter-country inequality also increases, as does absolute poverty. Increased social stratification seems to become a cornerstone for post-coronavirus capitalism (McNamara and Newman, 2020: E66–9).

Growing inequality is dangerous not only for the poor, but also for the better off, since it undermines social stability and democracy. High levels of immiseration and strongly rising social discontent may lead many people to flirt with authoritarian solutions. However, the crisis has also demonstrated that income-support policies can be designed in a way that actually reduce inequality and poverty, which is not necessarily the case with many welfare state instruments (see Chapter 3). This development should be utilized in order to intensify activities for the reduction of social inequality in the immediate future, since even (US) Americans that usually have a large tolerance for social inequalities tend to change their preferences towards redistribution when realizing the impact of the pandemic on class inequalities (Yildirim, 2020). Correspondingly, the post-crisis environment may be a unique opportunity to introduce policies that reduce social inequalities.

PART II

Domestic Institutions of Capitalism on the Demand Side

As we have seen in the case of welfare states, countries differ considerably in their ways to tackle economic challenges, with very different institutions in conservative, liberal and social-democratic welfare systems. The discipline of Comparative Political Economy focuses on these institutional differences, in contrast, for example, to approaches that focus on the commonalities of capitalism across economies understood as separate national entities (for example, Kaczmarczyk, 2020; Bruff, 2021).

To put it very simply, we can compare institutions on the demand and on the supply side of the economy. This section studies the macroeconomic institutions and policy choices on the demand side, whereas the subsequent section addresses the microeconomic institutions supporting different varieties of capitalism on the supply side. The most prominent contemporary Comparative Political Economy approach addressing the demand side of the economy is the 'Growth Models' approach (Baccaro and Pontusson, 2016; Stockhammer, 2020; Vermeiren, 2021). Its basic distinction is between debt-led and export-led and growth models, named after the main source of demand in the Global North, whereas the emerging research on growth models in emerging economies mainly distinguishes between two types of investment-led growth models, one fuelled by foreign direct investment and one by state-directed development (Schedelik et al, 2020).

During the pandemic, all economies reacted in a similar way. Central banks reacted with a highly expansive monetary policy (Chapter 8) and governments stimulated the economy with immediate fiscal impulses (Chapter 9). Even during the Global Financial Crisis, governments did not increase their budgets to such an extent. The reason for this unprecedented response was a unique feature of the crisis. The pandemic-related closures imposed by governments worldwide halted production processes. It led to laying off workers and therefore undermined private demand.

Correspondingly, public funds were needed to prevent the economy and society from collapsing, to keep both people and businesses alive, and to prevent suppliers from going broke. After the crisis, however, economies with different growth models will use different ways to recover the funds that were necessary for economic stabilization during the crisis: (1) they can extract funds from the private business sector and/or households via taxation or nationalization of companies (Chapter 10); (2) they can borrow from the private business sector and/or households via additional public debt (Chapter 9); or (3) they can ask the central bank to create money and use it to buy government bonds (Chapter 8). Hypothetically, there is a fourth option; namely, receiving financial aid from foreign sources, but in quantitative terms this is only relevant for some low-income countries and it is not the matter of major debates at the moment (but see Chapter 18 on Foreign Debt in the Global South). Finally, the strongly increased role of the public sector in the economy during the crisis may also have repercussions on the long-term sharing of tasks between the private and the public sector with regard to investment, possibly including a more prominent role for industrial policy (Chapter 11).

8

Monetary Policy: Democratic or Technocratic?

During the coronavirus pandemic (as during the Global Financial Crisis), central banks were instrumental in stabilizing the economy via highly expansive monetary policy. Arguably, central banks were at least as important as governments for overcoming the economic crisis. The range of their tasks and instruments has become broader than ever before in history. This raises crucial questions about the future of central bank independence. Can we continue considering central banks as neutral, technocratic institutions or do we need more democratic accountability via a stronger involvement of parliaments in monetary policy?

Monetary policy in different national growth models

The alternative options of central banks as technocratic or political (and therefore to be guided by parliaments) is closely linked to the preferences with regard to the direction of monetary policy. A conservative monetary policy prefers independent and technocratic central banks with a narrow mandate on the fight against inflation, a heterodox monetary policy gives central banks a whole range of targets, thereby increasing the need for democratic control, in order to adjucate between different targets. These preferences vary both between countries and over time.

Countries with different growth models have different preferences with regard to monetary policy (Vermeiren, 2021: 86–9): export-oriented growth models such as the German one clearly prefer a very strict ('conservative') central bank that focuses on keeping inflation rates very low. A low inflation rate helps in price-based export competition. Even in the case of an economic crisis, this central bank would not lower interest rates in order to stimulate the economy, given that export-led growth models seek additional demands from foreign, not domestic, markets. Domestic demand-led growth models, as for example in the US, the UK, France and the Mediterranean, in contrast, favour a much more expansive ('heterodox') central bank that fights recessions and unemployment via interest rate cuts or the utilization of even more heterodox instruments (to be discussed later). In the Global South, a third 'developmental' perspective on central banks with a focus on extensive administrative instruments to control banking can be found (Krampf, 2013). Some economies in the Global South also suffer from 'monetary dependency'; that is, they are unable to pursue an independent monetary policy (Koddenbrock and Sylla, 2019).

However, preferences towards monetary policy do not only vary between different national growth models, but also over time. Put very simply, the struggle is between a heterodox focus on 'full employment', or a conservative focus on 'sound money' (Vermeiren, 2021: 62–86). This struggle is not academic, but interwoven with massive distributive effects, with the former usually preferred by workers and the latter by rentier capital (that is, capital that primarily derives its income from financial assets). For post-coronavirus capitalism, this raised two related questions; namely, whether central banks should be independent and whether central banks should stick to their traditional instruments or may also utilize heterodox instruments.

Alternative approaches towards central bank independence and paradigms over time

Conservative economic theories assume that if central banks are independent from governments and parliaments, they target very low inflation because low inflation is assumed to be a public good that has no long-term costs and no distributive impact. According to this view, non-independent central banks, in contrast, will follow the short-term preferences of governments and parliaments, assuming that the latter often wish to stimulate economic growth by an accommodative monetary policy. Correspondingly, inflation will be much higher with the democratically closely controlled central banks. Conservative economic theories therefore have a clear preference for independent central banks. In spite of the powerful function of central banks, they see no need for a comprehensive democratic control, given that central banks have a clear and simple technical function to narrow-mindedly pursue a certain (very low) level of inflation. A conservative central banker prioritizes transparent and simple policy rules. Examples of such rules are the Gold Standard, in which the domestic currency is pegged to an external key currency or to gold, or the inflation-targeting regime described mentioned earlier, in which the purpose of monetary policy is to attain a very low and precisely defined inflation level.

A heterodox central bank prioritizes discretion and it highlights the existence of trade-offs and spillovers. Therefore, a heterodox central bank tends to take into account a large number of desirable economic objectives: in addition to price stability, it also considers growth, employment, export, exchange rates, financial stability – including global financial stability – and more recently also social purposes such as social equality, gender equality and the fight against global warming. The heterodox approach towards central banking draws more strongly on the Keynesian and post-Keynesian traditions (Dow, 2017). It also raises much bigger problems of democratic accountability, given that central banks lose their narrow technical function and have to weigh between different political targets – in democracies the prerogative of governments and parliaments.

Throughout history, the ideas that guided the behaviour of central banks changed markedly along with the conservative/heterodox epistemic pendulum and with regard to the emphasis on central bank independence. During the Gold Standard regime, the convention was that the central bank must be independent of domestic political pressure in order to maintain the pegging to gold and convertibility (Gallarotti, 1995). After the disintegration of the Gold Standard during the interwar period, a new international monetary regime consolidated, which shifted the emphasis from the monetary authority to the fiscal authority – to governments. In the post-WWII era, the role of (politically accountable) central banks was to exercise monetary policy to support the Keynesian welfare state (O'Brien and Williams, 2016: 227). Given that capital flows were restricted, central banks and governments had the capacity to respond to domestic economic and political circumstances, and adopt expansionary fiscal and monetary policies.

The stagflation era of the 1970s, associated with the spiralling inflation level and low growth rate in the Northern economies, brought an end to the expansion of the Keynesian welfare state and to a radical transformation in central banking ideas and practices: central banks became more independent and more conservative (Balaam and Dillman, 2014: 167). Amid the gradual but persisting process of financial liberalization, governments floated exchange rates, and central banks started to focus on inflation targets as their anchor for monetary policy. By the 1990s, the 'new consensus' in central banking dictated a reform of central bank mandate that made them even more focused on inflation targets (Krampf, 2019; Louca et al, 2021). This institutional change complemented a change in fiscal policies: governments tied their hands by legislating fiscal rules that forced budget restraint (see Chapter 9). This policy paradigm, characterized by fiscal austerity and sound money policies, prevailed for several decades, until the Global Financial Crisis (GFC).

Changes in monetary policy instruments since the GFC

Since the GFC, a new paradigm among central bankers emerged, according to which inflation was no longer the primary risk of global capitalism. Central bankers started to watch for a large number of economic objectives and risks, including capital flows, the exchange rate, the cost of financing public debt and long-term interest rates. They are embracing very unconventional monetary policy instruments, in particular quantitative easing; that is, the acquisition of large amounts of government debt via acquisitions from private banks (Louca et al, 2021). Central bank policy has become more heterodox and political, but central banks remain strictly independent in most countries. Correspondingly, central banking has become a combination of rather heterodox policies and a conservative institutional set-up. Conservative central bankers still are uneasy about the current situation. Next to fears about rising inflation they are worried about moral hazard problems: if governments take loans from a central bank (via private banks), would they actually pay back their debt? After all, it is like the state pays back to itself.

Central banks, according to the heterodox approach, sit at the apex of the hierarchy of money and provide backup to all other types of moneys, as liquidity providers of last resort. The central bank may provide liquidity to the government by purchasing of government bonds in the primary or secondary markets. In secondary markets, government bonds are first bought by banks and the central bank buys from the latter. Law in many countries forbids issuing debt by the government directly to the central bank via the primary market. This conservative law is a remnant of the legacy of the stagflation crisis in the 1970s. By requesting central banks to operate via private banks it should act as a brake on money creation – and, according to the theories dominant in the 1980s – on inflation. However, during the current situation, when states are in need of saving societies and they cannot rely on taxes or issuing bonds to the public, some central banks move even closer to the business of direct state financing and fuel discussions that go even further towards heterodoxy. Given that the central banks provide loans by money they create, one may argue that it is better to give up the 'show' of a so-called transaction via the buying of bonds, and let the bank create money for free – without debt – and transfer it to the government, to corporations or households. Transferring freshly created money to households is often called 'helicopter money' (Friedman, 1969; Masciandaro, 2020), since it may be compared to throwing out money from helicopters.

Transferring the money for free to the government has become a particularly hot topic with the rise of the controversial 'Modern Monetary Theory' (MMT) during the last years. The core argument of the theory is that states have no need to refinance their expenditures, because states create money. In this perspective, the central bank is part of the state and it can simply provide the government with money, without the detour via issuing public debt. This is not only hypothetical; the Bank of England, for example, offered the UK Government 2020 the option to temporary extend its 'Ways and Means' facility (Ehnts and Paetz, 2021: 202). MMT suggests that there is no limit to the central bank capacity to create money, besides the side effect of inflation. However, they further argue that printing money does not necessarily cause inflation, certainly no hyperinflation and that harm of a low level of inflation – below 10 per cent – has been exaggerated by the economic orthodoxy (Kelton, 2020). The key policy implication of MMT is that states should not be as anxious of their budget deficit and their public debt as the economic orthodoxy argues, it is thus in policy terms rather a theory of fiscal and not of monetary policy (see Chapter 9). Whereas MMT has a point in its criticism against the 'deficit myth', it ignores the international hierarchy of money; that is, the fact that for small states extensive money creation by the central bank could have devastating external implications in terms of the exchange rate and capital flows. Correspondingly, MMT-like practices may well be an option for the US – where it has gained some traction in the Democratic Party – and other countries with currencies high in the global hierarchy such as Japan and the UK, but hardly for most countries of the Global South. For the near future, it is also no option in the EU where it would require unanimous change of its fundamental treaties.

The consolidation of non-traditional instruments of monetary policy during the coronavirus crisis

A description of the Fed's response to the crisis demonstrates in an exemplary way how the response to the COVID-19 crisis replicated, institutionalized and enhanced the consolidation of the non-traditional approach in central banking, even if we can only cover a small selection of its measures (Cheng et al, 2021). The Fed cut the Fed funds rate, the rate commercial banks pay for overnight credit, from 1.5 per cent in March 2020 to zero. The Fed also offered forward guidance and guaranteed a future low-level interest rate. The Fed also supported the financial market through the purchasing of securities such as government bonds ('Quantitative Easing', see mentioned earlier). Between March and December 2020, the Fed holding of securities grew from US$3.9 trillion to US$6.6 trillion. To stabilize the banking system, the Fed eased regulatory demands, including eliminating reserves requirements.

A significant unconventional measure also was the support to private businesses, which went even further in terms of heterodoxy than during the GFC era. In March 2020, the Fed established the Primary Market Corporate Credit Facility and the Secondary Market Corporate Credit Facility. Both facilities were designed to tap money into the economy through loans to large corporations and to purchase corporate bonds. After being criticized during the GFC for supporting 'Wall Street' by taxing 'Main Street', during the coronavirus crisis the Fed established the Main Street Lending Program and the Paycheck Protection Program to support small and mid-size businesses. The Fed expects to offer US$600 billion in five-year loans. To support households, consumers and small businesses, the Fed activated the Term Asset-Backed Securities Loans Facility (TALF) designed to provide loans using asset-backed security with new student, auto or credit card loans as collateral. The Fed also provided a global financial safety network through international swap lines. During the crisis, the Fed lowered the interest rate it charges on swaps with the central banks of Canada, England, the Eurozone, Japan and Switzerland, and it created temporary swaps to the central banks of Australia, Brazil, Denmark, Korea, Mexico, New Zealand, Norway, Singapore and Sweden.

The case of the Fed's response to the crisis demonstrates the institutional and conceptual continuity between the GFC and the coronavirus crisis. In the recent crisis, the Fed used the same policy instruments it had used a decade ago. In that sense, COVID-19 was the last nail in the coffin of the conservative 'new consensus' on central banking that consolidated in the 1990s. The idea that central banks should focus one simple policy rule, such as the rule of inflation targeting, by using a simple response function, was discarded. However, at the same time, the coronavirus crisis and the response to it also demonstrated the limits of monetary policy, in the broad sense of the term. The sequencing of the GFC and the coronavirus crisis show that an active approach of central banks cannot substitute active fiscal policies by governments (see Chapter 10). Hence, since the outbreak of the coronavirus crisis we see accumulated evidence that governments abandon the norm of permanent austerity in favour of a bigger government in terms of demand management and public investment (see Chapter 11).

As with any monetary policy, the recent turn towards a non-traditional approach with a very aggressive stimulation of the economy by central banks is not without risks. Most prominent among the latter are the very high valuations for equities and real estate that have very problematic distributive consequences, given the uneven distribution of these assets in society. Hypothetically, the combination of active fiscal policy and heterodox monetary policy can even lead to a new wave of high inflation, as during the 1970s, although the currently high degree of underemployment clearly speaks against this tendency. In addition, inflation might be fuelled by rising prices caused through supply chain reshoring (see Chapter 17). Fighting inflation would require to close the levers in terms of heterodox monetary policies in much stronger ways as exercised after the GFC. However, this would be very difficult for central banks, given that the currently high valuations for equities and real estate rely on these levers. A powerful anti-inflation policy would not only lead to a drastic reduction of these valuations (and probably to a major financial crisis, particularly in countries of the Global

South with high levels of foreign debt), but also an extended recession and strongly increased unemployment.

The future of central banks after the coronavirus crisis: independence or parliamentary control?

The further consolidation of heterodox conceptions and non-traditional instruments of monetary policy poses the old question of central bank independence anew. With conservative monetary policy, one may make an argument in favour of central bank independence, given that its function is very narrow and technical, without much policy space. Both the increased importance of heterodox conceptions and of non-traditional instruments of central banking triggered by the succession of the GFC and the coronavirus crisis, however, give these institutions much more power and leeway for decisions. Correspondingly, central bank independence becomes more questionable than ever before, at least from the perspective of democratic legitimacy. The next step in the broadening of the mandate of central banks towards ever more heterodox practices has been announced already; namely, the utilization of central bank instruments for the fight against climate change (see Chapter 24), in the form of 'green central banking' (Dikau and Volz, 2021).

Given the ever increasing breadth of central bank mandates and policy instruments, as well as the growing distributive consequences of their operations, it does not come as a surprise that the democratic legitimacy of independent central banks has become heavily contested again (Epstein, 2019; Tucker, 2019; Braun, 2020; Dietsch, 2020; de Boer and van't Klooster, 2020). From the perspective of democratic legitimacy, there are two basic options: either countries return to conservative central banking with a narrow inflation rate mandate, narrow instruments and central bank independence. Alternatively, central banks continue with their broad mandate as well as a broad range of instruments – but then have to be put under direct democratic control via parliaments and elected governments again.

Towards democratically accountable monetary policy

The coronavirus pandemic has further consolidated non-traditional central bank instruments as well as a heterodox interpretation of central bank mandates. The conservative approach with its narrow focus on inflation rates and traditional instruments of central banking increasingly has been pushed in the back seat, even with central banks that have to cater for export-led and extremely inflation adverse economies such as Germany.

Given that it is very unlikely that central banks will ever return to their conservative style of operations, we need to put these extremely powerful institutions under democratic control. And even if a return to conservative central banking with a narrow focus on inflation control is on the agenda, this decision – with likely very severe economic consequences – should be taken by elected parliaments and governments and not by central bank technocrats, if we still want to speak of democratically legitimate economic policies.

9

Fiscal Policy: Absolute Ceiling or No Limits to Deficit Spending?

During the coronavirus pandemic, most governments have taken up additional public debt. As governments faced a pressing demand to increase public spending within very short periods, the only available source of funding was borrowing. One of the core questions with regard to the economic policies in post-coronavirus capitalism is how to deal with this debt level. Shall we bring the level of public debt – usually calculated in relation to gross domestic product (GDP) – quickly back to pre-corona levels, shall it remain on the increased level or shall we even increase it, in order to fund post-crisis restructuring?

Fiscal policies in different growth models

The discussion on growth models in Comparative Political Economy informs us why governments have different propensities to rely on debt-based funding. This discussion goes against claims that there is only one generally desirable level of public debt – an issue that has been a focus of contention among economists and politicians for decades. Conservative economists call for an absolute ceiling of public debt (for example, less than something between 60 per cent or 90 per cent of annual GDP), in order to avoid a decrease of economic growth (Reinhart and Rogoff, 2010). They further argue that without such a ceiling economies would be instable (for example, with regard to international financial flows), governments would be under the pressure of interest groups to spend in their favour and later generations would need to pay for high public debt today. Left economists, in contrast, argue that there should be no limit to public debt, as long as countries have their own central bank and are not at the bottom of the international currency hierarchy (see Chapter 9). They do not find any evidence that rates of economic growth slows down if debt transgressed 90 per cent of GDP (Herndon et al, 2014). In their perspective, fiscal policies are at the centrepiece of the democratic process, play an important role for safeguarding low unemployment and governments need not worry about intergenerational fairness, as long as public debt is used for productive purposes (investment).

From the perspective of Comparative Political Economy, the level of public debt a country prefers depends on the growth model (Vermeiren, 2021: 86–9; Schoeller and Karlsson, 2021: 199–200). Put simply, Northern economies pursuing an export-led growth model prefer a rather low level of public debt. If the government takes up much debt in order to increase public spending, it may trigger strong domestic growth that may lead to higher wages and prices. Higher prices, however, may negatively affect the price competitiveness of goods and services in international competition. Correspondingly, extremely export-led countries such as Germany prefer a low level of public debt. Northern countries pursuing a domestic consumption-based growth model, in contrast, have a much higher degree of tolerance towards high levels of public debt. Their domestically oriented sectors crucially rely on expansionary macroeconomic policies. Particularly during a recession, governments of these economies may consciously increase the level of public debt considerably, in order to get the economy going again. However, their ability to take on public debt depends on their position in the international hierarchy of money. Debt-driven economies with a strong ability to attract foreign financial flows – for example, because they are housing an international financial centre and an international reserve currency (for example, the US and the UK) – have a much stronger ability to take up foreign debt than those countries without.

Most countries of the Global South have a limited ability to take up public debt because of their more narrow financial markets. Unless governments do not intend to ask their central bank to directly finance public expenditures (see Chapter 9), they need parties that are willing to provide savings, a condition that cannot be taken for granted. For many small economies in the Global South, the capacity to amass funds from domestic markets is particularly limited, and they face pressures to issue debt denominated in foreign currencies, in order to attract foreign creditors. This move exposed them to completely new types of risks (such as currency valuations), which depends also on factors that the government has no control on (see Chapter 23).

Fiscal policy during the pandemic: at the centre of economic stabilization in the Global North

During the coronavirus pandemic, a strong expansion of fiscal policy via stimulus – next to the automatic stabilizers that kick in, for example, with higher payments for unemployment insurance – was at the centre of efforts to fight the crisis. Governments mobilized extremely high volumes of direct fiscal support and credit guarantees in order to keep business, workers and vulnerable groups afloat (Eurofound, 2020; Anderson et al, 2021; Makin and Layton, 2021). According to OECD estimates for 2020, an average OECD country took up discretionary fiscal measures to ease the pandemic of about 4 per cent of GDP; this is about twice the amount provided during the GFC 2008/09 (OECD, 2020a). Discretionary fiscal measures, however, are only a part of the budget deficit increase; they, for example, do not incorporate revenue losses or additional exposes via automatic stabilizers. The peak global deficit for 2020 is estimated of around 14 per cent of world GDP, about three times the deficit following the GFC, with particularly high increases for the rich economies (17 per cent) and much lower fiscal impulses in emerging economies and low-income countries (Makin and Layton, 2021: 343).

Northern governments took on additional debt in a situation where debt levels already were at a historical high. In the early 1970s, public debt to GDP rates in the OECD were merely around 40 per cent. They climbed to more than 90 per cent in 2011 (Menz, 2017: 178). After the resolution of the GFC and the Eurozone crisis, public debt to GDP levels in the major economies grew more slowly (and were even reduced in case of Germany), except for some large emerging economies, such as Brazil, China and South Africa (Naisbitt, 2020: 5). The coronavirus crisis, however, increased debt-to-GDP relations in many economies to the highest numbers ever seen, at least for the last decades. According to OECD estimates, government debt-to-GDP ratios at the end of 2022 will be 20 per cent higher than in 2019, and even 40 per cent higher in Canada and the UK (OECD, 2020a); these calculations were made before the Biden administration took office, with its massive public investment plans.

The fact that debt levels in the Global South increased much less is not a good sign – it rather reflects a limited ability to mobilize additional fiscal firepower and it will go hand in hand with far more severe economic hardship. The decision to go for expansionary fiscal policy (or austerity) in the rich economies of the Global North is mainly a question of the preferences of the policymakers (Romer and Romer, 2019). However, in the poorer economies of the Global South, expansionary fiscal policy during the pandemic, in contrast, was mainly a question of market access for the issuing of government debt, with limited market access going hand in hand with low credit ratings before the coronavirus pandemic; the previous debt-to-GDP level, in contrast, is hardly relevant (Benmelech and Tzur-Ilan, 2020).

Fiscal policy after the pandemic: further deficit spending or austerity?

After the coronavirus crisis, many governments will not only face much higher levels of public debt, but also strong demand for additional public spending; for example, for climate protection (Bahri and Singh, 2021). Unless additional public spending leads to very high inflation (see Chapter 8) and unless a government has a strong preference for a one-sidedly export-based growth model (such as large parts of German elites do), this would be feasible without major problems. In contrast, if governments generally shift to a very restrictive ('prudent') fiscal policy after the crisis, there is a high likelihood that debt to GDP relations will even get worse, given that this restrictive policy would harm growth in many economies, particularly those relying on domestic demand. Recovering depleted state coffers via taxation, the other side of fiscal policies, will be difficult, particularly in the short run (see Chapter 10). Supporting economies via aggressive monetary policies leads to a number of unintended consequences, such as increased wealth inequality (see Chapter 8). Correspondingly, many countries will need to operate with high levels of public debt for the foreseeable future, unless they want to risk a new recession.

As long as inflation rates are low, the economy does not run at full capacity and governments find productive usage for public investments where returns are higher than the interest rates at which they can borrow, substantially increased public debt is not a problem for most economies. They can grow out of their debt, as long as the interest rate they have to pay is lower than the growth rate of the economy (and their national central bank is willing to keep interest rates low). In the current environment with low safe interest rates for public debt – lower than growth rates, which is the historical norm – public debt may come without fiscal cost (Blanchard, 2019). After all, the public debt burden is measured as a ratio between the volume of public debt and the GDP – if the latter grows faster than the volume of debt, the debt burden de facto is reduced (Stern and Zenghelis, 2021). However, for two groups of countries the situation is far more complicated. One group is heavily indebted countries in the Global South (see Chapter 23) and the other is the member countries of the Economic and Monetary Union, given that they are bound to inflexible fiscal rules.

Post-pandemic public expenditure and fiscal rules

The likely need to continue – or even further increase – high levels of public spending will be a particular problem for many countries with fiscal rules in place. Most fiscal rules put a limit upon overall public debt or annual public deficits. While virtually unknown before 1990, more than 90 countries have introduced these rules since then (Kriwoluzky et al, 2020). Fiscal rules have substantial advantages with regard to keeping public deficits low – thereby increasing fiscal firepower in case of crisis – but can also have serious disadvantages, if they are inflexible and do not allow exemptions in a situation of a sudden crisis caused by an exogenous shock (such as the pandemic).

Fiscal rules can also have different degrees of flexibility with regard to the expenditures at stakes – some only look at overall debt; others exclude debt caused by public investment, in order to avoid that public investment is severely reduced in a situation of fiscal consolidation (Ardanaz et al, 2021). Given that most governments find it more difficult to implement austerity upon other types of expenditures (for example, defence, social support), public investment often is the first victim of fiscal consolidation, often leading to a substantial reduction of long-term growth potential.

Particularly severe are the fiscal rules within the EU (see also Chapter 28). The 1992 Maastricht Treaty on the establishment of the Economic and Monetary Union prescribes that annual public deficits may not transgress 3 per cent of GDP, while the accumulated public debt is limited to 60 per cent of GDP. These debt brakes in the European 'constitution' were introduced at the insistence of Germany (Schoeller and Karlsson, 2021). The German export-led growth model competes internationally not only on product quality, but also on prices. A low domestic inflation is very helpful in international price competition. However, it is somewhat difficult to enforce the Maastricht criteria – and the 1997 Stability and Growth Pact that makes these criteria operational – via the European level institutions and countries were still able to take up higher debt, if required by an extraordinary economic situation.

The situation has aggravated after the Eurozone crisis of early 2010. Given that Germany was in a particularly powerful situation during the crisis – Southern Eurozone economies required financial support, but did not have their own central bank anymore to provide the latter (see Chapter 8) and had to pay ever higher interest rates in order to float government bonds on international financial markets – the German government insisted on a more binding regulation of the Maastricht criteria. Germany insisted upon the introduction of debt brakes within national constitutions as a precondition for financial support, thereby generalizing a crucial component of its extremely export-led model to the whole Eurozone. The European Fiscal Compact based on these rules was ratified in 2012, as a precondition for the fiscal and monetary policy interventions that mitigated the Eurozone crisis, in particular the decision of the European Central Bank (ECB) to buy government bonds in very large amounts and the establishment of the European Stability Mechanism.

During the coronavirus pandemic, the debt rules of the Stability and Growth Pact have been suspended by the European Commission in March 2020 and many EU member countries have also suspended their national debt brakes, including Germany. Germany even agreed to the establishment of a fiscal recovery package at the EU level ('Next Generation EU'), due to rising concerns about loss of buyers for German exports to many European economies (Schoeller and Karlsson, 2021: 201; see also Chapter 28).

However, the expectation of the German government and the German public is that these rules would be applied again after the end of the pandemic and public deficits would be substantially reduced in 2022/23 already (BMF 2020; Schoeller and Karlsson, 2021: 202). If these ideas are put in practice in a comprehensive manner throughout Europe, this might lead to a strong contraction of demand and stagnation in the European economy.

Towards the abolition of contraproductive debt constraints

During the coronavirus pandemic, an extremely expansive fiscal policy has stabilized our economies which would have undergone far deeper recessions otherwise. This expansion of fiscal policy has led to a record increase of levels of public debt, particularly in the economies of the Global North. After the crisis, most economies will prefer to continue operating on a high level of public debt, in order to avoid another recession. However, two groups of countries will encounter problems in this regard: on the one side highly indebted low-income countries in the Global South and on the other side member countries of the Economic and Monetary Union, given the fiscal rules of the latter.

After the coronavirus pandemic, some governments will plea for a return to pre-pandemic public debt levels. This plea will be particularly intense in countries with a one-sidedly export-led growth model such as Germany. However, a better option would be to balance out Germany's growth model, with a somewhat less pronounced role for exports and a more important role for domestic demand, including public sector-induced demand (Nölke, 2021). Given that it will be difficult to substantially increase taxation − at least with regard to conventional sources (see Chapter 10) − and that monetary policy has become very heterodox − leading to grave questions about democratic legitimacy (see Chapter 8) − we will have to put up with high levels of public debt for the foreseeable future, unless we want to risk a new recession. The most urgent political task is to get rid of contraproductive overly strict debt constraints in the member countries of the Eurozone and to assist countries in the Global South with regard to their debt load (see Chapter 23). At the very minimum, debt brakes should exclude public investment and therefore allow net new credits up to the volume of public investments.

10

Tax Policy: Conventional or Unconventional Measures?

The countries at the top of the economic hierarchy – the US, Germany and a few other economies in the Global North – still have flexibility to increase their debt (see Chapter 9 and Chapter 23) and/or to rely on money creation by their monetary authority (see Chapter 8). However, the fiscal flexibility of most other economies is limited, and they will have to resort to tax policy to fill their treasuries in the medium to long run. During the coronavirus crisis, tax policy focused on tax relief and referrals, in order to support companies and stabilize domestic demand (Collier et al, 2020). After the crisis, however, the focus of policy debates rather will be on increasing taxation, given depleted public budgets. Tax increases, however, are very unpopular politically. The key question is whether governments will respond by finding unconventional new sources of revenue or whether they will rely on the conventional ones. Given that there is strong political opposition against increases of conventional taxation, governments might turn towards unconventional measures, such as nationalization of companies or international minimum company taxation standards. The latter option has received considerable media attention since the initiative of the Biden administration in spring 2021.

Taxation in Comparative and International Political Economy

Although taxation is an issue with a long tradition in Political Economy, it did not find much attention in recent decades, outside specialized circles. In Comparative Political Economy, issues of taxation were largely neglected in the company-focused Comparative Capitalism research programme (see Part III on Domestic Institutions of Capitalism on the Supply Side), although tax policy can be seen as a modern form of industrial policy, with different functions in different varieties of capitalism (Haffert, 2019). The macroeconomic research programme on Growth Models spends more attention on tax policies. After all, the latter have played an important role in the emergence of different country-specific models after World War II, with the export-driven Continental economies focusing tax policy on encouraging savings and investment, whereas the domestic demand-driven economies use tax policy to stimulate consumption (Haffert, 2019).

In International Political Economy, the core issue for researchers has been international cooperation between governments. The focus of established international tax governance was to avoid double taxation (Rixen, 2008). More recently, scholarship has focused on tax evasion, or double non-taxation, in particular based on huge amounts of data reported by investigative journalists, such as the 'Lux Leaks' and the 'Panama Papers' (Vlcek, 2019). Given that tax evasion by large multinational corporations has become an increasingly important policy topic before the coronavirus crisis (for example, based on the work of the OECD on 'Base Erosion and Profit Shifting'/BEPS), it is highly likely that it will also play a major role in post-coronavirus capitalism.

Different options for the extraction of financial resources by the state

To finance themselves, governments either use various means of monetary policy (see Chapter 8 and Chapter 9) or extract financial resources from the private sector and households. Taxing is the most conventional way of extraction. There are several types of taxes, each of which is imposed on different socio-economic groups, and therefore it has different economic and social consequences. Any mix of taxes has to be effective economically and stable politically. In the following, we discuss five means of extractions: income tax imposed on worker wages and company profits, capital (or financial) gain tax, wealth tax, tax on transactions (indirect tax), and nationalization. We illustrate current taxation levels with the cases of Germany and the US.

Taxes on income are the most common types of extraction in modern capitalism. Income tax – or direct tax – is imposed on the flow of wealth into the hand of individuals or organizations. Therefore, income tax is perceived as more consistent with private property rights, in comparison to other forms of extraction, which are imposed on stocks such as wealth. Income tax, so to speak, is imposed on newly created wealth before it has been appropriated by the appropriator, being a worker, a firm or an investor. In recent years, since the onset of globalization and liberalization of financial flows, tax competition led to a decrease in corporate tax levels worldwide, increasing the relative burden of income imposed on wages. Between 2010 and 2020, the tax burden on wages in the US increased from 34 to 42 per cent and in Germany from 29 to 33 per cent. During the same period, corporate tax fell in the US from 8 to 7 per cent, while in Germany it increased from 2 to 3 per cent (Jarass et al, 2017).

Financial gain tax differs from income tax as it is imposed on realized capital gains once the asset is sold. Still, authorities often calculate theses taxes as a type of non-wage income tax for asset holders. Non-wage income tax did not change considerably in the US and Germany, at the level of 7 and 10 per cent of total tax revenue in the two countries respectively (Jarass et al, 2017). Indirect taxes are imposed on transactions, such as the Value Added Tax. Taxes imposed on transactions are not progressive and, therefore, social activists endorse the minimization of indirect taxes. Economists, on the other hand, often endorse taxing transactions as they are more 'efficient' and easy to implement. In the US, the revenues from transaction taxes are around 25 per cent while in Germany they are about 42 per cent (Jarass et al, 2017). The different levels of these transaction taxes can be explained by the different growth models pursued, with transaction taxes bad for consumption-led economic models, but good for export-based ones (Haffert and Mertens, 2019).

Other taxes are imposed on assets – they include inheritance taxes and wealth taxes (not to be confused with capital gain taxes). Taxing wealth rather than income is considered a more intrusive way of extraction because it breaches private property rights of individuals, which is a fundamental principle – some would say 'sacred' – of liberal market-based economies. Libertarians, as well as many liberals, oppose taxing wealth because, they argue, wealth had been already taxed (by income tax). However, in recent years, the argument in favour of taxing wealth is getting more and more support, as wealth inequality has become more significant than income inequality, as growth levels – mainly in the Global North – are lower and as the tax burden on wages has grown.

Libertarians even argue that taxation is theft (or 'legalized extortion', according to Edward Troup, the head of the UK tax authority that later joined McKinsey as tax policy advisor). There is truth to it if one accepts the principle of private property rights as sacred. From this perspective, there is no difference between taxation and straightforward nationalization: in both cases, the sovereign confiscates private property. Moreover, nationalization (without compensation) can help to refill depleted public finances, if we think of the case of oil or gas companies that have been appropriated by the state in the Global South in the past. However, even today and even in liberal democracies, governments maintain their authority to nationalize property in states of emergency, such as in war situations or natural disasters. Therefore, when we consider alternative fiscal sources of governments, nationalization should be on the table too.

Tax policies after the coronavirus crisis

While the focus of tax policy during the coronavirus crisis was on tax referrals or tax exemptions (Collier et al, 2020; Megersa, 2020), after the crisis it will rather be on tax increases, given depleted public budgets. In Germany, for example, companies expect tax reductions during the crisis, but increasing tax rates thereafter (Bischof et al, 2021: 27). Tax increases are not only a matter of delicate timing – if you start too early, you may kill the economic recovery, but if you start too late, tax payers may have already forgotten the crisis that has made expensive public measures necessary – but also of delicate weighing of political support. Increasing taxation of wages, which is currently the main source of state funding, is likely to increase inequality between wage earners and capital owners. At times of economic slowdown and increased inequality caused by the crisis, this choice is highly unpopular and may lead to public protest, possibly further weakening the legitimacy of already battered political systems. Correspondingly, we do not expect a substantial increase in income taxes in the short to medium run. Increased taxes on transactions share many disadvantages of increased income taxes as a response to the coronavirus crisis. They reduce domestic demand and affect the broad population more than the rich. However, given that their distributional effects are less obvious than in the case of income taxes and that small increases of transaction taxes can lead to a very substantial resource extraction, they may become widely used options in the medium run; in particular, in the form of the taxation of negative environmental externalities as carbon taxes (Collier et al, 2020: 10).

In European and US public discourse, the idea of wealth taxes had become popular before the crisis, often in combination with stricter measures against tax havens (Cobham et al, 2020). The crisis has made these proposals – for example, based on the works of the French economists Thomas Piketty as well as Emmanuel Saez and Gabriel Zucman – even more popular (Collier et al, 2020: 9–10). During the early stage of the crisis, it was only supported by academics and activists, and did not enter the policymaking circles yet. However, it seems likely that it may receive broader support in the medium to long run. On the one side, it has fewer negative effects on domestic demand, if compared with general taxes on transactions and many forms of income tax. On the other side, the coronavirus crisis will markedly increase levels of inequality, thereby possibly mobilizing some social support for a stronger contribution by the richer parts of society. Both arguments may also speak in favour of an increase in financial gains taxes in the long run, given the strong concentration of financial assets with the rich.

International minimum standards for company taxation

The political opposition to balancing out depleted budgets by raising taxes on wages, wealth and transactions – and the likely negative macroeconomic consequences going hand in hand with some of these tax rises – have given a new impetus to the search for finding ways to tax the economic winners of the last decade; namely, the big companies of the digital sector (for example, Alphabet (Google), Amazon, Apple, Facebook, Microsoft or Netflix). This OECD-led project had already started before the coronavirus crisis, in the form of tax reform proposals particularly focused on digital companies. The latter cause considerable problems for cross-border taxation: under traditional international agreements, multinational corporations pay taxes where production takes place. However, for solely online businesses such as Netflix or Zoom, this gives no taxing right at all for most countries where only users are located (Collier et al, 2020: 14–15).

The coronavirus crisis has given additional impetus to the OECD project started in 2018, given that digital companies are the big winners of the crisis. At the same time, tax evasion by multinational corporations triggers a particularly strong public sentiment of unfairness during the crisis (Lafitte et al, 2020). Correspondingly, work on the two-pillar OECD 'Inclusive Framework' has intensified in 2020/21. Pillar One aims at making sure that multinational corporations are also paying taxes in countries with substantial business but without physical presence. Pillar Two seeks to establish a global minimum tax for business. This initiative has received a major boost when the US government proposed a minimum taxation of at least 15 per cent in 2021, although a minimum rate of 21 per cent would be preferable (Lafitte et al, 2020). A global minimum tax threshold for business is not only very important because it drastically reduces the most important business argument against higher taxes (that is, advantages for companies based in countries with low business taxes), but also makes sure that companies cannot avoid taxation by shifting profits to tax oases. Avoiding a race to the bottom in terms of taxation of multinationals is particularly important as many governments will seek foreign direct investments after the crisis, also by providing incentives based on low taxes (Heffron and Sheehan, 2020; see also Chapter 18). A minimum taxation for corporations would also be important for fiscal reasons. A 25 per cent minimum tax, for example, would increase corporate tax revenues in the EU by €170 billion in 2021, a more than 50 per cent increase in the current amount of company tax collected in the EU annually (Barake et al, 2021).

Fair taxation has received additional attention during the crisis, given that many companies that have received state support during the crisis still were involved in manifold strategies of tax evasion. Many countries have sought to link state support for companies during the crisis to the termination of tax avoidance, but this has proven to be difficult on political and legal grounds (Collier et al, 2020: 3–5). Windfall taxes on the winners of the coronavirus crisis can potentially take on very different shapes – they can be narrowly focused on companies of the digital sectors, but also more broadly applied to all companies that have done particularly well during the crisis, as a one-time 'excess profits tax'. Still, the practical implementation of the latter is quite difficult; for example, with regard to the exact calculation of excess profits or the fact that most of these companies are based in the US (Collier et al, 2020: 8–9). The 2021 initiative of the Biden administration has also to be seen in this context.

Nationalization as an alternative means to extract resources after the crisis

Nationalization became a legitimate state measure during the crisis for two key reasons. First, fiscal emergency packages implied taping huge amounts of public money into private hands. This time round – the first time was the GFC – liquidity channelled to production facilities, rather than only to the financial sector (see Chapter 12). Governments bought large amounts of equity of national companies particularly affected by the crisis, such as airlines. Complete nationalization, therefore, would be the logical next step to providing companies with public support. Another rationale for nationalization is exercising public control over strategic industries or crucial services, another motivation strengthened by the crisis. In India, we are witnessing demands for the government to nationalize healthcare services, to equalize difference in the cost of treatment incurred at government and private hospitals (Bhaduri, 2020: 5429). Even in Switzerland, a particularly liberal country, participants to a survey experiment strongly support renationalizing the health economy (Fossati and Trein, 2020: 17). For left-wing movements, the coronavirus crisis is an opportunity to call for a nationalization of the online food-delivery businesses or of Amazon, since they have become suppliers of public goods (Marx, 2020). In response, global law firms prepare advice for investors in order to defend against nationalization risks (BakerMcKenzie, 2020; see also Chapter 19).

There is no doubt the coronavirus crisis strengthened the rationale of nationalization. This does not necessarily mean that the balance already is tipped in favour of large-scale nationalization of private businesses. However, it will not be surprising if in countries which are characterized by less hostility to such ideas – in European countries, in Latin America and obviously in East Asia – governments will become more involved in the private sector. This allows them to pursue several aims at the same time, including creating incentives to localize production chains, to protect strategic companies and industries from foreign investors and to have more influence on strategic decision-making at the firm level. However, more importantly for the purposes covered in this chapter, nationalization can also help to extract resources from the economy, by providing profits of nationalized companies to public budgets. Some sectors that previously were in public hands, such as water provision, are highly profitable in many countries. Still, public ownership is no panacea and can also have negative repercussions on the broader public (Powell and Yurchenko, 2020).

The need to mobilize unconventional measures in tax policy after corona

During the coronavirus crisis, the focus on tax policy rather was on tax deferral and tax exemptions. However, given extraordinarily high level of public debt, many governments will be forced to consider tax increases after the coronavirus recession. Increasing income or wealth taxation will be politically unpopular, whereas transaction taxes will further increase economic inequality. Correspondingly, governments may turn to unconventional sources of taxation, such as carbon taxes, international minimum standards for company taxation or even nationalizations as a means to extract resources after the crisis.

During the last 40 years, the fiscal burden on workers has increased in many cases, while at the same time the public goods they received from the state often have narrowed. Therefore, it unlikely that governments will be able politically to amass the necessary fiscal sources by increasing income tax or transaction taxes, taxes mainly financed by workers. This is the reason why the idea of a higher level of taxing on wealth has made further inroads among economists, politicians and the lay public during the coronavirus pandemic. However, if politicians really endeavour to impose higher taxes on wealth, the small but politically very powerful upper classes will revolt. If countries also cannot (or do not want to) resort to higher public debt or even more aggressive monetary policy, they need to resort to unconventional policies of fiscal extraction. Nationalizations have hardly been used for resource extraction during the last decades. Still, the pandemic will make this option look more attractive in the long run. More feasible in the short run, however, is the implementation of initiatives for company minimum taxation that have been brought up during the late phases of the crisis. If implemented, these initiatives can make a contribution for refilling depleted public coffers without causing social unrest or negative macroeconomic consequences.

11

Industrial Policy: Laissez-faire or State Leadership?

The coronavirus pandemic has led to a massive increase in state activity in the economy. Correspondingly, we may wonder whether the state retains this role after the end of the crisis or whether it returns to its pre-crisis role. This is particularly relevant in case of industrial policy; that is, government policies for the upgrading of economies. While these policies can also have regulatory character, the focus here is on an active role in complementing private investment by state-led allocation of resources. This can be done in different ways, via as state-owned enterprises (SOEs), public investment banks or state subsidies to private companies. Industrial Policy is a very controversial topic for economic liberals – a recent IMF Working Paper (Cherif and Hasanov, 2019) even was titled 'The Return of the Policy That Shall Not Be Named: Principles of Industrial Policy'. Some parties consider it indispensable for economic upgrading, while others demand that the state should keep its hand off these allocation decisions and should leave the latter to the market.

The role of industrial policy in different growth models

Country-specific growth models do not only differ with regard to their fiscal and monetary policies, but also with regard to the role of industrial policy. Particularly governments that are not satisfied with the role of their economy with regard to their position in the global hierarchy of manufacturing (see Chapter 17) often are in favour of industrial policy. In the EU, for example, the necessity for industrial policy is felt most pressing in its Southern parts. Since the introduction of the common currency, we have witnessed a growing polarization of production structures within the Eurozone, where the private debt-led economies in the South have deindustrialized to a high degree, in contrast to the export-led economies around Germany. While the latter have accumulated the technological capabilities to compete on global markets for advanced manufacturing, the Southern European economies have increasingly been locked in lower tech and non-tradeable sectors (Gräbner et al, 2020).

Industrial policy is particularly prominent as a policy in economies of the Global South that intend to catch up in terms of industrialization. Particularly in East Asia, industrial policy was never 'dead' or 'outdated'. In other countries of the Global South, however, the structural adjustment programmes prescribed by the IMF often interdicted the use of fiscal resources for these policies (Eder and Schneider, 2020: 3). Correspondingly, these countries need external financial support for implementing this strategy – support that usually is not forthcoming from international institutions such as the WB (Cherif and Hasanov, 2019: 9). Industrial policy is particularly important in the Global South in order to avoid 'development traps', such as a too strong reliance on the exploitation of natural resources or of cheap labour (Aiginger and Rodrik, 2020: 201). Without comprehensive industrial policies (or the discovery of oil resources), the odds for countries of the Global South to move to high-income status are very low (Cherif and Hasanov, 2019: 5).

Within the broader term of 'industrial policy' we can find a whole range of different concepts. The most important basic distinction is between 'horizontal' and 'vertical' industrial policy, with the latter referring to the focus of this chapter. 'Horizontal' industrial policy focuses on general framework conditions for business across all sectors of industry. 'Vertical' industrial policy – also referred to as 'selective' or 'sector-specific' – focuses on the promotion of specific industries, companies or global value chains (Eder and Schneider, 2020: 3). This promotion mostly works via financial support, but can also have a regulatory focus; for example, by demanding certain maximum carbon dioxide levels for new plants, cars or machinery. Other typical aspects of contemporary industrial policy focus on the innovation and technology infrastructure, higher education and worker training, infrastructures and networks or long-term capital access (Andreoni and Chang, 2019). Moreover, industrial policy increasingly has to be coordinated with other policies, such as competition policy or trade policy. Industrial policy traditionally focuses on manufacturing, but more recently also covers services, particularly industry-based services (Aiginger and Rodrik, 2020: 191).

The industrial policy revival before the coronavirus crisis

The role of industrial policy not only varies between countries, but also over time. While industrial policy was a core topic of mainstream economic discourses – particularly with regard to economies of the Global South – during the 1950s and 1960s, it had completely fallen out of favour during the

1980s. Since the mid-2000s – and particularly after the GFC – there has been a revival of discussions about the necessity of industrial policy, as well as about its most important guiding principles (Cherif and Hasanov, 2019; Andreoni and Chang, 2019; Aiginger and Rodrik, 2020). These discussions have not only remained in the academic sphere but also have affected policymaking as witnessed by the IMF Working Paper, but particularly by the European Commission's communication about 'A New Industrial Strategy for Europe' (European Commission, 2020).

There are several reasons that have led to a revival of industrial policy during the last 15 years (Eder and Schneider, 2020: 3–4). The GFC has demonstrated the importance of stable industrial structures even in an era of financialization (see Chapter 12 and Chapter 13). The fight against climate change requires the development and marketization of new technologies. Particularly, small companies and start-ups cannot stem the latter without financial support. The same applies to the technical transformation of the 'fourth industrial revolution' that goes hand in hand with digitalization, automatization and artificial intelligence. Finally, the rise of China also in sectors with advanced technologies has triggered geo-economic motivations for keeping an edge, particularly in the EU (see Chapter 27).

Still, the need for industrial policy has remained controversial. Critics of industrial policy argue that it is a waste of fiscal resources, because governments are assumed to be much less qualified for picking the winners of future economic developments than private business. In addition, the assumption is that industrial policy support programmes fund activities that business would have undertaken anyway – a critique that seems to be valid in case of large and well-funded companies, in contrast to small companies (Criscuolo et al, 2019). However, many of these critiques are based on deeply held normative convictions (about the superiority of liberal markets for the allocation of economic resources), not on empirical study: 'The consensus among economists is that industrial policy usually fails, but the econometric evidence is surprisingly sparse' (Criscuolo et al, 2019: 49). Finally, the focus of industrial policy has changed during the last decades, making the typical liberal critique on the limited ability of the state to pick economic winners less convincing. Particularly, in the context of the fight against climate change, the focus now is on mission-oriented industrial policy; that is, as an instrument to realize politically set targets (Mazzucato, 2018; Aiginger and Rodrik, 2020: 192).

The revival continues: the after-coronavirus agenda in industrial policy

After the coronavirus pandemic, many of the reasons for the revival of industrial policy during the last 10–15 years have become even more pressing, while new reasons have emerged (Eder and Schneider, 2020). In the EU, the increasing tensions between the US and China, as well as the particularly fast recovery of the Chinese economy after the coronavirus crisis have intensified the geo-economic motivation for industrial policy, particularly under the heading of 'technological sovereignty'. The comprehensive turn towards digital companies such as Amazon or Zoom has further strengthened the impetus to support industrial development in related sectors. Moreover, the disruptions of global production networks during the crisis has triggered considerations to reshore some productions processes, particularly with regard to some vital products in the field of health, but also with regard to crucial components of many manufacturing processes such as semi-conductors or car batteries. Given that market processes alone do not provide sufficient developments in this direction, industrial policy becomes indispensable. Moreover, the coronavirus has made it usual practice in many countries that the state intervenes heavily into the economy via financial support. Against this background, industrial policy looks much less exotic than before the crisis. Finally, the pandemic did not end the strong political attention allocated to the fight against climate change and the related proposals for a 'Green New Deal'. The European Commission even has put a 'European Green Deal' at the centre of the economic reconstruction programme after the crisis.

However, there is also the possibility that industrial policy encounters a short spring in many countries, due to fiscal constraints. This possibility is particularly likely not only for highly indebted economies of the Global South, but also Southern European economies that are under strict fiscal surveillance by the EU (see Chapter 9). This would be very unfortunate. A study of economic transformation during World War II under US President Roosevelt – the last challenge of similar magnitude – indicates that these transformations succeed fairly quickly, if the state takes on a direct role, particularly with regard to its ability to guarantee long-term investment and to bear major economic risks (Bossie and Mason, 2020).

Towards a rejuvenation of international industrial policy via the UNIDO

Industrial policy has seen a revival in many countries even before the coronavirus pandemic. The necessity to rebuild economies after the crisis will strengthen the case for continuing in this direction, with a particular focus not only for support of digital and climate change technologies, but also the near-shoring of certain parts of global value chains. The most important factor that might work against the tendency for a rejuvenation of industrial policies could be the lack of financial resources in fiscally constrained economies (see Chapter 9). This could even lead to an increasing gap between wealthy and less wealthy economies.

In order to avoid this problematical development, we need an intergovernmental effort to fund industrial policies in less economically fortunate countries. A useful focus for these activities could be the United Nations Industrial Development Organization (UNIDO), an international organization that has been financially, intellectually and politically marginalized during the last decades in international development, but now could be given a second spring.

PART III

Domestic Institutions of Capitalism on the Supply Side

Comparative Political Economy does not only study country variation and macroeconomic policy issues on the demand side, but also institutional differences between countries on the supply side. The predominant approach here is called 'Comparative Capitalisms' (Clift, 2014; Menz, 2017; Nölke, 2019b). It analyses the differences between the economic institutions of countries at the company level. The focus is on country-specific comparative advantages for companies with regard to certain products and services that go along with these institutions. Among the most important company-level institutions are: the system of corporate governance (that is, who owns and directs a company); the financial sector (as the source for funding); industrial relations (that is, the relations with workers); and training systems, innovation and competition policy.

As we shall see, the coronavirus crisis has substantial implications with regard to each of these institutions. In order to stabilize companies during the crisis, many states have taken on a more prominent role within corporate governance; for example, via (partial) state ownership (Chapter 12). In contrast to the GFC in 2008/09, this crisis did not emerge in the financial sector. Still, the financial sector has contributed to deepening the crisis, particularly via private equity investments in the health sector (Chapter 13). While the crisis led to a short spring of 'covid corporatism' – that is, a close collaboration between companies, unions and the state – labour unions did not play a crucial role in economic reconstructions and may also be sidelined in their role within vocational training systems (Chapter 14). In terms of innovation, the pandemic stimulated two systems in particular: on the one side, it demonstrated the important role of state support for innovation (for example, with regard to vaccine development); on the other, it highlighted the useful role of frugal innovation (Chapter 15). Finally, the pandemic raises severe issues for competition policy, both with regard to the massive utilization of state aid and to the market power of US digital behemoths (Chapter 16).

12

Corporate Governance: Public Responsibility or Shareholder Value?

During the coronavirus crisis and the related recession, many governments have initiated massive public rescue operations for business, given that the latter was collapsing in sectors such as tourism. A prominent part of these operations was the increase in public control over companies. Increasing public control took different forms. Often, this meant increasing public (partial) ownership, directly via state bodies or indirectly via public banks or sovereign wealth funds. In other cases, governments introduced regulations with regard to preventing the takeover of prized companies by foreign investors. Government financial support measures during the crisis sometimes have led to controversial discussions about the behaviour on the side of business, in particular when the latter at the same time have used share buy-backs, provided dividend payments to shareholders or paid a massive bonus for top management. Critics argued that companies were using taxpayers' money for the enrichment of company owners and top management. Companies, in turn, defended the practice by highlighting their obligations towards shareholders or the need to retain top talent. Will post-corona capitalism focus on shareholder value or on the public responsibility of companies?

Corporate governance in different models and phases of capitalism

We can explain the competing rationales behind this controversy by linking them to various themes in Comparative Political Economy; namely, the discussions on financialization and on corporate governance in different types of capitalism (Clift, 2014: 230–56; Menz, 2017: 146–77; Vermeiren 2021: 118–46). The process of financialization of capitalism has unfolded since the late 1970s. Financial markets, actors within these markets and a financial market perspective on economic processes increasingly became important during the last four decades, affecting many aspects of the economy (see also Chapter 8, Chapter 13, Chapter 17 and Chapter 31).

In case of corporate governance, financialization means the rise of 'shareholder value' conceptions. These conceptions demand the maximization of short-term returns for the owners of the firm. In order to implement this target, companies have different instruments at their disposal. One typical instrument is share buy-backs; that is, companies using retained earnings or taking up a loan in order to buy their own shares. This will increase demand for the latter, drive up their notations on the stock markets and make existing shareholders richer. Another typical instrument of shareholder value capitalism is stock options. These options enable the company staff to buy shares of their own company for a set price – a very attractive option if these stocks note at a higher price on the exchange in the future. By issuing stock options, shareholders make sure that top management develops a strong material interest into the positive development of share prices. Alternative models of corporate governance usually are grouped under the heading of 'stakeholder capitalism'. In these alternative models, companies do not only have obligations to their current owners, but also to other stakeholders, most notably their employees, but also to, for example, their local communities or the state. Moreover, stakeholder capitalism also takes a more long-term view on companies. The long-term existence of the latter is prized; for example, with regard to substantial investments that reduce resource available for payments to current shareholders, but might benefit the company in the long run.

While financialization is a process that has been affecting all capitalist economies to varying degrees during the last decades, Comparative Political Economy also identifies typical differences between corporate governance practices along national lines. The identification of these differences stand at the centre of the 'Comparative Capitalisms' research programme (see also the other chapters of Part III). The most well-known approach within this programme is called 'Varieties of Capitalism' (Hall and Soskice, 2001). It poses the fundamental juxtaposition of 'liberal' and 'coordinated' types of capitalism. Corporate governance in the first type, modelled after the example of the US, already before financialization gave an important role to shareholders in principle, but in practice retained the most powerful role for management, due to the dispersion of shareholders and the related coordination problems. However, the process of financialization since the 1980s – triggered by financial liberalization, the growing importance of institutional investors (such as pensions funds) and an increasing amount of hostile takeovers (a threat for management) – shifted the power to shareholders and (transnational) capital markets. In the coordinated type of capitalism, modelled after the cases of Germany and Japan, capital markets are much less relevant. Instead, long-term coordination with stakeholders is very important, most notably including families and other block-holders (as concentrated ownership), 'house banks' as most important providers of financial resources and employees, as in the German institution of worker co-determination. More recently, the Comparative Capitalism research programme has widened its geographical focus towards emerging economies such as China, India or Brazil. In 'state-permeated capitalism' (Nölke et al, 2020), corporate governance is dominated by national capital, with an important role for the state.

Arguably, the Great Depression and World War II played an important role in the emergence of the different types of corporate governance systems. New Deal legislation in the US helped to protect outside investors, employee representation on company boards intensified stakeholder conceptions in Germany and the 'keiretsu' structure in Japan was the result of the break-up of family-owned corporations during US occupation (Gelter and Puaschunder, 2021: 13–16). Correspondingly, we may well ask what kind of changes may be the result of the coronavirus pandemic, arguably the largest economic and political crisis since WWII.

Corporate governance and the coronavirus crisis: moving away from shareholder value

Developments during the coronavirus crisis and the related recession indicate that corporate governance practices in many countries move away from shareholder value. More specifically, we can observe three developments that point in this direction (Gelter and Puaschunder, 2021). First, the crisis has highlighted the importance of corporate resilience. This has many companies to revise the trend towards financial leanness (for example, by share buy-backs) that may become a dangerous liability during a crisis. Second, the crisis has led to an increased tendency towards nationalism in corporate governance; for example, with regard to foreign ownership. Third, the pandemic, but also increasing concerns about climate change, have increased the importance of stakeholder considerations into corporate governance.

The coronavirus pandemic has led to considerable economic losses for many companies. This is particularly dangerous for those companies that had pursued a particularly pronounced policy of shareholder value. Similar to cross-border logistics and just-in-time production, companies that kept a very lean line financially by taking on a lot of debt and providing a maximum value for shareholders by share buy-backs and dividend payments were put in a more dangerous situation by the crisis. Those companies that kept a lot of cash on their books – instead of handing it out to shareholders – had a cushion for this situation of economic crisis (Ding et al, 2020). Correspondingly, the shareholder value orientation received a pushback, as for example a marked reduction of share buy-backs. In part this was also due to government regulations that reserved crisis support packages for those companies that do not repurchase shares or pay out dividends within a certain period of time (Gelter and Puaschunder, 2021: 20–38).

The second major corporate governance tendency during the crisis was the increased attention given to national security considerations and to option for companies to take on partial state ownership in order to stabilize during the crisis (Gelter and Puaschunder, 2021: 38–48). Empirical evidence indicates that state ownership of companies has increased quite substantially during the pandemic, particularly in sectors such as airlines. However, against the two general models provided by Varieties of Capitalism scholarship, state ownership already was a prominent feature before the crisis, not only in emerging economies, but also in countries such as France or Poland (OECD, 2020b). Correspondingly, it is not necessarily a new phenomenon, but in many countries a strengthening of existing tendencies. Moreover, next to providing cash injections – or loans/loan guarantees – states also reacted to the coronavirus crisis by introducing (or rather strengthening existing) regulations in order to prevent the takeover of firms by foreign buyers (UNCTAD, 2020a). The EU, for instance, introduced a framework for the screening of foreign direct investments in 2020. Very often, these regulations were implicitly directed against firms based in the People's Republic of China (see Chapter 18).

While increasing state ownership during the coronavirus pandemic has led to debates about the priorities companies with state support are supposed to pursue, this has also affected companies without the latter (Gelter and Puaschunder, 2021: 48–64). The pandemic has highlighted the need – and the opportunity – to address major societal challenges via intensified cooperation between the state and business. On the one side, the pandemic has further increased existing social inequalities (see Chapter 7), thereby increasing the need to address this major challenge. On the other side, the concerted efforts to combat the health challenge witnessed during the crisis have led to demands for an equally concerted effort with regard to climate protection after the crisis (see Chapter 24). In both cases, concepts of stakeholder capitalism have led to demands for problem-solving contributions by companies. Empirically, one of the most widely visible cases for these demands has been the annual letters that the CEO of Blackrock had sent to companies in 2020 and 2021, urging them to pay increased attention to issues of climate change and to stakeholder concerns – today called 'ESG' (Environment, Social, Governance) – in more general (Blackrock, 2021). Particularly, due to its management of numerous passively managed index funds (shares not selected by a manager, but simply mirroring an established index such as the S&P 500), most corporations can hardly risk to ignore demands articulated by Blackrock (or by Vanguard or State Street, the other 'Big 3' large fund management investors).

The future of corporate governance: struggles about companies' public accountability

Given strongly increased public support or even partial state ownership of companies during the crisis, it is unlikely that we will see a return to a system of corporate governance purely led by the principles of the maximization of shareholder value during the near future. This tendency away from shareholder value is also supported by the apparent dangers for financially lean corporations during the crisis and the increasing importance of ESG concerns that started already before the pandemic.

Increasing state ownership of companies creates important policy issues. In contrast to a shareholder value-based system where the purpose of the corporation is very clear and easy to measure, state ownership – and stakeholder-based models in general – raises questions about the balance between different company purposes. For example, how shall we weigh the concerns of the taxpayers against the concerns of employees and against climate change concerns? We have to choose between very different options here. The OECD (2020b), for instance, advises against 'political interference'; that is, for a passive role of state owners on company boards and rather favours temporarily very limited state ownership with a clear exist strategy, in order not to disadvantage other corporations. Alternatively, governments can use public ownership to impinge public priorities upon companies. Since increased public ownership of companies does not automatically lead to the maximization of benefits for society, we need to develop accountability mechanisms that ensure that companies receiving state support indeed follow public priorities to a certain degree, such as improving climate protection or avoiding lay-offs (or avoiding tax payments). As we have noted earlier for the OECD, this is a controversial issue, since it conflicts with the competing concept of shareholder value. Moreover, the exact design of these accountability mechanisms is important. Very often, increased public ownership leads to the appointment of public sector representatives on company boards. However, these representatives usually are not parliamentarians, but rather staff based in public banks, sovereign wealth funds or ministries of finance. Given the very indirect responsibility of these representatives to the voter, we may need a system where they justify their major decisions with regard to the steering of companies to the wider public.

13

Finance: Fragile or Stable?

In contrast to the 2008/09 Great Recession, the Northern financial sector was not the origin of the coronavirus recession. Still, it has been massively affected by the recession, although the emergency rescue operations by the central banks have avoided a major damage during the early phase of the crisis by providing massive injections of liquidity into the financial system. Still, its medium-term stability is not warranted, given the large number of highly indebted companies in the Global North as well as in the Global South in particular. A large number of credit defaults may create additional stress for banks and those non-banks that have acquired related financial assets. Given the strong transnational interconnectedness within the financial sector, these problems will not be limited to single economies but can easily spread globally, as witnessed during the GFC. How is potential destabilization of the financial sector possible in spite of the regulatory flurry of the previous decade that was meant to prevent a repetition of a major financial crisis? Scholarship on financialization in Political Economy is able to answer this question. The regulatory measures put in place after the last crisis did not reduce the strongly increased – and potentially highly fragile – role of the financial sector, but were limited to ironing out some of its more obvious inconsistencies. This raises the question whether post-coronavirus financial sector regulation should continue this path or opt for a substantial shrinking and national compartmentalization of the financial sector altogether.

Finance in different models of capitalism

The traditional 'Varieties of Capitalism' approach in Comparative Political Economy distinguishes between the financial market-based systems in Liberal Market Economies (LMEs) and the bank-based systems in Coordinated Market Economies (CMEs) (Hall and Soskice, 2001). Whereas the LME model is assumed to be able to quickly mobilize large volumes of finance for radical innovations, the CME model is assumed to have its strength in patient finance for long-term incremental innovations (Clift, 2014: 230–56; Menz,

2017: 146–77; Vermeiren, 2021: 147–73). The extension of this approach to emerging economies adds two alternatives for company finance: on the one side, the dependence on foreign direct investments and on foreign banks in the Eastern European Dependent Market Economy (DME) model (Nölke and Vliegenthart, 2009); and on the other side, the focus on national control via public (bank) support in the state-permeated capitalisms of China and India (Nölke and Claar, 2013).

However, during the last four to six decades, the financial systems in the Global North (and some of the financially more open emerging economies, such as Brazil, South Africa and Turkey) have changed substantially in the process of 'financialization' (see also Chapter 12). Although the process of financialization has become increasingly broad and multifaceted (Heires and Nölke, 2014; Mader et al, 2020), we can still broadly define it as 'the increasing dominance of financial actors, markets, practices, measurements, and narratives at various scales, resulting in a structural transformation of economies, firms (including financial institutions), states and households' (Aalbers, 2016: 2). Financialization affects not all economies to a similar degree – it is particularly pronounced in the US – and it is based on a global hierarchy, with a dominant role for the US dollar. During the process of financialization, the old distinction between financial market-based and bank-based systems of finance has become mostly obsolete, except for small local banks. Nowadays, savings deposits have become less relevant for large banks in formerly bank-based systems; these banks rather rely on the mobilization of short-term loans on money markets – a practice that is called 'liability management' (Beck and Knafo, 2020: 142–4).

Since the GFC, the process of financialization has increasingly been supported by the very liberal monetary policy of the Northern central banks. Ultra-low interest rates not only drive many households into the acquisition of shares (instead of maintaining conventional interest-bearing savings), but also allow financial market actors the acquisition of an increasing number of assets. These assets notably include real estate (Blakeley, 2021), but also (parts of) companies. A crucial ingredient of processes of financialization is the growing importance of the shadow banking sector. Shadow banking refers to financial sector companies that are not supervised by the banking authorities – and also are supposed to survive without the specific stabilizing institutions for the banking sector, such as deposit insurance and liquidity provision by the central bank lending facility (Wullweber, 2020: 28–34). Although much less well known than conventional banking, shadow banking has been the most quickly growing sector of finance for the last three decades, with higher profits and less regulation than investment or retail banking. For example, shadow banks do not require the large capital and cash buffers that are required for ordinary banks. Shadow banking is also less transparent than commercial banking, given that shadow banks mostly lack supervision. Finally, shadow banking also has become more controversial than conventional banking, given that it provides particularly high earnings to its owners and staff, while at the same time frequently putting much short-term pressure on workers' remuneration (Neely and Carmichael, 2021: 5–6).

Among the most important shadow banking institutions are private equity funds and hedge funds. Private equity funds typically invest in companies that are not listed on the (public) stock exchange – or in companies that are listed there, but are then taken private by these companies. Usually, they take up a lot of debt in order to finance these acquisitions – debt that the acquired company has to service. They strongly influence the management of the acquired companies, with the target to sell the latter at a higher price after some years. Hedge funds use similar strategies, but also target companies in public stock markets and usually operate on a shorter time horizon (Neely and Carmichael, 2021: 2).

Fuel for the crisis: private equity and the US health sector during the pandemic

Private equity funds have considerable activities in the health sector, including hospitals, urgent care and ambulances. Studying these activities in an exemplary way allows us to gauge the interaction between the financial sector and the pandemic. The classical private equity business model in the health sector is leveraged buy-outs; that is, the funds are buying one platform company and several small health providers, loading them with the debt necessary for the acquisition, combining these health providers into one large one with substantial market and price-setting power and then selling this combined health provider with considerable profits to major hospitals or insurance companies. This is a large-scale activity, with 885 deals and US$100 billion capital invested in the US in 2018 alone; in comparison, private equity investments in the health sector stood at less than US$5 billion in 2018 (Appelbaum and Batt, 2020: 3, 14).

Private equity investments in the US health sector increased inequality even before the pandemic in several ways. In spite of the economies of scales that go hand in hand with consolidation, private insurers had to pay strong price increases, due to the market power of the consolidated health providers vis-à-vis insurance companies and local healthcare systems. Although private equity funders claim that their activity in the market is indispensable with regard to injecting additional capital to fund new technologies and facilities, the focus of their management decisions rather was on maximizing the cash flow; for example, by exercising 'pressure on doctors to increase volumes of patients seen per day, to overprescribe diagnostic tests or perform unnecessary procedures, or to save on costs by using shoddier but less costly supplies and devices' (Appelbaum and Batt, 2020: 5). Typically, private equity firms set a tough '100 days' performance target for acquired firms that usually only can be reached by putting pressure on workers in terms of cutting hours or reducing payments. Given the high debt load, acquired companies are over-proportionally prone to financial distress or even bankruptcy.

On the other side, private equity (PE) deals are very profitable for the PE firm (such as Bain Capital, Blackstone or KKR) and the PE fund. The latter usually belongs to pension funds, sovereign wealth funds or very wealthy individuals; it is not open to small investors. Usually, the PE fund buys a company and uses the assets of the company as collateral for the credit to fund the acquisition, with roughly 70 per cent of the latter funded by credit and 30 per cent by an equity injection of the fund. The acquired company – not the PE firm, nor the PE fund – has not only to pay back the credit, it also usually has to pay a 'monitoring fee' to the PE firm. Often, the acquired company is asked to issue bonds – with 'junk' status, given the high company debt – in order to pay dividends to the PE firm and the PE fund. Usually, PE funds sell the acquired – or consolidated – company after three to five years, with 20 per cent of the gains going to the PE firm that has managed the deal (Appelbaum and Batt, 2020: 6–8).

Even before the pandemic, private equity activity in the US health sector – via a massive debt overhang – had negative repercussions on health provision in many – mostly rural – regions in the US; for example, by causing the need to sell or even close hospitals to reduce debt (Appelbaum and Batt, 2020: 28–41). Another problem caused by private equity investments in the US healthcare sector is related to their strong investments in the urgent care sub-segment. Private equity funds focused on the consolidation of these centres in favour of wealthier suburbs of Sunbelt cities, given the highest concentration of well-insured patients in these locations. As a result, the distribution of urgent care clinics in the US has become extremely skewed. As of 2019, 78 per cent of these clinics were based in suburban parts of large metropolitan areas and only 5 per cent in small towns and rural areas, where they would have been important to provide good medical care to people with limited access to the latter (Appelbaum and Batt, 2020: 44).

During the pandemic, the hollowing out of the US health system via private equity investments backfired in a deadly way (Neely and Carmichael, 2021: 7–9; see also Chapter 1). Due to limitations on investments, health workers had insufficient stocks of personal protective equipment (PPE). Moreover, pressure to reduce staff costs made it very hard to fill shifts when staff caught the virus. Women (particularly women of colour) have suffered particularly severely from PPE shortfalls and understaffed health facilities, given that they make for 9 out of 10 nurses and nursing assistants, the most vulnerable group among the thousands of healthcare workers that died from COVID-19. The consolidation of the sector also has cut off many rural areas from any access to healthcare, while other hospitals developed a high risk of bankruptcy, given that the pandemic prevented their usual income based on elective surgeries based on insurance. Normally, private equity funds should have made major losses during the pandemic, due to the very fragile financial situation of their medical investments even before the crisis. The Fed, however, rescued the private equity sector by setting up a major acquisition programme for junk bonds.

The state–finance nexus: financial sector stabilization via monetary policy 'firepower'

Many observers expected that the pandemic would lead to a massive financial market crisis, comparable to the GFC. Not only states, but also many companies and consumers had accumulated huge debt. Particularly risky debt loads for consumers are recorded in the case of car loans and student loans, whereas for business the focus of major risks is on the leveraged loans and junk bonds mentioned earlier. Vulture capital funds that acquire distressed debt in a crisis in order to sell it at a higher price afterwards already were preparing for major acquisitions. Banks had to calculate with high numbers of non-performing loans, given that many companies – particularly in the services sectors – did not find any customers anymore. Indeed, financial sector actors reacted with a massive run for safety and liquidity in February/March 2020 (Wullweber, 2020: 49–54).

However, the expected major crisis did not (yet) take place, at least in most countries of the Global North, although non-performing loan projections for the countries of the Southern and Eastern EU are worryingly high (Kasinger et al, 2021: 14–15). Governments and central banks stabilized the Northern economies with massive doses of fiscal and monetary policy (see Chapter 8 and Chapter 9). Whereas fiscal policy was particularly important for households and business, for the financial sector, the support via monetary policy was crucial, based on an extremely close cooperation between central banks and financial market players (Wójcik and Ioannou, 2020: 393). The US Federal Reserve even went so far to buy up junk bonds by shadow banks, although shadow banks such as private equity firms operate in an unregulated environment and are supposed to carry their losses themselves; this is also why they normally should only be open to super-rich investors who can afford these losses. Given the Fed intervention, investors rediscovered their interest in junk bonds, even leading to a record inflow into the segment in early April 2020 (Wullweber, 2020: 54). Correspondingly, very loose monetary policy during the pandemic again fuels the process of financialization, leading to further wealth inequality between those who have access to cheap loans (notably, financial sector actors) and those who don't (Blakeley, 2021: 91–3).

The global financial hierarchy: emerging economies and speculative flows

Not all countries were able to shield their financial sectors with massive injections of fiscal and monetary support during the coronavirus crisis. Most countries of the Global South did not have the fiscal means and the monetary credibility for this type of activity. The coronavirus pandemic has seriously affected many of these economies by reducing their export revenues and remittances. Moreover, emerging economies suffered a second challenge; namely, massive speculative financial outflows (Sokol and Pataccini, 2020: 6). Some years after the GFC, speculative flows into emerging markets had increased very substantially, particularly because of the low interest environment in the Global North (and the much higher rates in the Global South). At the onset of the pandemic, however, financial investors panicked and withdrew huge amounts of speculative investments from emerging economies, in favour of US dollars (Wójcik and Ioannou, 2020: 389). In order to stem against the outflow, some emerging economies have increased their reliance on foreign currency debt (for example, Argentina, Turkey and Ukraine), thereby increasing their future vulnerability to shifts in external financing conditions (IMF, 2020: 21; see also Chapter 23).

The speculative back and forth has very negative economic repercussions on emerging economies, the multi-year inflows leading to currency overvaluation (a major hindrance for domestic industry), the sudden outflows leading to large currency depreciations and increasing spreads for government bonds. Ironically, the problem of massive speculative flows towards and away from the Global South will probably return. Given the very aggressive monetary policy by the Northern central banks, investors again take up cheap loans and speculate upon the much higher interest rates in the Global South. The later tightening of monetary policy in the Global North then may lead to another financial crisis in the Global South, given that it provides an incentive to withdraw speculative investments in the latter.

Towards a reversal of financialization

During the coronavirus pandemic, we have seen how the process of financialization – particularly leveraged buy-outs in the health sector by private equity firms – has aggravated the crisis. Operations by private equity companies have contributed to the severity of the pandemic and have deepened socio-economic inequalities in the US. Financialization – for example, by shared buy-backs and share options – strips companies of the capital they require in a crisis. Normally, this would have led to broad waves of insolvencies and non-performing loans, but the coordinated intervention by the fiscal and particularly by monetary policy has prevented this wave in the Global North. The Global South was somewhat less fortunate, due to more limited fiscal and monetary firepower, but also due to speculative financial flows. Post-coronavirus capitalism will remain fragile, unless the process of financialization is reversed.

Although the central bank interventions have prevented a worse financial crisis, it comes with highly problematical side effects, in particular with further deepening the grave inequalities caused by the process of financialization. Given that the coronavirus crisis is the third major crisis in two decades that would only be limited by massive monetary policy interventions – the same was necessary after the burst of the 'dotcom bubble' and the GFC – and that the flurry of regulatory activity after the last crisis did not make these interventions superfluous, it is high time for a drastic reversal in the field of finance. After the coronavirus crisis, we should generally limit the process of financialization that has made our economic systems ever more crisis prone during the last four decades. Tighter banking regulation alone is not sufficient, given that the sector is notorious for finding loopholes. Most importantly, we need to break the central bank–shadow banking nexus (Braun and Gabor, 2020). Future economic stabilization programmes during a major crisis should rather focus on fiscal policies, by allowing central banks in the Global North to support governments – or citizens – directly, instead of taking the monetary policy detour via the banking system (see Chapter 8).

14

Industrial Relations and Training: Strengthening or Weakening of Unions?

The coronavirus health crisis has highlighted the importance of many forms of low-paid labour for our societies. At the same time, many people have acknowledged the miserable working conditions of these people; for example, Amazon warehouse and delivery workers and workers in the meat industry, but also of bus drivers and retail assistants. It has also led to quite substantial changes in the relations between employers and employees. How will the crisis affect the relationship between the latter in the long run? For example, will the more widespread practice of working from home during the health crisis lead to a weakening of labour unions? Or will the latter be strengthened because gig workers have realized their vulnerability during the crisis and become organized in trade unions? And how will the education and training systems of young people be affected by the crisis – will the role of unions in the latter be marginalized or strengthened?

Industrial relations and training systems in Comparative Capitalism

In order to develop a more precise idea of how these questions can be answered, it is again useful to turn to concepts of Comparative Capitalism and their treatment of industrial relations and training systems (Menz, 2017: 100–45; Nölke et al, 2020: 187–90; Vermeiren, 2021: 90–117).) Industrial relation systems and the related systems of Vocational Education and Training (VET) are a core topic of Comparative Capitalism approaches and their distinctions between Coordinated and Liberal Market Economies in the Northern economies and between the Hierarchical and State-permeated Economies in the South as well as the Dependent Economies in Eastern Europe. Industrial relations and VET are closely connected: both depend on the power balance between employers and unions; both are crucial for incomes and career trajectories for large parts of the population (Menz, 2017: 100). More specifically, the combination of industrial relations and training systems is assumed to be crucial for the attainment of crucial institutional advantages in different types of capitalism. For example, sector-wide wage-setting and vocational training not only enables the development of crucial skills for incremental innovations in CMEs, but also helps to avoid the problem of poaching where companies hire workers trained by competing companies (Vermeiren, 2021: 101–5).

In the ideal type, industrial relations in CMEs feature corporatist and rather consensual relations between capital and labour, based on comprehensive agreements between strong labour unions and strong business associations on the sectoral and national level. LMEs, in contrast, showcase pluralist, market-based and often confrontational industrial relations with few collective agreements. Emerging market types of capitalism range somewhat in-between. Whereas Dependent Market Economies (DMEs) still contain some comprehensive company-based agreements in order to appease skilled labour with good working conditions, industrial relations in the Latin American Hierarchical Market Economies (HMEs) and in the Asian State-permeated Market Economies (SMEs) are strongly segmented, ranging between small well-protected segments on the one hand and large informal sectors on the other (Nölke et al, 2020: 185–96). In perspective, Germany and other Central, Western and Northern European economies that are close to the CME type are an outlier, due to the powerful role of unions and employer associations. However, the latter economies also have witnessed some changes during the last three decades – most notably a tendency towards decentralization of wage bargaining, the weakening of unions as well as employer associations and the emergence of a large marginal employment sector, particularly in Germany (Menz, 2017: 109–17; Vermeiren, 2021: 105–9).

The core dividing line between different types of capitalism with regard to VET is on the question whether the latter is based on a comprehensive formal system based on sectoral cooperation between the social partners (employers and unions) or rather on individualistic qualification measures based on short-term company requirements. Whereas the former is typical for CMEs (usually long-term workplace-based apprenticeships for specific vocations), the latter is prevalent in LMEs (Menz, 2017: 137–44). Emerging markets' models of capitalism rather range in-between, with comprehensive training for small groups of workers in the formal sectors and the large majority of workers – particularly in the informal sector – receiving very little formal training or none at all (Nölke et al, 2020: 189–96).

Of course, the development within specific countries does not necessarily stick to the theoretical models. For example, some employers in Germany became hostile to 'over-training' in the traditional system and demanded more often to focus more clearly on company-specific training, whereas privatization processes in Latin America led to a reduction of comprehensive VET provided by parastatal enterprises (Avis et al, 2021: 1–2). Moreover, an increasing number of the young prefer a university education over vocational training, leading to a smaller pool of highly qualified applicants for apprenticeships (Menz, 2017: 143). Finally, both CME- and LME-type vocational training is also challenged by Marxist critics. In their perspective, the focus of VET on 'human capital formation' is wrong in principle and should be replaced by a completely different approach: 'In this instance VET stands as a public pedagogy that refuses a narrow instrumentalism and exclusionary associated with waged employment. It would be able to address the needs of the unpaid and those excluded from waged employment but who are nevertheless engaged in really useful labour' (Avis et al, 2021: 13).

From 'Covid Corporatism' to further marginalization of labour unions

Comparative Capitalism perspective would expect very divergent developments in industrial relations systems, depending on the type of capitalism. Strongly increasing unemployment might weaken the negotiation position of labour in the LMEs, but also in the HMEs and SMEs of the South, driving in the latter even more people into informality. In CMEs, fairly strong unions would prevent this increase in unemployment, but would give in in terms of payment, in order to preserve the competitiveness of companies.

At least during the early phase of the crisis, empirical developments did not always fit with these expectations. A particularly striking example is the case of the UK. As one of the archetypical LMEs, one could have expected a further weakening of labour, due to increasing unemployment after the crisis. Instead, we witnessed 'fiscal activism on a gargantuan scale, instituting an economy-wide wage subsidy and openly contemplating rescuing, and possibly even nationalizing, large swathes of the private sector. ... At the company level, firms and their workers have been cooperating, amidst the pandemic on adjustments to employment patterns, wage freezes and arrangements for social distancing' (Coulter, 2020: 534). Economies leaning towards the CME type, however, rather followed the predicted pattern. Germany has revitalized its 'Kurzarbeit' (short-time working) scheme that already has stabilized the economy during the GFC, whereas unions and employers in countries such as Belgium and Denmark collaborated with each other (and the government) in order to preserve jobs. In the Global South, scarce financial means for income-support programmes have limited opportunities for corporatist collaboration. Moreover, particularly in Arab states, tripartite dialogue between governments, trade unions and employers associations was more limited in comparison with Europe and 'trade unions operating in countries with less consolidated industrial relations ... expressed their dissatisfaction regarding social partners' insufficient involvement in decision-making processes' (ILO, 2021: 24).

How can we explain the deviance of the UK from the expected pattern? A crucial argument is that governments were seeking consensus during a situation of deep crisis in order not to cause even more social unrest, in addition to the unrest already caused by the harsh public health measures put in place to combat the pandemic (Coulter, 2020: 534). Some of the labour-friendly measures obviously were motivated by macroeconomic concerns. Without, for example, furlough schemes the recession would have been even deeper and unemployment broader, due to domestic demand reduction. Additionally, the more positive assessment of stakeholder concepts of the corporation (see Chapter 12) may have supported a more constructive engagement with the representatives of labour. And in other cases, reasons may have been idiosyncratic, as with the UK Tory government's attempt to retain the labour-leaning constituencies won during the last elections.

However, many of these factors are temporary and 'Covid Corporatism' may prove to be a short fad. We can see this tendency already in Australia. While the pandemic initially led to intense collaboration between the government, trade unions and business and to the setting up of a wage subsidy scheme (JobKeeper), later developments indicate that the government rather intends to use the crisis for a deregulation agenda (Forsyth, 2020). When governments lose their interest in the crisis-soothing support by labour unions, the latter have to rely on their membership in order to extricate concessions via collective bargaining. Union membership and collective bargaining, however, has been constantly waning since the heydays of corporatism in the 1960s and 1970s. Moreover, most of the 'labour-friendly' measures put in place during the pandemic have been put in place without substantial involvement of labour unions, rather based on a unilateral government decision. For the EU, a comprehensive study notes that 'it is striking that over 50 per cent of legislative measures contained in the Eurofound COVID-19 EU Policy Watch database are reported to have been passed with no agreement or involvement from the social partners' (EUROFOUND, 2020: 13).

Temporary labour-friendly policies do not make for corporatism. In particular, the increasing importance of the 'gig economy' threatens to further undermine the ability of labour unions to powerfully negotiate on behalf of workers in the future. In the gig economy – examples range from Uber drivers to services contracted via online platforms – workers directly compete against each other, thereby making collective action even more difficult than in traditional employment relations. Again, the self-employed and casual workers of the gig economy were among the most affected and vulnerable workers during the pandemic, together with healthcare, informal and migrant workers (ILO, 2021: 3–5). Finally, the increasing role of working from home also makes collective organization by labour unions more difficult, given that the latter traditionally has been strongly focused on the workplace.

Sector-specific vocational training eroded between technical atomization and public pedagogy

The coronavirus pandemic obviously had immediate repercussions on vocational training: training very often has been interrupted or suspended altogether, due to lockdowns. And many companies have cut back on apprenticeships, particularly with regard to the post-pandemic recession (OECD, 2020c). Correspondingly, the pandemic will have negative repercussions on the youth labour market in many countries. Disadvantaged young people, including those with a migrant background, will probably suffer most (Avis et al, 2021: 9). For example, young people have to very different degrees access to the digital platforms that have been utilized to replace the traditional VET education.

However, more important for post-corona capitalism are the structural changes stemming from the crisis. These changes indicate that the 'social-democratic' sector-specific vocational training typical for Germany and other CMEs may increasingly be eroded. On the one side, the liberal perspective as, for example, put forward by the OECD, takes the pandemic as point of departure to argue in favour of online courses for more general skills via fast-track licences, micro-credentials and foundational digital competences (OECD, 2020c). At the background of these suggestions are typical LME-type ideas that focus on the education of an atomized, flexible workforce with general skills that can be employed anywhere. Moreover, these systems are also much cheaper than the comprehensive CME system. On the other side, critics on the left argue in favour of expanding VET into some kind of public pedagogy, a comprehensive education of citizens with regard to becoming 'active, critical citizens and integrated members of society' (Avis et al, 2021: 7), given that the pandemic in many economies will lead to even more surplus labour and lack of adequately paid work.

Whither the marginalization of comprehensive industrial relations and training systems

Developments during the pandemic do not bode well for labour unions. 'Covid Corporatism' seems to be a temporary fad, if established at all. Labour unions did not play a major role in the design of economic stabilization policies, even where the latter were favourable to workers. The expansion of the 'gig economy' and of remote working increases the challenge of collective action for unions even further. This tends to strengthen a long-term process where the role of unions in industrial relations and in vocational training systems has increasingly been eroded. The latter particularly affects sector-specific vocational training systems typical for coordinated market economies.

While both the liberal focus on general transferable skills and the Marxist focus on citizenship education have important merits, one may wonder whether it is a good idea to further marginalize the CME model of sector-specific skill formation based on a close collaboration between unions, employers and the state. Even if empirical developments in Germany and other economies close to the CME ideal type tend to undermine the role of labour unions, further erosion of collective organization may lead to the loss of institutional advantages that are difficult to (re-) build from scratch. Similarly, the political marginalization of labour unions in most capitalist systems during the pandemic may also backfire in the end; for example, with regard to more adversarial labour relations and social unrest. While a move (or return) to a macro-corporatist system is highly unlikely (and not necessarily desirable), we may still want to strengthen labour unions in their ability to substantially participate in wage negotiations and skill formation, particularly if embedded in comprehensive sector-wide or even national systems.

15

Innovation: Frugal or Radical?

The coronavirus pandemic has demonstrated the importance of technological innovations in a very forceful way; for example, with regard to vaccine development or digital services. Still, the economic crisis may negatively affect the innovation capacity of many companies. Countries will differ widely in their ability to support innovative activities. Which innovation system is best suited for post-corona capitalism? Apparently, two types of innovation systems do particularly well in the context of the pandemic – the frugal one in a context of very limited resources and a state-led radical one, particularly in liberal rich economies.

Innovation systems in Comparative Political Economy

In traditional Comparative Political Economy research on the 'Varieties of Capitalism' (Hall and Soskice, 2001; Vermeiren, 2021: 137–9), the core distinction is between incremental and radical innovation. Incremental innovation processes make small improvements to existing products in a continual manner. CMEs, such as Germany and Japan, are famous for this type of innovation activity, with a particular focus on well-established industrial sectors, such as automobile and machinery production. This innovation system is based on a high degree of stability, with regard to stakeholder-oriented corporate governance (see Chapter 12) and long-term bank credit, as well as consensual labour relations and massive investments in vocational skill formation (see Chapter 14). Radical innovation processes invent completely new products; for example, in biotechnology or IT. LMEs, such as the US and the UK, are assumed to be particularly successful in this regard, inter alia based on the important role of venture capital in their capital markets-based financial systems (see Chapter 13).

In many countries of the Global South, however, a third type of innovation is very important. This innovation is called 'frugal', since its focus is on 'good enough' robust and affordable products that increase the standard of living for consumers with limited financial resources (Zeschky et al, 2011).

Comprehensive regulatory standards, in contrast, do not play a major role for this kind of innovation. Frugal products are made for environments with poor infrastructures and utilize readily available resources – their design is rather simple and technologically less sophisticated. Very often, frugal products are environmentally friendly, since they minimize resource usage (Corsini et al, 2021: 196–8).

The pandemic and its stimulating impact on frugal innovation

Frugal innovations haven been given a boost during the pandemic. As the saying goes, 'necessity has been the mother of invention' (Harris et al, 2020). In the health sector, for example, the sudden explosion of cases for hospital care not only overtaxed staff capacities, but also required improvisation with regard to technical resources. ICUs urgently needed huge amounts of new ventilators, thereby overtaxing the available resources. This has led to the mass production of simple and inexpensive ventilators based on open-source technology (Dave et al, 2021). In contrast to high-tech ventilators, these designs come without unnecessary features and are easy to use for staff not trained in an ICU environment.

Frugal innovations also have made inroads in lifestyles in the Global North. Here, frugality is 'defined by a considerate and prudent use of resources' (Herstatt and Tiwari, 2020: 24). A focus on frugal innovations works well with a movement that does not see economic growth as core target and rather prefers a moderate lifestyle – a movement that has been fuelled by the crisis (see Chapter 25). Still, frugal innovation of this type fits also with capitalist business models, as demonstrated by the 'blue movement' by Bosch-Siemens Hausgeräte in the Netherlands. The latter provides consumers with household appliances on a temporary basis for a rental fee, similar to a car-sharing system. This reduces resource utilization, since it gives an incentive to construct very robust machines that are not artificially aged – a typical feature of many household appliances (Herstatt and Tiwari, 2020: 23–4).

Given that makeshift improvements with limited resources have proven to be very useful during the crisis, there is a high likelihood that they retain their popularity afterwards (Harris et al, 2020: 814). One example is the various activities of 'digital makers', where digitalized machines are used for customized products, for example via 3D printing (Corsini et al, 2021; Vesci et al, 2021). During the last decade, these technologies have spread widely in the Global North as well as emerging economies such as China and India. During the pandemic, they have been put to highly productive use; for example, by quickly producing safety valves for ventilators and assisted breathing in Italy or face shields in India. Given the use of 'high tech' such as 3D printing, the 'Maker' movement is not the most obvious case of frugal innovation, but still shares many core features, such as quick responses to new problems based on limited resources.

The importance of state support within systems for radical innovation

During the coronavirus crisis, countries with a focus on incremental innovation did not make it to the news with regard to disruptive new projects. Companies working on mature technologies in a bank-oriented financial system mainly achieved process innovations; in particular, with regard to organizational matters such as dealing with home offices and teleconferences (Lecossier and Pallot, 2020). Economies based on radical innovation systems, in contrast, at first sight seem to be the big winners of the coronavirus crisis. Particularly, US digital platforms such as Amazon or Zoom have benefitted tremendously from pandemic-related lockdowns. However, these economic gains are based on innovations developed during pre-pandemic years. During the crisis, however, radical innovation systems also have demonstrated crucial weaknesses. A comparison with the experience of the GFC demonstrates the strong procyclicality of innovation investments in firms. In the UK, for example, the share of firms that was innovating fell by a third during the GFC and took four to six years after the crisis to return to its original level. The coronavirus pandemic seems to have led to similar effects (although the liquidity constraints now stem from reduced turnover, instead of commercial finance), particularly for small companies that had to reduce their research and development activities because of financial weakness (Roper and Turner, 2020). Correspondingly, governments are well advised to support these companies. This also relates to technology-based high-growth enterprises that rely on venture capital in order to reach profitability, given that venture investors may focus on existing investments during the crisis and may be unwilling to fund new companies (Mason, 2020).

Governments have become active with regard to particularly innovative small companies already during the crisis. Here, the issue is the protection of these companies against acquisitions – or even relocations – by foreign buyers. A particularly well-known case was the acquisition of a substantial share of the German vaccine producer CureVac by the German government (Guderian et al, 2021: 233). Another important government support instrument for innovations during the crisis was the massive use of public procurement agreements – particularly, in the form of advance purchases that heavily reduced uncertainty for innovative companies – that even have replaced the traditional demand incentives based on the patents for big private companies. The US government was also by far the most important funder of corona-related biomedical research globally, particularly through the National Institute of Health. The success of innovation support during the pandemic may even lead to a reconsideration of the typical set-up of public research support in liberal market economies, given that it has demonstrated that this support does not only work well for fundamental research, but also for applied activities – traditionally the remit of private companies (Sampat and Shadlen, 2021). This could also reduce the problems encountered with regard to intellectual property rights for life-saving treatments during the pandemic (see Chapter 21). Some governments even went a step further with regard to public support for research and development. Particularly, South Korea was very successful in coordinating the national response to the pandemic, including the development of health technologies. This also helps to avoid the deep structural inequalities – for example, with regard to research on the causes for the disproportionate impact of the pandemic on people of colour – that are typical for the US innovation system (Parthasarathy, 2020: 106–7).

The need for both frugal and state-supported innovation in post-coronavirus capitalism

If success during the pandemic is a criterion what will be utilized in post-corona capitalism, two innovation systems stand out. On the one side, frugal innovations typical for emerging economies such as China and India have not only flourished, but also found their way into economies of the Global North. On the other side, systems based on radical innovation have been able to make massive profits based on innovations developed before the pandemic.

However, in both of these systems small firms and technology-based high-growth enterprises may suffer from financial resource constraints for the development of new innovative products. Future innovation policies may be well advised to make used of both tendencies, particularly with regard to the intensification of financial support for small-scale companies and public-venture capital. Generally, the pandemic has forcefully highlighted the importance of massive state support for successful innovation.

16

Competition Policy: Economic Concentration as Vice or Virtue?

Next to the tendency towards digitalization, the coronavirus crisis also has led to increasing concerns about economic concentration. This pertains to not only the strengthening of major digital companies such as Alphabet (Google holding company), Amazon and Facebook on the one side, but also the destruction of many small companies (for example, in retail) on the other. Is this an inevitable development or should governments interfere? Moreover, most competition authorities liberalized their usual cartel laws in order to allow companies to cooperate intensively for the production of scarce goods, particularly in the health sector. Will this lead to intensified cartelization in the future? Finally, the massive size of some governments' stabilization policies for domestic business have led to concerns about unfair competition; for example, vis-à-vis companies based in fiscally less well-off economies. Shall we interdict rich governments to support their companies during the pandemic and the related recession, in order not to bias economic competition?

Competition policy and Political Economy

Most observers of modern economies agree on the usefulness of competition for economic well-being. They assume that competition in the market safeguards efficiency and innovation. Lack of competition, in the form of monopolies and cartels, in contrast, often is perceived to lead to wasteful behaviour and the unjust collection of rents (Büthe, 2019). Competition policy traditionally is a topic mainly studied in Economics and Law. Economists, for example, study the effects of economic concentration on consumer prices. Law scholars, for example, establish whether certain forms of inter-company cooperation have to be qualified as an unlawful cartel. More recently, however, competition policy has become an increasingly prominent topic in Political Economy.

We can distinguish two fields of competition policy. For one, competition authorities try to prevent the abuse of market dominance by single companies or a small group of companies. Core instruments include merger control; that is, checking whether the fusion of two companies or the takeover of one company by another leads to too much market power, and antitrust; that is, checking whether one company has already a too powerful position and investigating whether companies have formed cartels to the disadvantage of competitors or consumers. Companies involved in cartels can be fined; too powerful companies can be broken up as happened, for example, to John D. Rockefeller's Standard Oil in 1911 or AT&T in 1982; Microsoft barely avoided this fate in 2000. The second field of competition policy looks at activities of the state that might distort market competition. A classical case would be a state subsidy handed out to selected companies, but this can also relate to loans by public banks or state ownership of companies (see also Chapter 12).

While there is a fairly broad agreement on the usefulness of healthy market competition, there are very different perspectives on how to attain this competition and how to weigh it against other economic concerns. Put simply, we can distinguish three traditions of thinking, linked to three basic types of capitalism (see also Chapter 12 and Chapter 14). The first of these traditions can be called the Chicago School tradition of competition policy, linked to the liberal or US model since the 1960s (Wigger and Nölke, 2007: 492–3). In the perspective of this tradition, public market interventions should be avoided as far as possible. This not only relates to state subsidies, but also to antitrust and merger control. Only under exceptional conditions, the state may intervene. The yardstick for this intervention are the short-term effects upon consumer welfare. If economic concentration leads to low prices – for example, based on economies of scale – it can be permitted. Collusion between companies, in contrast, is seen very critical, since it may lead to cartels, with very negative effects on consumer prices. While state aid to companies goes against the liberal, market-leanings principles of the US model, in practice it exists at any level: federal, state and local, but without an overarching regulatory framework as in the EU (Wood, 2013).

The second tradition of competition policy has its origins in German ordoliberalism and sometimes is called the Freiburg School (Wigger and Nölke, 2007: 490–2). This tradition takes a broader view of economic competition, focused on long-term efficiency. Competition policy does not only pursue one target (that is low consumer prices), but several. On the one side, it should avoid the misuse of excessive market power or the restriction of competition for the disadvantage of third parties. On the other side, it should also allow for those forms of inter-company collaboration that seem acceptable or even desirable. One example for the latter is the well-established cooperation between German companies for the development and promotion of technological innovations. Correspondingly, the ordoliberal approach is somewhat more open to collusion between companies, but more critical towards economic concentration than the Chicago approach. State interventions such as state aid is legitimate, if it does not lead to a biased competition (Clift, 2013: 108–9).

There is no linkage to a specific (university) location for the third tradition of thinking on competition policy that has been developed in many emerging economies striving for catch-up industrialization, but we may call it the 'Beijing School' for lack of a better term. The governments of these economies usually are more lenient with regard to economic concentration and large domestic companies, often called 'national champions'. The latter are supposed to be more robust and stable in tough international competition than a competitive economic structure based on small companies. Concentrated economies provide particularly small emerging markets with more robustness and with economy of scale that improve the competitiveness of large corporation in global markets. This advantage comes with the cost in terms of aggregated economic and political power for the 'tycoons' and the large business families. Also with regard to state aid to companies, the third tradition is more lenient than the first two. It is also not exclusive to emerging economies, but can also be found in European economies, in particular in France, with its long tradition of 'dirigisme' (Clift, 2013).

Corona and market power

The coronavirus crisis has intensified concerns about the market power of some US-based multinationals, at least within the rich economies. At the core of these concerns were big digital platforms such as Amazon, Facebook or Google. The growing importance of these companies in a digital economy was already a major concern before the pandemic. Social distancing during the pandemic has further increased the demand for the services of these platforms.

The responses to concerns about the further rise of the US digital behemoths dependent on geopolitical location. In the US, calls for more powerful antitrust policies became increasingly frequent, including a breaking up of very large companies or even nationalization (Liu, 2020). These demands were particularly acute for those companies playing a major role in political communication, such as Facebook. However, concerns about all-powerful 'superstar' companies were not only reserved for US companies, but also related to Chinese companies. In the latter case, the major concern rather related to telecommunications companies such as Huawei that were the obvious choice for the construction of 5G mobile networks, but also raised security concerns.

In the EU, these concerns were shared, but also combined with a higher degree of tolerance towards economic concentration on the side of European companies, in order to be able to compete with the US digital behemoths, but also to defend European companies against potential acquisitions by state-backed Chinese ones. The quick recovery of the Chinese economy after the pandemic – and the slow recovery of the European economy – further intensified geopolitical concerns that already had been cultivated in the years before the crisis (Meunier and Mickus, 2020: 1081). During the pandemic, traditional concerns about economic concentration quickly gave way to a highly a permissive stance on antitrust matters. Similarly, strict rules governing the collusion between companies quickly were relaxed, in order to allow cooperation between companies dealing with the emergency (Meunier and Mickus, 2020; Schinkel and d'Ailly, 2020).

However, this greater tolerance towards rising firm size and crisis cartels may have very detrimental implications for the global economy and society in the end. The pandemic-related recession will lead to many cases of weakened companies being taken over (Schinkel and d'Ailly, 2020). Even before the pandemic, we have seen a tendency towards rising market concentration. The latter, however, has led to the emergence of 'abnormal' or 'surplus' profits that are much higher than usual company profits. Even before the outbreak of the pandemic, a United Nations Conference on Trade and Dealing (UNCTAD) study has found that 'the share of surplus profits in total profits has increased from an average of 7 per cent in 1995–2000 to 25 per cent in 2009–2015, and from 24 per cent to 42 per cent for the 1 per cent most profitable companies' (Bouhia, 2020: 1). Similar concerns about the problematical consequences of increasing market power for the concentration of profit markups with very large companies have been articulated by the IMF (2019). The coronavirus pandemic most likely will intensify this tendency. Therefore, it does not come as a surprise that emerging economies such as South Africa have focused competition policy during the pandemic on the control of excessive pricing (Boshoff, 2021).

Corona and state aid

A second major battlefield in competition policy was state aid policies, at least within the EU. Again, traditional restrictive rules with regard to state aid to companies were quickly shelved, in order to stabilize ailing companies. The European Commission quickly suspended its system of individually (and restrictively) assessing state aid measures by its member states. Subsequently, it allowed a broad range of measures, including direct grants to companies, tax rebates and loan guarantees. By early June 2020, the European Commission already had accepted state aid measures for more than €2 trillion (Meunier and Mickus, 2020: 1079).

Some member economies such as Germany or Austria weathered the first phase of the health crisis better than others. They already recorded a better economic development as the Southern European economies in the years since the GFC. However, the post-coronavirus recession threatened to affect their export-led economies very badly. In order to minimize the economic damage, they were using their solid fiscal situation for very large assistance programmes to domestic industry. Southern European countries were unable to counter this strategy, also because of much higher health damages during the early phase of the crisis. This threatens to deepen the deep gap between economic developments in the North and the South of the EU. The asymmetric recovery threatens to further fuel political tensions within the EU (see Chapter 28). In a global perspective, this development may even be worse, given that many countries of the Global South have even less fiscal means at their disposal than Southern European economies.

Finally, state aid policies during the pandemic were not only a concern in an international, but also in an intersectoral perspective. Many governments treated ailing sectors in very unequal ways. The Netherlands is a case in point (Sullivan and Wolff, 2021): while the Dutch government handed out loans amounting to €3.4 billion in order to support the KLM aviation company, the domestic hospitality sector – with its multitude of small companies – has been denied any substantial support, although both sectors have been prime victims of the crisis.

The way forward: towards global coordination of competition policies

The coronavirus crisis has intensified the 'arms race' towards economic concentration, often with state support. Concerns about economic concentration, about collusion between companies and about unfair state aid to selected companies at least temporarily have been relegated to the background. Small companies and consumers may become victims of this race in post-coronavirus capitalism. Similarly, the divergent ability of rich and poor governments to provide massive state aid to their companies during the coronavirus pandemic deepens economic inequalities. While there are frequent warnings with regard to this trend, these warnings quite easily are rebuffed by hints towards the advantages accruing to other economies if domestic companies would be treated by a more restrictive competition policy.

Clearly, there is a need for a greater degree of political and social engagement with issues of competition policy that so far have largely been relegated to a small community of economists and law scholars. Another option to improve the problematical situation would be to intensify the global coordination of competition policies. Traditionally, competition policy is pursued on the national or on the European level at most. The establishment of an international competition policy regime failed when the US Congress did not ratify the treaty for an International Trade Organization in 1950. The latter later was replaced by the much weaker General Agreement on Tariffs and Trade (GATT) (see Chapter 20) which did not contain regulations on competition policy (Büthe, 2019). Only during the last two decades, a loose network of global competition authorities (International Competition Network) has slowly emerged. While it looks unlikely that the very different 'Beijing', 'Chicago' and 'Freiburg' traditions may be harmonized in the foreseeable future, a more frequent exchange about the different perspectives towards competition policy and of the experience collected with applying the various instruments may be highly useful, in order to avoid the issues raised during the Coronavirus pandemic.

PART IV

The International Institutions of Capitalism

International (or Global) Political Economy deals with the co-constitution of economic and political processes on the global level. Its core topics include global production, trade and finance, as well as global economic governance and more specific issues such as development and health (Balaam and Dillman, 2014; O'Brien and Williams, 2016; Shaw et al, 2019; Andersson, 2020; Ravenhill, 2020). A core concern is the question of the extent of global cooperation and the role of the international institutions of capitalism in order to support this cooperation. Although a full understanding of these international institutions requires the incorporation of its co-determination with the national institutions of capitalism (Kalinowski, 2019; Nölke, 2019b), the focus subsequently is on the global level.

The coronavirus crisis has substantial repercussions with regard to many issue areas of International Political Economy, although not all are equally affected. In contrast to the GFC, for example, the crisis did not have major repercussions onto the field of global financial regulation. Similarly, the global institutions of development assistance also seem stable. Other issue areas witness important developments. Among the most visible changes in the context of the pandemic is the increased attention given to the stability of global production networks (Chapter 17). The crisis has demonstrated the fragility of these networks in a very visible way, particularly for medical products. Correspondingly, many companies and governments contemplate the reshoring of production – a step that has important repercussions on foreign direct investments; for example, with regard to restrictions for the acquisition of domestic companies by foreign buyers (Chapter 18). These and other government interventions into the economy likely will trigger a wave of investor–state disputes, with potentially massive fiscal implications (Chapter 19). Similarly, the coronavirus pandemic has caused a series of protectionist policies, particularly with regard to the export of medical supplies. Does this indicate a general turn to protectionism or will liberal trade policies prevail (Chapter 20)? A particularly controversial part of the global trade regime was the protection of intellectual property rights with regard to vaccines (Chapter 21). The limited solidarity of the vaccine producer economies in the Global North with the Global South also is mirrored in global health governance which was unable to safeguard an equitable distribution of vaccines (Chapter 22). At least in case of external public debt of low-income economies, the crisis has led to a demonstration of some solidarity, but this still poses the question whether temporary debt relief for some countries is sufficient or whether we need permanent write-offs (Chapter 23).

17

Global Production Networks: Diversification or Reshoring?

One of the most visible features of the coronavirus crisis is the importance of global production networks. In particular, with regard to medical supplies, the vulnerability of national economies in a world where more than 60 per cent of trade takes place with intermediate goods in global production networks has become more than obvious (Strange, 2020: 459). In global production networks, goods are not manufactured completely in one country and then sold in another country, but the production process of the goods takes place across borders, with some parts produced in one country, others in another, maybe to be assembled in a third. In the case of the coronavirus crisis, this distribution of tasks has not only made the quick production of vital medical products very difficult, but also brought other production processes to a standstill; for example, because an intermediate product was missing that was produced in China's Wuhan province. More generally, the coronavirus pandemic has highlighted numerous weaknesses of global production networks, including staff that is important for the operations of these networks not being allowed to cross borders, international air travel strongly being reduced, health checks delaying border crossings and increasing political scepticism about free trade (Strange, 2020: 460). As a result, many producers now contemplate about decreasing their dependence on these networks by bringing production back to the home economy ('reshoring') or by relying on intermediate products from more than only one country ('diversification'). Political Economy theories about global value chains can inform us which of the two options is a realistic perspective.

Theories of global value chains

The patterns of global production have changed substantially in the three decades before the GFC. While international trade has been with us for centuries and multinational corporations roughly since the 1920s – think, for example, of manufacturing sites of American companies such as General Motor and Ford in Europe – the complexity of global value chains has increased drastically during the last four decades. We can measure this quite broadly by looking at the volume of global foreign direct investment (FDI) inflows that increased from US$59 billion in 1982 to US$1,697 billion in 2008 (Thun, 2020: 176–8). A better illustration for the cross-border complexity that goes hand in hand with modern production is the data for just one company in 2019: 'Nike has approximately 74,400 direct employees, but … its projects were being manufactured by 1,069,674 workers in 527 factories in forty-one countries' (Thun, 2020: 176).

Moreover, the nature of cross-border production has changed. The core feature is the tendency to split up the production process of a good or service – a global value chain – in a number of separate activities that often take place in different countries. The crucial issue then is where to locate individual activities and how to govern the global value chain (Thun, 2020: 182–8). The latter takes place between the two poles of pure market relations for the acquisition of intermediate goods at the one end and the hierarchical control within one company (FDI) at the other; in-between are different types of network governance. Usually, lead firms govern global value chains via performance standards (for example, with regard to quality of components or delivery schedule), either as buyers (for example, retailers or supermarkets) or as producers. Lead firms cream off most of the value in these chains, either based on pre-production activities such as research and development or on post-production activities like branding and marketing (Gereffi, 2020: 289). In terms of location, the core question is whether companies outsource production to other companies in the same country or offshore this production to another country, with a strong preference for the latter choice during the last decades. Offshoring to other countries is chosen if the latter's economy offers competitive advantages. Among the most important advantages driving offshoring during the last decades was cheap labour.

Political Economy studies on global value chains – and the closely related concepts of global commodity chains and of global production networks – have identified the conditions that made the extension of global value chains possible during the last decades. These conditions include political processes of economic liberalization, as well as technological developments; in particular, with regard to transport and the modularization of production (Thun, 2020: 178–82). Of course, trade liberalization (see Chapter 20) was a very important factor. When trade barriers are high, multinational corporations may set up production facilities in a protectionist economy in order to gain access to its market, but they will hardly use this economy for the production of intermediate products that will have to be integrated in complex value chains. In terms of technology, container shipping, the digital revolution and the modularization of production, where units are produced individually, but still can work as a integrated whole, are the crucial factors.

While the evolution of global value chains was a global phenomenon, one country played a particularly important role; namely, China (see Chapter 27). During the last four decades, China – and East Asia in more general – has mutated into the factory of the world. Typically, China imports components from neighbouring economies, assembles these components into complete goods and then exports these goods globally (Thun, 2020: 188–94).

Global production networks in the medical sector during the coronavirus crisis

Given this analytical background, we can situate early evidence during the coronavirus pandemic in a more meaningful way. Media gave most attention to medical supplies such as PPE (for example, facemasks, surgical gloves and medical gowns), testing kits and vaccine ingredients, but also more complex products such as ventilators and other medical devices were at stake. Governments increasingly became concerned about the implications of very fragmented global value chains for national security.

Given the drastic increase of demand for PPE and medical devices during the coronavirus crisis, shortages were unavoidable, even if global production had expanded quite substantially before the crisis, due to the general demand increase by the ageing populations in the Global North, but also some of the emerging economies in the Global South. Moreover, the crisis took place against the background of a US–China trade war. Finally, a very large number of countries introduced export restrictions for coronavirus-related goods during the first months after the outbreak of the pandemic. Correspondingly, the governance set-up of global value chains was not the sole reason for shortages of products during the coronavirus crisis (Gereffi, 2020: 290–1).

A case study of the provision of N95 masks in the US during the first half year of the coronavirus crisis confirms that it was not only the management of global value chains that has led to a drastic shortage of this type of masks. At least as important were policy failures of the Trump administration that underestimated the pandemic at first and then pursued contraproductive interventions in trade policies, as well as US industry demands for liability waivers before shifting mask production from industrial to medical utilization. Still, the emergence of global value chains has contributed to the severity of the problem – nearly 90 per cent of US mask production was moved abroad in less than a decade – as did the related just-in-time business model that focuses on lean production and limited inventories, in order to maximize margins (Gereffi, 2020: 292–6).

A more comprehensive study comparing the global value chains for seven PPE products comes to similar conclusions, warning against both an ending of global value chains and keeping global value chains (GVCs) as they are. Whereas most GVCs adapted well to the early single-country crisis in China, the later global crisis often led to a breakdown of these chains, not the least because of activist public policies; in particular, trade restrictions by the EU. Moreover, countries like the US were very fortunate that China quickly recovered from the crisis; GVC breakdowns for PPE products would have been much more severe otherwise (Dallas et al, 2021).

Reshoring or diversification: early evidence during the coronavirus crisis

The medical sector, however, is unusual – high salience for national vulnerability, a strong role of public regulation and oligopolistic structures (Felbermayr and Görg, 2020: 10) – and we need to study other types of products as well, in order to establish whether recent experience with GVCs will lead to a reshoring of production more generally. Here, we can see that the expansion of these chains in manufacturing already had run out of steam before the coronavirus crisis, after a very strong expansion in the two decades before the GFC. One of the main reasons for the latter was the sudden expansion of supply of cheap and skilled labour after the breakdown of the Eastern Bloc and the opening up of China, not to be repeated any time soon (Antràs, 2020: 5–15, 26–32). Instead, rising labour costs in many countries of the Global South and the ongoing tendency towards automation and robotization work against this trend, to be boosted by the coronavirus. After all, 'robots do not get the coronavirus' (Brakman et al, 2021). During the crisis, global FDI flows predictably collapsed, by more than 40 per cent in 2020 (UNCTAD, 2021; see also Chapter 18).

Still, there are no indications for a fundamental reduction of production in transborder value chains in the long run. A core reason for the latter is the considerable sunk costs that go hand in hand with the integration into value chains. Lead firms have invested a lot of effort in identifying suitable producers (or production locations) for components. The producers of components, in turn, have invested a lot of capital in production facilities to match the requirements of a specific lead firm. All of these investments would be lost if a relationship is abandoned (Antràs, 2020: 22–6). In addition, a substantial reduction of reliance on transborder production chains in favour of more resilience is expensive. Even if managers consider a reduction of this resilience useful, competitive pressures may act as a brake for its implementation (Butollo, 2020: 41). In some sectors such as garment production or the manufacturing of simple electronic goods, the cost advantages of the Global South are simply too large for reshoring (Dünhaupt et al, 2021: 21). More likely scenarios thus include the diversification and replication of GVCs (to decrease the reliance on individual companies and countries), together with a limited degree of regionalization and reshoring; all of these processes had already started before the pandemic (Elia et al, 2021).

Moreover, there are also forces at work that will assist the integration of additional companies in GVCs. Particularly, the further rise of digital technologies is important here. For example, global digital platforms will assist in matching buyers and sellers from smaller economies. Companies from countries with bad physical infrastructures – but decent access to high-speed internet – may integrate by focusing on the production of digital services instead of physical goods (Antràs, 2020: 21). The marked increase in working from home (WFH) during the crisis has indicated that many services can be rendered remotely – in-country, but also globally (Brakman et al, 2021).

Based on these observations, post-coronavirus capitalism may well witness a stagnation of production in transborder value chains, but a wholesale retreat from these production networks seems unlikely – unless political decisions lead to a massive increase in protectionism (see Chapter 20). A bifurcation into US- and China-centred spheres of production appears to be the most likely case for this type of political decision (Linsi, 2021; see also Chapter 27).

Options for more robust global production systems

The coronavirus crisis has demonstrated the vulnerability of GVCs in a very forceful way. Correspondingly, companies and governments are seeking ways to reduce this vulnerability in the future. However, this does not mean that we are necessarily heading towards an isolationist international production system where each country tries to manufacture as much as possible in-country. It rather implies that the configuration of global production networks and domestic production systems will be adjusted gradually in order to increase their robustness, at least for crucial goods as in the medical sector. The over-reliance on national competitive advantages, extreme specialization, just-in-time production and highly complex global production networks made the system very vulnerable to various sorts of instabilities. The more complex these networks are – increasingly mutating from simple supply chains via supply networks into intertwined supply networks (Ivanov and Dolgui, 2020) – the more likely is an interruption.

Several options are available to reduce this instability without completely turning away from global production networks, both for companies and governments. The latter would be a disaster, particularly for many workers in the Global South. Generally, a diversity of sourcing options is important for companies. In the future, companies should be reluctant to source all components from one country and one company. They should also source particularly important components at the domestic level, if possible. Companies will also need to cut back on super lean just-in-time production and minimal inventories. Another useful option is nearshoring; for example, relocating production into the region of the company (for example, Eastern or Southern Europe in the case of German companies and Mexico in the case of the US), in order to reduce transport risks. The latter has become abundantly clear when in March/April 2021 the container ship Ever Given grounded in the Suez Canal and blocked large parts of global trade for nearly a week. The need to decarbonize the economy will further strengthen arguments for reshoring or nearshoring (see Chapter 24). Not only companies but also governments need to act in order to prevent similar problems in the future. The coronavirus pandemic is not the first crisis that has demonstrated the fragility of globalized economies. Challenges to this fragility have become more frequent during the last years, including the GFC, the advent of populism-related trade wars and now the coronavirus pandemic. Citizens expect that governments reduce the vulnerability of their economies with regard to GVCs, not only by stockpiling reserves of vital medical goods. Governments should also protect by various means of industrial policy; for example, by preventing strategical companies against foreign takeovers, making public procurement dependent upon a certain volume of domestic content or using regulatory policies for retaining the production of crucial components (Dullien, 2021). If governments do not succeed in reducing fragility, the next crisis may indeed lead to isolationism and a fundamental reversal of globalization.

18

Foreign Direct Investment: Promotion or Restriction?

Similar to other large recessions, the coronavirus pandemic has led to low valuations of many companies in distress. Foreign investors may utilize this situation for acquisitions. As we will see, this is not a hypothetical consideration during the coronavirus crisis. Particularly, Chinese companies were quite active with regard to foreign acquisitions. This leads to the question whether the government of the country with the target company appreciates this initiative (as a much-needed rescue operation) or rather harbours concerns regarding the latter (as sell-out of a national treasure). More generally, will post-coronavirus policies for the regulation of inward FDI rather promote or restrict the latter?

FDI policies and International Political Economy

FDIs refer to the practice that companies invest outside their home country. If they set up a completely new facility, this is called 'greenfield investment'; if they buy an existing facility, this is called 'brownfield investment' (usually summarized under 'mergers and acquisitions'). A second major distinction is between FDI proper and 'portfolio investments' – in the latter case, the focus is not on the control of facilities in other economies, but on financial investments. Of course, portfolio investments can morph into proper FDI, if the investor uses 'creeping acquisitions' in order to increase its shares of the target company until it acquires control of the latter (Das, 2021: 2). Although FDI (and trade) policies are closely related to the issue of global production networks (see Chapter 17) – they can either facilitate or restrict the latter – these policies warrant a treatment of their own. Put simply, governments decide about FDI and trade policies; companies decide – on this basis – whether they produce (or source inputs) in only one country or spread the production process across several national economies.

Although the debate on the advantages and disadvantages of FDI is not as extensive as the debate between free-traders and protectionists (see Chapter 20), it still has become quite comprehensive, usually with the implicit perspective of a government confronted with the option of inward FDI. Among the most important potential advantages of inward FDI range from the access to additional resources (both financial and technological), the mobilization of tax revenues and employment as well as the transfer of management techniques. A more critical perspective, in contrast, highlights that FDI can outcompete (and destroy) domestic companies, lock in the target economy in a sub-optimal international division of labour (for example, as a one-sided commodity exporter) and can even reduce the taxes collected domestically, by using mechanisms of transfer pricing that shift tax payments towards low-tax environments (O'Brien and Williams, 2016: 130). Moreover, the benefits of FDI are distributed very unequally, with FDI equity income particularly benefitting the top 1 per cent of households in the advanced economies (Joyce, 2021).

Related to these arguments, governments have developed manifold investment policy instruments (UNCTAD, 2020a), next to the inclusion of regulations on investor–state dispute settlements in trade agreements (see Chapter 19). On the one side, there is a broad set of policies to encourage FDI. Most of these policies focus on the attraction of inward FDI via tax rebates, the provision of infrastructure or the mobilization of a skilled labour force, but we can also observe outward FDI policies, usually pursued by the governments of emerging economies such as China. In this case, governments encourage domestic companies to set up shop abroad in order to improve the access to foreign talent and technologies, as well as markets. Host-country governments have developed policies for the screening and potential interdiction of inward FDI, due to the concerns mentioned earlier.

Whereas a selective screening of inward FDI traditionally is a policy pursued by powerful emerging economies such as China, it has become increasingly common with Northern economies more recently. UNCTAD counts 29 countries with specific FDI screening mechanisms before the coronavirus pandemic (2020a: 8). The US, for example, gave additional power to its Committee on Foreign Investment in the United States (CFIUS) in 2018. More generally, UNCTAD reported an increasing trend towards 'more rigorous screening of investment in strategic industries on the basis of national security considerations' (2020b: xi). Screening both focuses on investments in specific economic sectors with strategic significance and certain multinational home economies; it has moved from a rare exception to a regular tool, already before the outbreak of COVID-19 (Gertz, 2021).

Inward FDI screening during the coronavirus crisis: a focus on Chinese acquisitions

How did governments adjust their FDI policies during the coronavirus pandemic? At least in the established economies, the focus clearly was on restrictions for inward FDI, not on the promotion of the latter. For example, the EU, EU member states, Australia, Canada and India introduced restrictive measures (UNCTAD, 2020a: 8; Kowalski, 2020: 140–6). More specifically, the attention of most governments was on brownfield FDIs that originated in China. China had faced the pandemic earlier than other countries. It also fought the pandemic with more draconian measures than most other countries. Correspondingly, the Chinese economy had recovered from the pandemic-related recession much earlier than other industrialized economies. Some Chinese companies attempted to utilize the situation to acquire Western companies, particularly with regard to access to technologies. Given the different institutional background of Chinese companies in comparison with most Northern companies – in particular, a closer proximity to the national government (Nölke and Taylor, 2010; Nölke, 2014) – this raised some concerns in the Global North.

Chinese companies had started to invest in other economies on a big scale after 2004, inter alia based on the accumulation of large foreign exchange reserves. The volume of Chinese outward FDI increased quickly, from less than 1 per cent of global FDI to 12.7 per cent in 2016, with some limitations thereafter (Fang et al, 2021: 12). Among the most well-known Chinese outward investment strategies ranges the 'Belt and Road' initiative, but the lion's share of these investments go to Europe and the US. While many countries of the Global South generally welcome these investments with open arms, some countries in the Global North are somewhat more reserved. For the latter, the disadvantages of inward FDI mentioned earlier sometimes outweigh the advantages, with a special focus on national security concerns and the close relationship between Chinese multinationals and the Chinese government. Particularly, during the Trump administration in the US (2017–20), frictions between the US and China also affected the treatment of Chinese FDI into US companies. The US government has set up a so-called 'Entity List' of Chinese companies that would only allow acquisitions of US companies based on an explicit approval by the US government. This list includes many important companies, such as Huawei, the leading Chinese chip producer SMIC and the world's biggest drone-producing company DJI. China has retaliated by setting up its own 'Unreliable Entity List' in 2020.

Concerns about FDI from China increased during the coronavirus pandemic. The EU introduced its first FDI mechanism in October 2020, although some of the poorer member states generally are quite positive about Chinese FDI. In addition, several EU member states' governments tightened their national regulations, such as those in Germany and Italy (Das, 2021: 3). The government of India followed with restrictive measures in April 2020 after learning that the People's Bank of China had utilized the massive pandemic-related share downfall of HDFC – the holding company of India's largest private bank – in order to increase its ownership of the latter company (Das, 2021: 2). It now requires approval for any inward FDI by businesses from any neighbouring country; of course, the latter notion mainly refers to China. The government of Japan even went further and has set up a US$2.2 billion support plan encouraging Japanese manufacturers to move production out of China (UNCTAD, 2020a: 6).

Restrictions towards outward-bound Chinese FDI to the established economies undoubtedly will strengthen the inclination of the Chinese government to become technologically independent as soon as possible and to further its 'connectivity politics', 'understood as an approach to diplomacy and foreign policy that aims to proactively connect the rest of the world to China while only selectively integrating with existing international norms and principles' (Kohlenberg and Godehardt, 2020: 1). Due to the increasing restrictions towards FDI from China in some Western economies, the relative share of FDI going to countries involved in the Belt and Road initiative among Chinese outward FDI increased considerably in 2020 (Fang et al, 2021).

The quantitative development of FDI during the coronavirus crisis

Due to the economic crisis, but also due to increasingly restrictive policies, the overall volume of FDI during the crisis decreased, by 42 per cent in 2020 alone (UNCTAD, 2021). Western economies were affected in a particularly massive way, including a halving of FDI into the US and a reduction of FDI into the EU by two thirds. The reduction of FDI into the established economies was much stronger during the coronavirus pandemic than during the GFC. Inflows to these economies amounted to only US$229 billion in 2020, in contrast to US$714 billion in 2009. This has led to a record share of countries of the Global South in global FDI inflows in 2020 (72 per cent). Given that lockdowns and border closures were still in place in 2021, a recovery of global FDI flows will start in 2022 at the earliest. But even then the recession will lead to the re-evaluation of planned investments (UNCTAD, 2021). Moreover, the trend towards more resilient GVCs will reduce FDI into economies of the Global South (see Chapter 17).

Towards more selective FDI screening policies

The coronavirus pandemic has led to a substantial reduction in FDI levels. However, a reduction in FDI during the crisis does not necessarily mean that FDI has to remain low after the crisis. Many observers expect a strong rebound after the end of the pandemic and the related recession, although the tendency towards reshoring of production may dampen this rebound. Moreover, the restrictions for inward FDI introduced during the crisis are here to stay. Many governments have introduced FDI screening policies during the crisis, with a special focus on acquisitions by Chinese companies. China has retaliated with its own list of unwelcome companies. Post-coronavirus capitalism will see increasing attempts for an economic decoupling between China and the US, particularly with regard to FDI in technologically sensitive sectors.

It is the legitimate right of each national government to decide about FDI policies. Still, an increasing number of inward FDI restrictions very likely inhibits economic cooperation and leads to global welfare losses. Inward FDI screening may become particularly problematic if individual domestic companies in industrialized economies learn to play these restrictions for keeping foreign competition out of the country and to mobilize monopolistic rents. Governments of the established economies, therefore, should strive to limit these restrictions to cases where national security concerns undoubtedly are at stake. Correspondingly, it would be important to have transparent and predictable policies on FDI screening in place. For economies of the Global South, the core issue continues to target inward FDI in a way that it contributes to technology transfer towards domestic companies, similar to the practices the Chinese government has utilized to treat inward FDI during the last decades in order to industrialize (Nölke et al, 2020: 180–4). While the negotiation position of individual Southern governments will be much weaker than those of the Chinese government (with the strong incentive of access to the very large Chinese domestic market), they may consider using regional integration schemes in order to negotiate favourable FDI deals.

19

Investor–State Dispute Settlement: Business as Usual or Moratorium?

Mechanisms for the settlement of disputes between foreign investors and national governments are among the most controversially discussed topics of contemporary investment and trade agreements. Opposition to the latter often is primarily based on 'investor–state dispute settlement' (ISDS) issues. During the coronavirus pandemic, hundreds of non-governmental organizations (NGOs) have asked for a moratorium on ISDS operations (S2B Network, 2020), so far in vain. Instead, informed observers expect a major wave of new ISDS claims triggered by the crisis. Why does the pandemic raise additional concerns about ISDS? Can we continue with this practice or do we need a moratorium?

Political Economy and ISDS mechanisms

ISDS mechanisms have emerged since the 1950s, triggered by the increasing amount of international investments. Before their emergence, foreign investors had to rely on two unattractive options when they considered themselves to be treated in an unfair way by host-country governments. One option is to make use of the court system in the host country, but the latter often was considered to be biased in favour of its national government. The alternative option for companies is to appeal to their home-country government to take up the issue with the host-country government, but these diplomatic channels were also of limited usefulness, given that investment concerns often ranged among low priorities if weighed against other foreign policy issues.

The establishment of independent dispute settlement mechanisms originally was targeted against newly independent governments of the Global South after decolonization that threatened Northern companies with expropriation; for example, in natural resource extraction sectors. From the millennium onwards, however, ISDS cases have become an increasingly salient issue between multinational corporations and governments in the Global North. In part, this was because of the movement towards remunicipalization of local services, such as energy and water supply, that previously had been privatized, also to the favour of foreign multinationals. In part, this was triggered by environmental or health policy reversals, such as the German '*Energiewende*' that demanded a shutdown of nuclear reactors, again partially owned by foreign companies such as the Swedish Vattenfall. Correspondingly, concerns over ISDS have become a central issue in major trade negotiations, contributing substantively to the failure of the Trans-Atlantic Trade and Investment Partnership (TTIP) and the crisis about the ratification of the Comprehensive Economic and Trade Agreement (CETA) between Canada and the EU.

The opportunity to address an ISDS mechanism usually is included in trade agreements or investment treaties; in particular, in bilateral investment treaties between two countries, multilateral investment treaties – such as the Energy Charter Treaty (with a focus on European investments into Eastern Europe and Russia) – and free trade agreements. The resolution of company claims against foreign governments is negotiated in the context of specialized institutions, most prominently the International Centre for Settlement of Investment Disputes (ICSID) set up by the WB, but also the International Chamber of Commerce (ICC), the United Nations Commission on International Trade Law (UNCITRAL), or specialized bodies set up in London and Stockholm. Individual cases are decided by three judges – one appointed by the investor, one by the government and the third by the other two judges. Negotiations are not public and there is no central register of cases (Weghmann and Hall, 2021: 4–6). Estimates assume that more than 1,000 claims have been filed, mentioned earlier half during the last decade. Payments based on these claims can be quite high, for example US$6 billion to be paid to one foreign investor by the government of Pakistan based on a case settled in 2019 (Skovgaard Poulsen and Gertz, 2021: 2).

Currently, the ISDS topic ranges among the most controversial topics with regard to investment and trade in Political Economy. Critics argue that the threat to be sued by international investors creates a 'regulatory chill'; that is, governments will fail to introduce legislation in order to solve regulatory issues, or at least water down this legislation considerably (Tienhaara, 2011). Correspondingly, the impact of ISDS far transgresses those cases where companies actually have won compensation. Moreover, critics point to the fact that ISDS gives multinational corporations power over the democratic decisions of sovereign states, with 'corporate liquidity taking priority over community welfare' (S. Schmidt, 2020). ISDS can also distort competition between foreign and domestic companies, because the latter cannot resort to this mechanism. Furthermore, the impartiality of judgments is cast into doubt, inter alia based on the observation that foreign investors benefit very often and that most arbitrators also work as lawyers preparing claims against governments in other cases (Weghmann and Hall, 2021: 4). Finally, critics also point to the unpredictability of the existing ISDS mechanisms, in combination with their costly and lengthy proceedings. Given that arbitration tribunals – in contrast to domestic courts – are not bound by case precedence in the past, their judgments can be quite inconsistent (Nikièma and Maina, 2020: 4).

Liberal proponents of ISDS, in contrast, argue that this critique is 'populist', by pitting corporations, law firms and arbitrators as part of a corrupt elite. They highlight the importance of reliable investment conditions for companies that are active across borders. Moreover, they contest that the diagnosis of regulatory chill can be measured in any meaningful way, given that policy proposals always are contested between different socio-economic interest groups, thereby making the causal attribution of regulatory chill to ISDS very difficult (Ranjan, 2020).

Before the coronavirus pandemic, social mobilization against ISDS, but also the increasing number of cases against Western governments has led to the exclusion of this institution from several investment treaties and trade agreements. Among the most well-known cases for this reversal is the renegotiation of the North American Free Trade Agreement (NAFTA) towards the United States–Mexico–Canada Agreement (USMCA), now basically excluding ISDS. Moreover, major emerging economies such as Brazil, India, Indonesia and South Africa have begun to renegotiate or even terminate their bilateral investment treaties, in order to get rid of ISDS mechanisms. The majority of EU member states went even further and agreed on a treaty for the termination of intra-EU bilateral investment treaties. The EU also has proposed an international court system to replace ISDS and has excluded the latter mechanism from its recently negotiated agreement with Mercosur. Countries such as Australia and New Zealand also restricted ISDS in their existing trade agreements (Weghmann and Hall, 2021: 9–11).

The coronavirus pandemic and the potential wave of ISDS cases

While it is yet too early to estimate the number of disputes caused by the coronavirus pandemic, there is a broad consensus on the very high likelihood that this will become an important phenomenon during the next years. Critics and proponents of ISDS share this consensus (Ranjan, 2020; Ranjan and Anand, 2020). Among the latter, international law firms and speculative third-party funders (that fund litigation and arbitration based on a share of damage payments in case of success) have been preparing for additional litigation opportunities (Simson, 2020; Freshfields Bruckhaus Deringer, 2021). On the side of the critics, more than 500 NGOs have signed an appeal for a moratorium on ISDS (S2B Network, 2020). Not only existing ISDS cases and payments should be stopped, but also any coronavirus-related cases should be interdicted permanently, according to the appeal.

There are several reasons why the pandemic most likely will lead to a wave of dispute settlement cases. Lawyers working on related matters list the following coronavirus-related causes:

- 'Revenue losses due to restrictions on the freedom of movement;
- state price regulations ensuring the affordability of drugs, tests and vaccines;
- financial relief measures supporting overburdened health systems;
- rental price controls and relief from mortgage payments;
- suspension of energy bills;
- debt relief for households and businesses;
- implementation of moratoriums on export contracts;
- suspension of the issuance of dividends, share buybacks, executive bonuses;
- suspension of the collection of fees on privately run national toll-roads; and
- requisition of private hospital facilities, nationalization of private hospitals or mandating the production of ventilators by designated manufacturers' (S. Schmidt, 2020).

International law firms started to threaten claims for investor protection a few months after the emergence of the crisis. In Peru, for example, they questioned (on behalf of the concession-holders) the adequacy of the suspension of the collection of tolls on the country's road that had been initiated in order to allow the transport of essential goods in a situation when many people had lost their income (Olivet and Müller, 2020). Previous crises also have led to a wave of ISDS claims; for example, the economic emergency in Argentine during the 2000s or the Arab Spring in Egypt (Ranjan and Anand, 2020: 227). Correspondingly, ISDS cases could place a heavy burden on the governments of less well-off countries during and after the crisis, both in terms of administrative capacity and financial obligations. This could inhibit an adequate response to the health and economic crisis.

However, liberal proponents of ISDS argue that most of these cases will be won by governments. Given the dimensions of the pandemic, governments such as the Indian ones that have brought the economic activities of foreign multinationals to a standstill should be able to defend their cause in ISDS arbitration (Ranjan and Anand, 2020). Furthermore, they openly oppose the proposed moratorium on ISDS, because the broad range of drastic measures undertaken by governments around the world speaks against any effect of regulatory chill. Moreover, the administrative overburdening argument is cast into doubt, because the agencies dealing with ISDS claims would be quite different from those dealing with the pandemic and its economic consequences. Similarly, the financial consequences of ISDS settlements usually are limited, according to this position. For liberal proponents of ISDS, the latter are even held as an important antidote to authoritarian developments during and after the crisis (Anand, 2020).

The pandemic as accelerator for the reform of the ISDS system

Before the coronavirus crisis, growing social opposition to ISDS has led to an exclusion of the latter institution in a series of investment treaties and trade agreements. This exclusion was part of the growing tendency towards protectionism that also can be observed with regard to trade (see Chapter 20) and FDI policies (see Chapter 18). The fight against the pandemic, however, gives ample munition for new cases among the existing dispute settlement systems. Therefore, reform of the ISDS system is more prominent than before, with the target of narrowing down the rights for investors given by these mechanisms. This reform process had already started before the crisis. Given that governments – in contrast to investors – widely agree on the shortcomings of the existing system, it is likely that the coronavirus crisis will speed up this reform process; for example, with regard to the creation of an appellate mechanism and to a more qualified selection of ISDS tribunal members.

However, even if no new agreements with ISDS would be negotiated, the existing stock of more than 3,000 investment treaties would still give ample access to this mechanism. Correspondingly, we should make use of the coronavirus-related attention to the issue of ISDS for not only constraining (or abolishing) ISDS in future investment treaties, but also reforming the system for existing ones. However, the individual renegotiation or termination of existing treaties is very costly. Alternatively, governments that are parties to specific treaties could articulate interpretative statements on how ISDS tribunals should apply these treaties, in order to narrow down the opportunities under which investors can ask for compensation by states (Skovgaard Poulsen and Gertz, 2021).

20

Trade Policy: Liberalism or Protectionism?

Even in a world of global production networks, trade policies remain important for capitalist economies. They regulate the conditions under which goods and services may cross borders; for example, by imposing tariffs or regulatory norms. Countries can choose more liberal or more protectionist policies. With the onset of the coronavirus crisis, several governments have implemented protectionist policies; in particular, by limiting the export of medical supplies. Moreover, we can observe increasing indications of a public discourse that turns against trade liberalization. Political economy approaches help us to identify the motivations behind these policies and declarations, as well as the consequences for the institutions of global trade governance. Should we continue on this path to a somewhat increased protectionism or move back to trade liberalism?

Trade policy and International Political Economy

International trade policies are the most established topic in International Political Economy scholarship. Each textbook features at least one comprehensive chapter on the topic; some, a whole series of chapters (Oatley, 2019). While there is a long list of trade policy instruments and institutional settings, as well as a great variety of theories on how to explain trade policies, the core issue always is the juxtaposition between free trade and protectionism.

Proponents of free trade claim that a specialization of countries based on their comparative advantages leaves everybody better off. While Adam Smith highlighted the importance of specialization for enhancing productivity due to economies of scale, David Ricardo demonstrated that trade can also improve overall welfare when one country has absolute advantages on the production of all goods and services. Modern trade theories added that this does not only relate to labour productivity, but also to factor endowments such as capital, land and labour. Correspondingly, some countries are supposed to focus on agricultural production and others on labour-intensive industries. Liberals despise protectionist measures because they limit overall welfare. Moreover, they assume that protectionist measures are put in place in order to increase the profits of individual companies, because these measures limit competition (O'Brien and Williams, 2016: 104–5).

Critics of free trade argue that the latter has strong distributive consequences. Some countries – and some groups within countries – gain much more than others. In particular, countries that focus on agriculture – or the exploitation of other natural resources – will always stick to that specialization if they adhere to free trade. A specialization in manufacturing industry, however, is much more promising in terms of value added and employment. In order to move to manufacturing, however, you need to protect infant industries temporarily before they can compete on the world stage. Correspondingly, protectionism can be highly useful, if applied selectively and temporarily. Ha-Joon Chang (2002), for example, demonstrates that today's highly industrialized companies all have used protectionist measures in their history, but preach free trade to today's industrializing economies – they are 'kicking away the ladder'. Moreover, empirical research demonstrates that the gains from free trade are distributed very unevenly in societies. While free trade may be beneficial to economies as a whole, it also produces losers; for example, workers in industries closed down due to foreign competition. This problem could be overcome if the winners of free trade compensate the losers, but this rarely takes place. Finally, there is a national security argument in favour of protectionism. If countries pursue free trade policies, it could well be that they are lacking strategic goods in a crisis, such as food, medical goods or weapons. Correspondingly, certain vital industries need protection, in order to prevent a country becoming too vulnerable (O'Brien and Williams, 2016: 105–8).

However, International Political Economy work on trade policy is not limited to these general considerations on protectionism versus free trade. Other important topics are the fate of the major institutional arrangements in order to regulate trade – in particular, the global system of the World Trade Organization and the various (inter-) regional or bilateral trade arrangements (Andersson, 2020: 63–82) – and the various trade policy instruments, from regulatory harmonization (Claar and Nölke, 2013) to border issues; in particular, various forms of import restrictions. While the major trade institutions take some time to change course – if at all – the discussion of trade policy instruments can help us to make sense of changes caused by the coronavirus pandemic. In this case, export curbs were a widely used instrument; many observers also expect an increased use of ISDS mechanisms in the future (see Chapter 19).

The proliferation of export curbs during the pandemic

The core issue during the early phase of the coronavirus pandemic was medical supplies. Countries were in need of a wide array of goods, from disinfectants to medical masks and from test kits to ventilators. The governments of countries where companies produced these goods very often decided to ban their export. They were afraid that they otherwise might not be able to protect their own population during the crisis – or they were worried that they would lose their legitimacy if parts of the population would suffer shortcomings in this regard. By 21 March 2020, 54 governments had implemented export curbs (Evenett, 2020: 830). Not all of these restrictions were straight bans; governments also used more subtle means such as imposing a government agency with exclusive access to the relevant goods. Corona-related goods were not the only staple affected by export curbs. Many countries also imposed the latter on food, because they were worried about food shortages, again with highly problematic repercussions on other countries (see Chapter 26).

These decisions were not self-evident. Governments took these decisions in spite of the awareness that they might deny other countries in need of vital resources. A liberal observer has called this practice 'sicken-thy-neighbor' (Evenett, 2020), in association to the famous dictum by Adam Smith that mercantilist countries 'beggar-thy-neighbor'. He also argues that these decisions may be counterproductive, at least in the long run. Export bans reduce the incentives for domestic companies to invest in expanding production for these goods.

Leaving these textbook liberal arguments aside, export bans have the potential to throw sand in the gear of GVCs for the production of these goods (see Chapter 17). The production of ventilators, for example, often requires parts that are produced in different countries. If any of these countries imposes an export ban, fewer ventilators can be built in total (Evenett, 2020: 831–2). Governments of the economies affected can deplore this praxis, fight against these bans – or decide to require domestic companies to start production domestically, thereby leading to a drastic shortening of global production chains, with the concurrent loss of efficiency advantages. Generally, the promotion of global production networks is based on the assumption that trade policies continuously lower trade barriers – an assumption that looks increasingly out of date (Curran et al, 2021: 7).

A measure for improving access to medical goods during the pandemic in line with a liberal free trade agenda would have been to reduce or abolish import taxes (tariffs/duties), in order to make these goods more affordable domestically. Import taxes on relevant goods were fairly frequent before the crisis. And indeed we can find an abolition of these measures during the crisis, with low- and medium-income economies being particularly active

(Curran et al, 2021: 10). However, this form of trade liberalization had no substantial impact in practice, because there were hardly any goods available on global markets that could have been imported (Curran et al, 2021: 10).

Public discourses on trade policy during the coronavirus pandemic

Next to the practical measures implemented during the crisis, we have the general discourse on trade policies. Does it indicate liberalism or protectionism in the future? Liberal-minded observers are deeply worried about protectionist-leaning discourses triggered by the early phase of the coronavirus pandemic and argue 'why turning inward won't work' (Baldwin and Evenett, 2020). Orbi and de Ville (2020) have studied the debate on EU trade policies during the first three months of the crisis based on 172 sources. Although they record many articulations with regard to a reshoring of production to Europe and to the protection of strategic industries, they doubt that these changes will amount to more than small policy adjustments in the direction of protectionism on the side of the EU, a particular stringent advocate of liberal trade. A more comprehensive study of the Australian public discourse on trade policies between February and June 2020, however, indicates a strong turn towards protectionism (Branicki et al, 2021). The coronavirus crisis has triggered latent deglobalizing discourses, particularly with regard to China: 'COVID-19 has arguably materialized the pre-existing antagonism within the Australian–Chinese relationship and in doing so has precipitated the early warning signs of future trade boycotts and the potential for economic de-regionalization' (Branicki et al, 2021: 12). Later in 2020/21, these discourses did not remain discourses only, but materialized into a massive Australia–China trade conflict (Pan and Korolev, 2021).

The weakness of the WTO during the coronavirus crisis

Although we cannot predict how far the process will go, the coronavirus pandemic undoubtedly has led to a wave of protectionist articulations and measures. Who could have imagined the imposition of export controls even between European economies? Globally, the initial trade policy reaction to the coronavirus pandemic was even more protectionist than after the GFC: 'the crisis has led to a widespread and intense instigation of potentially WTO incompatible measures over a very short period of time. This is unprecedented in post-war history' (Curran et al, 2021: 12). Moreover, these measures were initiated in a context that already had become very protectionist before the crisis. Particularly, the US–China trade war had weakened the liberal trade agenda already before 2020, as did the refusal of the US to nominate new Appellate Body members at the WTO Dispute Settlement Body and the withdrawal of the US from trade agreements such as the Trans-Pacific Partnership (TPP) (Curran et al, 2021).

The coronavirus pandemic further intensified the crisis of the WTO, also in a broader view. It has demonstrated the power of 'weaponized interdependence' (Farrell and Newman, 2019). Whereas this exploitation of vulnerabilities of other states by key states such as China and the US had been used rather rarely before, the pandemic not only exposed the powerful nature of this weapon, but also demonstrated the weakness of the WTO to prevent its utilization (Narlikar, 2021).

How to manage protectionist tendencies wisely

In a comprehensive perspective, the coronavirus pandemic has met an international trade system that has seen a decade of norm erosion, norm evasion and norm abuse in the international trade regime, with 'erosion' pointing to its ability to address new challenges, 'evasion' referring to the non-implementation of earlier commitments and 'abuse' highlighting the direct defiance of existing rules (Albertoni and Wise, 2021). Correspondingly, the handling of the coronavirus pandemic in the Global North will strengthen the case for protectionist trade policies in the South. Many countries have learned that they cannot rely on the free trade gospel preached by Northern governments and the international organizations dominated by the latter. Increasingly, this looks like a fair-weather policy that is pushed aside if vital interests are at stake.

While a turn towards more protectionist trade policies seems unavoidable, this does not necessarily have to let to a disaster for all parties concerned. As mentioned earlier, some positions in International Political Economy argue in favour of selective protectionism, from the perspective of the less industrialized Global South. After all, the wave of protectionism in the North during the 1930s has led to a massive step of industrialization in the South, based on the paradigm of 'import substitution industrialization' (Clapp and Moseley, 2020: 1409). Still, there is 'good' and 'bad' protectionism. The IPE discussions mentioned earlier highlight that a progressive form of protectionism embeds the latter in a coherent strategy for catch-up industrialization (and national security in a few selected areas), whereas a degressive form of protectionism misuses trade policies for the rent-seeking of individual companies that simply are keen to collect monopolistic profits. Export curbs on medical supplies as witnessed during the early phase of the pandemic certainly would qualify as another case of degressive form of protectionism, if applied outside very short-term emergencies.

21

Intellectual Property Rights: Global Commons for Vaccines or Private Property?

During the coronavirus crisis, the fast production of pharmaceutical products to detect, prevent and heal virus infections has become an issue of utmost urgency. At the same time, this has led to the question why products related to similar diseases have not been produced much earlier. Some observers have argued that this neglect is due to the limited financial incentives for the pharmaceutical industry, particularly with regard to vaccines. Moreover, after the development of vaccines, their mass-scale production arguably was limited because pharmaceutical companies were worried about the loss of their intellectual property rights. Whereas the one side argued that patent protection should be relaxed or even abolished in order to make vaccines quickly available to as many people as possible – most notably including the global poor – the other side warned that this proposal would weaken the incentives for pharmaceutical companies to invest resources into vaccine development in the future. Which side has the better arguments?

Intellectual property rights in global trade institutions

During the last decades, the pharmaceutical industry has been a prime topic for students of International Political Economy, particularly because of the controversial debates on the protection of intellectual property rights by international institutions such as the agreement on Trade-Related Intellectual Property Rights (TRIPS) of the World Trade Organization (WTO). At the background of these debates are four fundamental trends that have increased the importance of intellectual property during the last decades (Balaam and Dillman, 2014: 238). First, it has become increasingly obvious that economic growth and political power today more and more depend on knowledge and human capital in fields like engineering and ICT, instead of traditional resources such as control of land. Second, profits increasingly do not accrue to those who manufacture a product, but rather to those that develop, design and market products (think, for example, of the distribution of iPhone profits between Apple and manufacturing companies such as Foxconn). Third, although the flow of information is difficult to control, most governments try to make sure that their knowledge economies flourish, based on the investment of substantial resources, but also the desire to reserve as much as possible the resulting economic benefits for themselves and their national companies. Finally, there is a growing tension between those powerful companies that own intellectual property rights (IPR) and those numerous individuals and NGOs arguing that the utilization of this property should be free to the world.

Owners of intellectual property – patents, copyrights and trademarks – argue that only if this property is soundly protected, creators have incentives to invest time and other resources into their development. Without protection, other firms would have unfair advantages; for example, by offering the same products cheaper, without expenses for research and development. This free-riding would lead to less innovation in the future. Moreover, IPR protection also makes sure that products are safe and of high quality – an important consideration in the case of vaccines. Intellectual property protection requires two steps (Balaam and Dillman, 2014: 239): first, this protection has to be upheld by national law (and law enforcement). Second, governments have to make sure that other governments also respect and enforce IPR held by foreign owners. The second – and arguably more challenging – step usually is based on bilateral or multilateral treaties, including the TRIPS agreement mentioned earlier.

Opponents of IPR protection argue that the universal access to knowledge is a basic human right. Moreover, they argue that strict IPR protection limits the ability of countries of the Global South to catch up with the Global North; for example, due to the prohibitively high costs for foreign technologies. A particularly controversial issue are the conditions for compulsory licences for patented medicines. Governments can issue this type of licence to a domestic company or government body in order to allow it to produce and sell a generic medicine without the consent of the owner of the IPR in case of an emergency. This became a major issue, for example, during the AIDS pandemic, because of the very high prices of US-developed drugs and the high number of poor patients in countries such as South Africa (Balaam and Dillman, 2014: 255–7). Other North–South conflicts on IPR protection relate to the patenting of traditional knowledge of indigenous peoples; for example, on plant uses, by Northern companies. Finally, states play a very important role for financing important components of intellectual property via research and development (R&D) funding or the public procurement of innovative products (whereas companies often focus on the commercialization of the results of this R&D, see Mazzucato, 2011). Correspondingly, the results of public funding should accrue to all citizens (at least of this state), according to IPR protection critics. The development of vaccines against the coronavirus mirrors the classical debates in International Political Economy in great detail.

Over the last decades, these debates mainly have played out around the TRIPS agreement established in 1994 (Balaam and Dillman, 2014: 250–60). This agreement is widely seen as a major achievement in favour of the creators of intellectual property, since it makes the protection of IPR obligatory to all members of the WTO, including its binding mechanism for dispute resolution, even if many bilateral and regional trade agreements negotiated by the US feature even more stringent regulations for IPR protection. Pharmaceutical companies – together with companies producing audiovisual content, software and agricultural chemicals – were among the driving forces for the TRIPS agreement. The agreement only allows exceptions from the requirement to put in place stringent rules of IPR protection for the least developed countries (LDCs) until 2033. Hardly any LDC was able to make use of this development-friendly rule – due to the still fairly high technological requirements – with the exception of Bangladesh which has developed a vibrant industry for generics medicine (Gay and Gallagher, 2020).

The neglected development of drugs to prevent and fight coronavirus infections before the crisis

For informed observers, the pandemic was not a surprise. A major wave of coronavirus infections was expected (Florio, 2020: 6–7; Rutschman, 2020). This expectation for once was based on certain features of this virus strain; in particular, its frequent mutation. Moreover, there were several warning shots. The first was SARS/Severe Acute Respiratory Syndrome-CoV-1, an epidemic in 2002, caused by a coronavirus. Another epidemic struck in 2012, again based on a coronavirus (MERS/Middle East Respiratory Syndrome). In spite of these clear warnings, the pharmaceutical industry did not invest major efforts into the development of drugs to prevent and fight coronavirus infections. Although there were substantial public grants for vaccine development against coronaviruses, only six clinical studies were recorded by the World Health Organization (WHO) before the outbreak of the pandemic. The same neglect applied to the development of antiviral drugs that might assist the treatment of infected patients. Both efforts would have been very helpful for fast vaccine and drug development when COVID-19 finally broke out.

Why was the pharmaceutical industry not interested to invest into research and development of drugs to prevent and fight coronavirus infections? In order to answer this question, we have to understand its business model (Florio, 2020: 7–9). The focus of the industry is on the development of drugs for the treatment of chronic pathologies (for example, diabetes or hypertension) and cancer, not on infectious diseases: 'In 2019 the Top 20 Pharma companies were busy carrying out research into about 400 new drugs, half of them anticancer drugs (which currently sell for an average of US$195,000 per treatment) but only 65 projects into any type of infectious disease' (Florio, 2020: 7). The development of drugs for infectious diseases is less attractive for pharmaceutical companies, either because these diseases mostly happen in areas with low spending power or because the market could be too short-lived, if the disease is eradicated. Furthermore, pharmaceutical companies have to expect massive political and social pressure to relax their IPR in the case of vaccines, as witnessed during the coronavirus pandemic. Most pharmaceutical companies follow a strongly financialized business model (see Chapter 12), with a focus of maximizing the returns to shareholders and a very limited concern for stakeholder considerations, thereby making the development of vaccines quite unattractive (Fernandez and Klinge, 2020). In order to make up for this neglect, two public–private partnerships have been set up – the Global Alliance for Vaccines and Immunization (GAVI) established in 2000 and the Coalition for Epidemic Preparedness Innovations (CEPI).

Even a pandemic such as the coronavirus outbreak would not have led to a massive research and development effort by the pharmaceutical industry: 'people recover and become immune or they die within a relatively short period of time. It is not a stable market to invest in, unless governments offer pharmaceutical firms substantial subsidies to encourage them to do research' (Florio, 2020: 8). Well, the governments did exactly that. The US government alone provided more than a billion US dollars for this research. Still, the pharmaceutical sector succeeded in placing a ruling that explicitly interdicts the US government to limit prices on pharmaceutical drugs patented with regard to the coronavirus – instead of controlling the prices of drugs and vaccines developed with public assistance (Florio, 2020: 8). This is even more striking given the massive involvement of the US National Institute of Health in vaccine development with Moderna and AstraZeneca (Rutschman, 2020).

The restrictive protection of IPR on vaccines throughout the coronavirus pandemic

After vaccines against the coronavirus had been developed with great speed, based on massive public support, the fast production of vaccines became the core bottleneck for fighting the pandemic on a global scale. Production was hampered by limited production facilities held by those pharmaceutical companies that had successfully developed vaccines (for example, BioNTech/Pfizer, AstraZeneca, Moderna). Moreover, rich countries were able to safeguard a very large share of the vaccines produced in the first months of 2021, to the detriment to low- and medium-income economies.

Even before a vaccine had been developed, demands were articulated to forego giving IPR to these pharmaceutical companies and make the vaccines globally available without IPR protection. This demand was based on a number of arguments. IPR make for the largest part of vaccine prices – only by waiving these rights they would become affordable to poorer countries. Waiving IPR protection would make the large global generic manufacturing capacities available for vaccine development and therefore speed up vaccination – in all economies. Moreover, quick vaccine development only was possible because extremely high contributions to research and development by the public sector, which does not fit well with IPR held by private companies. Finally, there is also the fear that rich countries will lose interest in the development and distribution of affordable treatments as soon as their population has been vaccinated (Acharya, 2020). A formal proposal to temporarily suspend IPR related to the coronavirus repeatedly tabled by India, South Africa and other Southern economies has not been accepted by the WTO, due to opposition by European and North American governments (Usher, 2020), although the US government reversed its stance in 2021.

Given the powerful nature of the global institutions for trade-related IPR, global affordable access to coronavirus treatments and vaccines faced powerful opposition. This opposition largely was successful, as indicated for the case of the US mentioned earlier. Among the arguments successfully forwarded in order to keep IPR with the pharmaceutical companies were not only the investments of the latter (which could have been refunded by governments and international organizations), but also the point that waiving IPR protection would set a dangerous precedent for further pharmaceutical product development. This would limit incentives for innovations in the future. Finally, the production of biological vaccines against the coronavirus is technically quite challenging and may not always be feasible for low- and medium-income economies. Instead, the vaccine requirements of Southern companies should be covered by the temporary Northern-funded COVAX initiative that is supposed to procure and distribute vaccines for poorer countries. The GAVI initiative COVAX (COVID-19 Vaccine Global Access Facility), however, has large difficulties not only with regard to mobilizing enough funding, but also with acquiring vaccines, due to the exclusive agreements rich countries had made with vaccine-producing companies (Usher, 2020).

An option for the future: vaccine production as global public good

The business system of the pharmaceutical industry is set up in a way that works against the development of drugs and vaccinations to prevent communicable diseases as caused by the coronavirus. In order to undertake the latter with great spend, it has relied on massive subsidies by governments. Still, considerations about the protection of IPR for the pharmaceutical industry have put a break on the dissemination of vaccines against the coronavirus towards the global poor. This has led to many demands for a relaxation of this protection in the face of the global pandemic. Still, the very fast and successful development of these vaccines by the major pharmaceutical companies has made initiatives to dilute IPR very unpopular in the Global North. Correspondingly, it is highly unlikely that we can expect a relaxation of IPR in post-coronavirus capitalism.

An alternative option for overcoming global health crises would be to use a global public goods approach towards the expensive and risky development of vaccines against the coronavirus and related diseases, still leaving the much bigger sector of lifestyle drugs to pharmaceutical companies. In this case, vaccine development as well as distribution would be undertaken by the public sector in an international, centralized and permanent way, predominantly based on funding by the Northern economies (Florio, 2020; Rutschman, 2020). International initiatives for organizing these activities are already in place (for example, CEPI, GAVI, see Chapter 22), but yet are underfunded and temporary. Massively increasing this funding based on public budgets in the North will be popular in the short term, but may, however, run into increasing opposition by Northern taxpayers in the medium to long term.

22

Global Health Governance: Intergovernmental or Private–Public Networks?

With regard to global governance, the most striking development during the coronavirus crisis was the decision of President Trump – withdrawn by President Biden – to leave the WHO, based on an allegedly too prominent role of the Chinese government in this organization. Later during the pandemic, limitations of global health governance became an issue because it turned out to be very difficult to safeguard an equitable global distribution of scarce vaccines and global health institutions were unable to prevent 'vaccine nationalism'. For some observers, finally, global health governance has been fundamentally flawed for many years, because of the prominent role of private actors such as the Gates Foundation. Do we need to return to the intergovernmental system of the WHO or should we proceed with giving a major say to private–public networks?

Concepts of global economic governance

The study of global economic governance provides us with ample analytical instruments in order to put these developments in place. For uninformed observers, the WHO may look like the powerful global authority on all health issues. International Political Economy scholars, however, are well aware that the power of the WHO – like that of all UN organizations – is severely circumscribed.

International organizations such as the WHO fulfil two main functions. On the one side, they act as meeting points of national governments for the development of common rules and activities. On the other side, the secretariats of these organizations have important functions for the impartial collection of data, research and recommendations on global best practices. In both cases, they rely on the cooperation by its member governments

(O'Brien and Williams, 2016: 300–1. International organizations only very rarely have power over its member governments. This usually is only the case if they have a huge amount of financial resources and member states are in financial distress, as for example in the case of structural adjustment programmes designed by the IMF and the WB during the 1980s and 1990s (O'Brien and Williams, 2016: 303–4). As we shall see, the WHO has been crippled by conflicts between its member governments and has been starved financially, thereby limiting its abilities during the last decades.

While the different priorities of Northern and Southern governments regarding UN organizations is a well-established phenomenon, it has recently been complemented by another 'North–South conflict'. Large emerging markets such as China demand a larger say in the institutions of global economic governance; for example, the IMF and the WB (O'Brien and Williams, 2016: 307–10). They also have set up their own club – Brazil, Russia, India, China and South Africa (BRICS) – and their own international institutions (for example, the New Development Bank). In the case of global health governance, the conflict between China and the US is particularly important.

Another recent topic in studies of global governance is the growing role of private actors such as NGOs, companies and philanthropic foundations (O'Brien and Williams, 2016: 305–7). As we will see, the issue area of global health governance in general – and the coronavirus pandemic, in particular – is a field where this is particularly prominent. Whereas traditionally international cooperation has been based on national governments and international secretariats only, we see a massive proliferation of private actors in global governance. Shall we be happy about the proliferation of private initiatives and public–private networks? It has advantages and disadvantages. Among the former ranges the mobilization of additional resources, among the latter the loss of democratic legitimacy, by giving powerful economic interests a major say about global policies (Nölke, 2003a, 2003b).

Global health governance regarding the pandemic: the UN paralysed between North and South

Officially, the highest body in global health governance is the annual meeting of WHO member state health ministers in the World Health Assembly. De facto, the influence of the World Health Assembly is limited. For many years, the WHO has become a focal point for North–South struggles. Governments of the Global South use their majority in this assembly for articulating their demands. Governments of the Global North, in turn, put limits on the regular budget of the WHO. The classical budget of the WHO (Assessed Contributions), a percentage of each member country's GDP, covers less than 20 per cent. More than 75 per cent of the WHO's budget is based on voluntary contributions by member states and private actors. Less than 4 per cent of the latter is made up of 'core voluntary contributions', meaning that the WHO has full discretion of the use of funds (WHO, nd). Correspondingly, the core business of the WHO is severely limited by underfunding and lack of flexibility. At the same time, the Northern governments effectively decide about the most important funding decisions, according to their own priorities.

The financing of vaccines for countries in the Global South follows the established pattern. At its centre stands the Covax Facility that pools the procurement of vaccines, in order to realize economies of scale and a good negotiation position. Covax is mainly funded through official development assistance by Northern donors and is meant for those countries in the Global South that have difficulties to finance their own vaccination programmes. It buys vaccines from the vaccine suppliers (via 'advance purchase agreements') and delivers it to Southern countries later, in order to vaccinate the high-priority populations in these countries (for example, health workers or old-age citizens). While Southern governments appreciate the provision of vaccines – in the early phase of the pandemic, nearly all vaccines have been bought by Northern governments – they are also critical that Covax operates in the Northern-dominated mode of strict protection of IPR and high prices for vaccines (see Chapter 21). Southern demands for relaxing IPR protection or lower prices have been turned down (Legge, 2020: 384–5). Moreover, relying on voluntary assistance by Northern donors is a very different mode of global governance than having a powerful international organization for a 'truly universal global initiative' (Gostin et al, 2020a: 1617).

The powerful role of private agents in vaccination campaigns: the 'Access to COVID-19 Tools Accelerator'

A particular feature of global health governance is the powerful role of private actors. Both transnational corporations and philanthropic foundations play a much more important role than in most other fields of global governance. Arguably, the WHO has ceased to be a conventional intergovernmental body and has mutated into some kind of 'multi-stakeholder public private partnership' (Legge, 2020: 383). Correspondingly, the most important global decisions with regard to fighting the coronavirus pandemic have not been taken within the official body of global health governance, but in a rather intransparent network of collaboration between public and private actors.

The creation of the 'Access to COVID-19 Tools Accelerator' (ACT-A) is a case in point. Its purpose is to make diagnostics, medicines and vaccines against the coronavirus available globally. Covax (see mentioned earlier) is the vaccination financing pillar of ACT-A. The organizational leadership in this pillar, however, is with CEPI and GAVI. CEPI is a public–private partnership set up at the World Economic Forum in Davos in 2017, by the governments of India and Norway together with the Bill and Melinda Gates Foundation, the British charity Wellcome Trust and the World Economic Forum. GAVI is another public–private partnership founded at the World Economic Forum, in this case already in 2000 and with the Bill and Melinda Gates Foundation as initial funder. The Gates Foundation and the Wellcome Trust are charged with managing the coronavirus treatment pillar of ACT-A, together with UNITAID, another public–private partnership. And the third pillar, on coronavirus testing, is managed by the Foundation for Innovative New Diagnostics (FIND) and the Global Fund to Fight AIDS, Tuberculosis and Malaria (Global Fund), again two public–private partnerships.

Normally, the organization of a campaign to confront a global threat such as the coronavirus would be led by the global organization in charge; namely, the WHO. In this case, it is a public–private alliance where the WHO is participating, but only in a very marginal role. The involvement of the private sector mobilizes additional financial resources, but also limits the accountability to national governments and the national democratic process. This may be less severe during the coronavirus pandemic with its massive public and media attention. But in other cases of global health governance, a strong influence of private actors is having negative repercussions on global health governance; for example, with regard to 'preventing and controlling noncommunicable diseases driven by commercial determinants of health, including alcoholic beverages, sugar-sweetened beverages, tobacco, and unhealthy foods' (Gostin et al, 2020a: 1617). Giving companies a say in these matters does not seem to be healthy.

The WHO Secretariat and the fight against the pandemic on the national level

Even if the role of the World Health Assembly and its global rule-setting is limited, the WHO still is a very important player in global health governance. Its importance is less based on the ability to make globally binding decisions by votes of national ministers of health, but rather on the technical authority of its staff and its impact on the national level (see Chapter 2). This authority was particularly important in the situation of great insecurity during the early phases of the coronavirus crisis. Governments – and their societies – were not sure about the severity of the health threat and about the most suitable measures on how to counter it most effectively. They looked towards the WHO for authoritative statements on the nature of the challenge and the most suitable counter-actions. Preliminary assessments regarding this role of the WHO during the coronavirus pandemic are more on the positive side: 'The WHO has done an outstanding job at the global level in convening expert groups, providing technical guidance, procuring and distributing medical commodities, working with news media, providing online education for health professionals and policy officials and distilling complex issues into meaningful slogans (solidarity, testing, human rights)' (Legge 2020: 386). Arguably, a feature of the WHO that usually attracts a lot of criticism – its decentralized structure – proved to be an asset during the crisis, in terms of data gathering and adapting advice to regional circumstances (Debre and Dijkstra, 2020: 12).

Still, even the technical work of the WTO has been compromised by fighting between its member states – in particular, China and the US (see Chapter 27). The core issue here was the origin of the pandemic, with the US attributing this origin to China and China intending to cast doubts on this claim. The same conflict had already blocked the UN Security Council with regard to a swift reaction to the crisis. It has taken six months for only a first resolution on the coronavirus pandemic and also has subsequently blocked a cooperative UN response (Gostin et al, 2020a: 1616). The US under President Trump even sought to withdraw from the WHO altogether, due to claims of undue proximity to the Chinese government. Indeed, the WHO was very reluctant with its official declaration of a 'Public Health Emergency of International Concern (PHEIC)' and only declared the latter by 30 January 2020. It neither investigated into earlier unofficial information on the coronavirus outbreak in China (admittedly, difficult to implement for an intergovernmental organization), nor took an immediate decision after the very late official information by the Chinese government on 31 December 2021 (Gostin et al, 2020b: 379).

Making the fight against communicable diseases a global public good

The coronavirus pandemic has demonstrated that money spent on the prevention of communicable diseases is money well spent, not only from the perspective of countries in the Global South. Moreover, it has become obvious that the current set-up of global health governance is not fully functional. We did not see much activity on the global pooling of expertise and joint development of vaccines during the early phase of the pandemic. Instead, in order to increase the global availability of protection against the coronavirus, many governments have banned exports of relevant material. The WHO often is paralysed between the Global North and the South, although it still is important as a technical authority. Moreover, its authority has been eroded by numerous private actors and public–private partnerships, as well as the China–US rivalry more recently.

These observations make a strong case for reforming global health governance with a focus of declaring the fight against communicable diseases a global public good. This should convince taxpayers in the richer economies of the Global North to agree to higher payments for the regular WHO budget. Subsequently, it should be possible to make a 'deal' where Northern governments increase their fixed financial contribution and Southern governments refrain from using their majority for politicization, thereby giving way for the fundamental reform of the organization that has been on the cards for decades. Increased core spending by WHO member states, finally, would also reduce the controversial influence of private actors in global health governance. Making the fight against communicable diseases a global public good does not mean, however, to give the WHO more power to supervise and intervene into member states. The coronavirus pandemic has illustrated how national governments safeguard their sovereignty in a crisis. This would be a lost cause (Hanrieder, 2020: 535–6). It also does not mean restricting the WHO to fighting pandemics. The idea rather would be to focus on the most popular part of the organization, in order to win back the ability to act in a meaningful way – and to address other concerns in a comprehensive way later.

23

Foreign Debt in the Global South: Permanent Write-off or Temporary Relief?

During the coronavirus crisis, governments have raised massive debt in order to combat the health emergency. However, many countries of the Global South already had high levels of public debt before the coronavirus crisis. Correspondingly, we may witness a new global debt crisis soon. Led by the G20, the IMF and the WB, creditor governments have reacted to this problem by temporarily relieving low-income governments from debt service. The question is whether this is enough or whether they have to permanently write off some Southern debt. International Political Economy scholarship provides us with a number of analytical instruments to tackle this question.

Why do governments get into debt crises? Between original sin and export competition

Taking up public debt is not necessarily a bad idea for countries of the Global South. Processes of economic catch-up often require huge amounts of public funds, often much higher amounts that are available domestically via tariffs, taxes and other public sector sources. Correspondingly, governments sell securities and bonds in order to raise additional resources. Depending on the income group of the country, governments address different sources for foreign debt. Upper-middle-income countries usually have a good access to international capital markets; that is, private creditors. For lower-middle and particularly low-income countries, both international organizations – in particular, multilateral development banks such as the WB – and Northern governments (via bilateral cooperation) are more important sources of loans.

In most cases, debt is issued in the currency of the debtor country. Other governments, however, have denominated their debt in foreign currencies (for example, the US dollar), due to the need to pay imports with these currencies. Moreover, the interest rates they have to pay for debt issued in, for example, US dollars is considerably lower than for debt in their own currency, because creditors do not have to face the risk of a devaluation of their credits denominated on the debtor country. The latter risk, however, is shifted to the debtor-government side. If the currency of the latter depreciates against, for example, the US dollar, its debt service (calculated in national currency) becomes much heavier. Serving huge foreign-denominated debts with a strongly depreciated currency puts a heavy strain on these economies. Due to this risk, taking up debt in foreign currency is called 'original sin'.

High volumes of sovereign debt are already a big risk in normal times. In a major recession – such as caused by the coronavirus – it gets much worse. A recession requires high public spending and does not allow for major tax increases, therefore limiting the available public funds – or increasing government debts. At the same time, indebted countries will try to boost their exports, in order to service their foreign debt. Unfortunately, many of the least well-off countries in the Global South have rather similar export profiles, often in the field of natural resources. This competition for exports often leads to a downward turn in the prices of export products (too much supply for an inelastic demand), thereby counteracting the debt service effort.

How are international debt crises tackled? Between London and Paris, between Beijing and Washington

Given the difficulties for highly indebted countries of the Global South to exist in the debt quagmire, creditors have developed several institutional solutions. Since the 1950s, creditor governments meet with debtor governments in the so-called Paris Club, in order to restructure the obligations of Southern countries with debt problems. Private creditors meet separately in the so-called London Club. Debt restructuring usually includes modifications to the date when debts are due – they will be postponed to the future – but often also a reduction of the overall debt volume. Multilateral institutions such as the WB receive preferred creditor treatment; they are the first creditors to be repaid. Originally established in order to assess the likelihood of repayments of financial obligations by business in the Global North, rating agencies also play a major role for managing the debt of Southern countries by providing their assessments on the likelihood that governments are able to service their obligations.

A major precondition for debt restructurings by one of the clubs – but also for access to many currency swap arrangements (to be discussed later) – is an agreement between the debtor government and the IMF. Particularly since the 1980s, the Fund has taken on a pivotal role in global public debt management. It has become a lender of last resort for those governments that have difficulties accessing conventional sources of credit. Credit by the IMF, however, often comes at a massive price. The IMF usually only provides credit to debtor governments in distress if the latter comply with the Fund's conditionality. While the conditions of the IMF vary over time and between countries (Krampf, 2015), a typical conditionality for a 1980s or 1990s structural adjustment programme includes policies such as raising taxes, cutting back public services (including the health system!), devaluing currencies, privatizing public assets and liberalizing tariffs (Balaam and Dillman, 2014: 183–4).

Although these conditions are very painful, debtor countries hardly default on their debt in an abrupt manner. If debt servicing becomes impossible, sovereign defaults usually are being engineered in an orderly way, in order to make sure that most debt is serviced, even if delayed. An unorderly default, in contrast, means that a country will be cut off from external credit for many years. This is very unpopular with the business and political elite in the debtor countries and – together with the powerful coordination and centralization of decision-making on the creditor side – responsible for the low number of defaults (Roos, 2019). Given that the debt load for low-income countries sometimes has become unbearable, but that the latter also should avoid an unorderly debt default, the international debtor community has developed a number of debt restructuring programmes for this group of countries, including some debt cancellation for particularly poor countries.

The dimension of the debt problem in the Global South during the coronavirus crisis

Even without the coronavirus crisis, we would have had a debt problem in some countries of the Global South. Particularly, booming prices of natural resources before the GFC have led to increasing public expenditures in the Global South. The bust of the commodity bubble after 2010 has forced many countries to take up debt in order not to drastically reduce these expenditures. Due to the very expansive monetary policy in the Northern economies, many investors were willing to lend, given the substantially higher interest rates in the South. Moreover, China has offered considerable amount of credit to Southern governments in order to finance (and build) infrastructure projects during the last decade, substantially contributing to debt build-up in some economies. Correspondingly, public debt in the Global South was a massive problem even before the coronavirus crisis. For example, for lower-income countries the average public external debt service (without domestic debt service) has increased from 5.5 per cent of government revenue in 2011 to 12.4 per cent in 2019; it would have further increased even without the crisis (Jones, 2020). The WB before corona even spoke of a fourth global debt wave, larger, broader and faster growing than the last three (Kose et al,

2021) – each of the latter led to a major financial crisis (the Latin American debt crisis, the Asian financial crisis and the GFC).

The pandemic has made matters much worse. On the one side, the health crisis has affected most countries of the Global South much more than most countries of the Global North. On the other side, most governments of the Global North had much higher financial resources available in order to fight the coronavirus recession (see Part II on Domestic Institutions of Capitalism on the Demand Side). Correspondingly, the recession is much worse in the Global South. Given that the debt load of an economy usually is measured against the GDP of the latter, the GDP reduction alone has increased the debt load in the affected economies. In addition, many governments have taken on additional public debt, in order to finance health, social or economic measures. This will further drive up the relationship between debt and GDP.

The problem is particularly acute for governments that are indebted in foreign currencies. These governments need to mobilize substantial amounts of liquidity in foreign currencies in order to meet their obligations. Access to foreign currencies, however, has become scarce due to several factors including outflows of speculative financial (portfolio) investments and decreased FDIs, as well as reductions in trade financing, tourism revenues and remittances that all started quickly after the outbreak of the pandemic. Correspondingly, the exchange relationship of the affected Southern currencies has been weakened, further aggravating the debt service problem (Kharas and Dooley, 2020: 2). Moreover, most Southern governments – except for Brazil and Mexico – do not have access to bilateral swap lines with the Federal Reserve of the United States; that is, cannot temporarily exchange substantial amounts of their local currencies with US dollars. The liquidity resources available for Southern economies at the IMF, as well as in the South's internal swap arrangements (next to the Chiang Mai Initiative Multilateralization in East Asia this most prominently includes the Contingent Reserve Arrangements of the BRICS group) are by far inadequate for covering the liquidity requirements of the Global South (Gallagher et al, 2021: 141).

Foreign debtors have realized that many of the least well-off Southern governments may experience difficulties servicing their debt. After the outbreak of the pandemic, only one sub-Saharan African country was given access to the sovereign debt market for raising additional debt. Very quickly, 36 countries have been downgraded by the credit rating agencies with regard to the likelihood of debt repayment (Kharas and Dooley, 2020: 2). However, in terms of overall volume, the largest share of debt service is due to the comparatively rich upper-middle-income countries. Within this group, countries differ considerably between economies whose debt is investment grade – such as China or Colombia – and easy to refinance and economies whose debt is highly speculative or even substantially at risk. Some of the countries in the latter group already have defaulted in 2020, such as Lebanon and Zambia (Kharas and Dooley, 2020: 4–7).

Too little too late? Debt service suspension during the coronavirus crisis

Given the precarious situation of many countries of the Global South, the G20 governments (notably including China) quickly have started a 'Debt Service Suspension Initiative' (DSSI). This suspension was agreed upon for all countries that are eligible for International Development Association (IDA) credits (plus Angola). IDA is the soft loan window of the WB that provides subsidized credit to currently 74 particularly poor countries that are unable to borrow on credit-market terms. Between May 2020 and April 2021, the initiative has suspended payments of around US$5 billion for about 40 countries (World Bank, 2021).

The temporary suspension of debt-service payments – not involving any debt cancellation – is not scheduled to take place until the end of 2021. It is limited to debt relationships with creditor governments and neither includes private creditors nor international organizations such as the WB as creditors. However, with delayed payments of about US$5 billion (and a maximum of additional US$7.3 billion), the DSSI only covers a small part of debts due. Countries participating in the DSSI have the option to participate in the more comprehensive 'Common Framework for Debt Treatments beyond the DSSI' set up by the G20 in November 2020. This would not only entail debt suspension, but also debt relief (and would possibly also involve private creditors), but so far countries have been very reluctant to appeal to this initiative, because the rating agencies react with sudden debt downgrades for those countries asking for a restructuring of debt with private creditors (EURODAD, 2021). Moreover, its volume is limited, if compared with the volume of the 'debt pandemic'. The Brookings Institution calculates that low-income countries owe US$356 billion for public debt service due in 2021 and US$329 billion in 2022. It also alerts us to the fact that some US$500 billion in private debt are due and that during earlier debt crises these obligations often also had to be met by governments (Kharas and Dooley, 2020: 3).

The situation in these economies is hardly tenable. A massive debt load leads to considerable economic and social problems. In addition, the permanent need to restructure debt causes a lot of administrative and political stress for the governments involved. However, the most straightforward alternative, simple debt forgiveness, also is not without problems. First, creditor-country taxpayers and benefits recipients would not be particularly happy with the corresponding burdens on Northern public budgets. Moreover, debt forgiveness can bring problems of its own, including moral hazard (that is, an incentive for reckless borrowing in the future), a wasteful utilization of public funds for private means and creditor reservations towards future credit for these countries (Kharas and Dooley, 2020: 3).

Options on how to deal with the debt pandemic in the Global South

Four alternative options are available in order to deal with this difficult situation. The first option would be to continue the current course and hope for a quick economic rebound in 2022 and thereafter that takes place in heavily indebted economies. This would mean that private creditors to countries of the Global South would continue to keep out of any debt suspension and the moratorium by bilateral official creditors ends as planned. However, this only seems to be an option for countries with investment-grade debt. It is highly unlikely that the most indebted economies are able to service their obligations, nor will they be able to raise new funds to cover this debt service (Kharas and Dooley, 2020: 7).

The second option, preferred for example by the Brookings Institution (Kharas and Dooley, 2020), is to reserve debt restructuring (that is, debt forgiveness with similar shares of all relevant parties in exchange for the implementation of structural adjustment programmes) for a few particularly hard-hit countries. Otherwise, creditors should focus on the provision of liquidity (that is, the rollover of principal repayments at acceptable conditions) for the large majority of countries in the Global South, in order to allow these economies to grow out of their debt difficulties. By issuing additional and reallocating existing Special Drawing Rights for countries in need of foreign currency, the IMF could play an important role for this liquidity provision that comes along without the usual IMF conditionality (Kharas and Dooley, 2020). In April 2021, the IMF governors agreed to increase special drawing rights (SDRs) by US$650 billion, but without reallocation only US$7 billion will be available for low-income countries (EURODAD, 2021).

The third option is to comprehensively strengthen the global financial safety net. Next to the activities of the second option this would, for example, include broadening the coverage of bilateral and regional swap facilities to be used by countries of the Global South and decoupling the latter from the condition of a parallel IMF programme, allowing the IMF to set up a multilateral currency swap facility and interdicting credit rating agencies to downgrade debt during the ongoing emergency (Gallagher et al, 2021). Moreover, support for debt-ridden Southern economies should not only be borne out by Northern governments (and taxpayers), but should also involve private creditors that have mostly been free-riding in terms of debt reduction so far.

A fourth option for poor countries and emerging markets could be to default on their sovereign debt, based on a coordinated debt strike. While this course of action has been rarely chosen in the past, the desperate situation in the current debt crisis, combined with the absence of a hegemonic power (see Chapter 27) that usually organizes collective action on the side of creditors, may change the odds. Mass foreign debt default, however, could put additional strain on many domestic financial systems in creditor economies (see Chapter 13).

Towards a global financial safety net for heavily indebted countries

The coronavirus pandemic has massively intensified the debt problem of many economies in the Global South. This problem was already a major cause for concern before the outbreak of the coronavirus crisis. The global creditor community has reacted with an initiative for temporary debt service suspension for low-income debtor countries. However, this initiative only deals with the tip of the iceberg in terms of countries involved. It also does not help in the long run. While upper-middle-income countries' governments may be able to refinance their debt on global financial markets and low-income countries' governments benefit from creditor initiatives, particularly lower-middle-income countries will face considerable constraints in the future.

Given these circumstances, Northern governments are well advised to agree to substantially strengthen the global financial safety net. Actions such as issuing additional SDRs at the IMF and allowing the latter to set up a multilateral swap facility do not cost much, but considerably improve the situation of many Southern countries. We should not forget that debt crises can be deadly during the pandemic – not only because of underfunding of health systems but also because heavily indebted countries may avoid life-saving lockdowns in order to limit the economic costs of the latter (Arellano et al, 2020).

PART V

Anthropocene Capitalism

The greatest challenge of our generation is global warming. Given that the latter process is closely connected to the expansion of industrial capitalism, it has become an important topic for International Political Economy. Core topics include the linkage between economic globalization and climate change and the role of business in negotiations on climate change limitation (O'Brien and Williams, 2016: 250–8; Dauvergne, 2020). Moreover, International Political Economy has started to engage with the more general debate between 'ecocentric' and 'technocentric' approaches to sustainability, particularly on the feasibility of planned 'degrowth' in order to overcome the global environmental crisis. The degrowth idea also moves against the global agribusiness food system and pleads for a return of agriculture as local community support.

The coronavirus pandemic has touched on all of these topics. It has demonstrated the close linkage between economic growth and climate change – pollution was heavily reduced during the core recession – and has given some indications on the salience of the climate change agenda during the period of economic reconstruction (Chapter 24). It has also brought the prospects for degrowth forcefully to the table and has given us an opportunity to gauge the attractiveness of the degrowth concept within society at large (Chapter 25). Finally, it has highlighted the dangers of a further expansion of the global agrifood system; for example, with regard to the frequency of zoonotic diseases and the ability of local production to support the need of the local population in a situation of crisis (Chapter 26).

24

Climate Change: Cheap Dirty Energy or Green New Deal?

During the coronavirus crisis, the use of disposable gloves and plastic containers for goods surged. In the mindset of many people, the war on the environment took the backseat for a while. But will it return to the front seat in the era of post-corona capitalism? Among environmental activists, the coronavirus crisis gave rise to hope, that this crisis is an 'opportunity', a trigger, for change. But will it be a change in the 'right' direction? Work on global environmental change in International Political Economy helps us to answer these questions in an informed and structured manner (for discussions in Environmental Studies with relevance for Political Economy, see Chapter 25).

International Political Economy and climate change

In contrast to other issue areas in International Political Economy such as trade and finance, the epistemic authority of scientists is particularly relevant with regard to climate change. It took not only this authority to get the topic of climate change onto the international agenda at all, but this authority became to a surprising degree contested. The questions whether climate change exists, whether it is dangerous and whether it is man-made still are contested by sizeable minorities, in spite of the overwhelming scientific evidence that answers these questions affirmatively (O'Brien and Williams, 2016: 250–1, 256). As we shall see, this problem returned during the coronavirus pandemic. When people agree on the highly dangerous and man-made nature of climate change, this leads to the question where it exactly it is coming from. From an International Political Economy perspective, the role of economic globalization for the causation of climate change is particularly relevant (Dauvergne, 2020: 386–9). How did the temporary retreat of globalization during the pandemic affect climate change?

After clarifying what causes climate change, the question is what we can do about it. This has been the focus on decades of international negotiations about agreements to limit climate change. From an International Political Economy view, a core question in order to discuss the likelihood of successful agreements is the political power of business vis-à-vis other social forces (O'Brien and Williams, 2016: 256–8; Dauvergne, 2020: 389–94, 400–10). How does the coronavirus pandemic affect the balance of forces in these negotiations? Next to lobbying governments with regard to national laws and international agreements, business also affects climate change by voluntarily adjusting its behaviour; for example, not only with regard to the profitability of investments in fossil energies, but also in the context of corporate social responsibility for sustainable development (O'Brien and Williams, 2016: 253–6; Dauvergne, 2020: 394–400). Does the coronavirus pandemic intensify corporate activities with regard to the latter or does it strengthen the argument for binding public regulation?

Coronavirus crisis and expert authority: lessons for the climate debate

During the coronavirus crisis, the expertise of doctors and epidemiologists was central for public debate and mostly also for policymakers, although autonomous health agencies in some countries were pushed aside by governments (see Chapter 2). Can we assume that this will also assist the epistemic authority of climate researchers and lead to more stringent climate protection policies in the future? Students of global environmental politics are sceptical. They point towards the more authoritative character of the medical community in comparison with the community of climate scientists, given that the latter has been highly politicized during the last decades and that 'the degree of trust in experts is closely related to the amount of public dissent over crisis response' (van de Ven and Sun 2020: 17).

From a Political Economy perspective, one may add that there are much stronger incentives for parts of the business community – particularly, those in the fossil fuels sector – to cast doubts on the expertise of climate scientists, given that more stringent climate protection policies may drive them out of business. Companies with strong interests in petroleum and chemicals, such as ExxonMobil and Koch Industries, are the main funders of conservative think tanks that are leading the effort to cast doubt on climate change issues (Roper et al, 2016: 779–80). In the case of the coronavirus, the negative impacts were less concentrated and more diffuse, thereby reducing the incentive for business to politicize the epistemic authority of doctors and epidemiologists. Moreover, in the rich countries of the Global North, fiscal policy was able to limit the losses for (large) companies.

Climate change during the coronavirus recession

During the coronavirus crisis, the slowdown of economic activity has led to substantial gains with regard to the reduction in pollution. Even early during the pandemic, we were able to measure a dramatic fall in pollution; for example, due to a reduced utilization of coal-fired power stations and the reduced burning of oil going hand in hand with reduced transport. Correspondingly, emissions of nitrogen oxide and greenhouse gasses went down (Hepburn et al, 2020: 5–6). GDP growth (or reduction) and emissions still seem to be coupled very tightly (Helm, 2020: 23). Moreover, the coronavirus pandemic has given new impetus to the fight against air pollution, given that the combination of high levels of pollution and infection by the coronavirus appears to be particularly deadly (Kuzemko et al, 2020: 9).

In addition, the temporary deglobalization during the pandemic also has reduced climate-unfriendly emissions, by reducing pollution from shipping and aviation (Helm, 2020: 31–2). It also may reduce the need to expand the supporting infrastructures such as airports and ports in the future, if reshoring becomes a major trend (see Chapter 17). Correspondingly, post-coronavirus reshoring may have an additional advantage for climate protection by relocating production into the EU where production is more climate-compatible than in China, particularly because of higher carbon prices. Introducing a border carbon tax in the EU would further increase incentives to produce in a more climate-friendly way (Helm, 2020: 32).

During its emergence, the coronavirus recession – in particular, in the Global North – also has led to an 'unprecedented fall in energy demand', particularly for oil (Kuzemko et al, 2020: 4). Since this has also led to a fall in fossil fuel prices, it makes investments into the exploration of further oil and gas reserves less profitable. This context provides for a unique opportunity, if post-pandemic recovery programmes are combined with a low-carbon conditionality, also given that 'state subsidies for fossil fuels continue to far outstrip support for sustainable energy' (Kuzemko et al, 2020: 5). A survey of rescue packages, however, indicates that conditionalities of this kind were absent in the first round of fiscal measures, with 4 per cent of supported policies 'green', 4 per cent 'brown' and the remaining 92 per cent maintaining the status quo (Hepburn et al, 2020: 6).

Finally, it makes a big difference whether the post-recession reconstruction and climate protection programmes follow the usual 'Green New Deal' recipes (public investment, public procurement, social policies, research and development) or whether these programmes will be partially financed by financial market actors within public–private partnerships. Whereas countries of the Global North may fiscally afford the first option more easily, some countries of the Global South will be pushed towards the second, due to more limited fiscal resources. The involvement of global institutional investors in climate financing via public–private partnerships – Gabor (2021) calls this the 'Wall Street Consensus' – can become very detrimental for climate protection, given that it incorporates the latter into the fluctuations of global financial markets, including the option that capital outflows will have very negative repercussions on the financing of climate protection policies in the Global South (Dafermos et al, 2021: 9–10).

Politics during the coronavirus pandemic: implications for climate change politics

During the coronavirus crisis, governments have demonstrated their ability for massive regulation of the economy. Does this allow for the conclusion that policies against climate change will be more powerful and effective during post-corona capitalism? Many climate policy activists and scholars assume that this will be the case, particularly if the lessons from the coronavirus crisis are well heeded (Howarth et al, 2020; Klenert et al, 2020; Malm, 2020; Heyd, 2021). Others, however, argue that the climate and the coronavirus crises are quite different and that inter alia the pronounced immediacy, visibility and universality of the coronavirus pandemic, as well as its transience, explain the more swift and far-reaching response if compared with the climate crisis (Lidskog et al, 2020; van der Ven and Sun, 2020). One could also argue that people will be tired of extraordinary measures after the coronavirus pandemic and keen to return to their normal life, instead of starting the next set of major changes.

Moreover, a deep global recession after the pandemic will severely reduce the amount of attention and resources for climate protection policies – and increase the hunger for cheap (dirty) energy. Survey research has demonstrated that an increase in unemployment decreases both interest in global warming and the belief that the latter is happening at all (Kahn and Kotchen, 2011). Strongly increasing income inequality and poverty after the pandemic (see Chapter 7) may limit social support for intensified climate protection, if the latter goes hand in hand with a higher price for carbon dioxide emissions and poor social groups will not be generously compensated for these price increases. Even in Germany, a country that has weathered the coronavirus recession very well, a survey indicates a strongly reclining importance of climate protection in public opinion between 2019 and 2021, whereas economic and social concerns become more important (FAZ, 2021).

The need to combine post-corona reconstruction with massive public investments in climate protection

During the coronavirus recession, we have witnessed a substantial decrease in climate-related pollution. This observation should help to convince those people who still doubt that climate change is man-made. However, this observation also strengthens the tension between the protection of the environment and the creation of employment via economic growth (see also Chapter 25). Moreover, many poor households will need years to recover from the economic losses during the pandemic. They will not like the perspective to pay substantially for climate protection, via high prices for carbon dioxide emissions.

Given this situation, it seems highly advisable to combine post-corona fiscal reconstruction packages with the fight against climate change ('Green New Deals'), by investing in climate-compatible technologies and public infrastructures (Hepburn et al, 2020: 13–15; see also Chapter 9 and Chapter 11). We urgently need to decouple economic growth and climate change via these investments and by a partial reshoring of production. Alternatively, the only option to save the climate would be to turn to 'degrowth' (see Chapter 25).

25

Degrowth: Necessity or Fantasy?

Many people see the outbreak of the coronavirus pandemic as a more or less necessary consequence of capitalism and its inherent growth imperative. Correspondingly, they perceive the pandemic not only as an urgent warning sign, but also as a unique opportunity to overcome the focus on economic growth. This is assumed to be even more pressing, given the climate crisis and the close linkage between economic growth and carbon dioxide emission (see Chapter 24). Is degrowth a realistic perspective or is it a fantasy that cannot be realized, due to economic or political reasons?

Degrowth in debates of International Political Economy

Traditionally, discussions about degrowth did not play a major role in IPE debates. However, during the last decades IPE scholars have started to engage with debates in Environmental Studies between 'technocentric' and 'ecocentric' approaches to sustainability (O'Brien and Williams, 2016: 246–9). Both perspectives agree on the urgent need to protect the environment, but they disagree on the relative weight of this objective against other objectives. From a technocentric perspective, the main function of the economy is to satisfy human needs. In an ecocentric perspective, human needs are balanced with the concerns of all living organisms. A technocentric perspective assumes that economic growth is possible without ecological degradation in principle, even if it has been tightly coupled so far. Crucial instruments would be taxes on carbon dioxide emissions and technological innovations. An ecocentric perspective is deeply sceptical of modern industrial growth and assumes that it is incompatible with ecological preservation.

The 'degrowth' concept is a particularly prominent articulation of ecocentric approaches. The basic assumption of the degrowth movement is that, sooner or later, the climate change crisis will lead to natural disaster, which entails much loss of human life. Therefore, human societies will not have a choice, but to take drastic measures to lower their economic footprint and to abandon their belief in the feasibility of endless growth, in favour of a 'steady-state economy' and a more frugal lifestyle. Most contemporary degrowth academics and activists share two beliefs: first, that it is impossible to have economic growth without environmental destruction; and second, that the necessary transformation has to be capitalism-critical, based on female emancipation, non-violent and deeply democratic (Eversberg and Schmelzer, 2018: 251–2). Whereas the first embodies the core of the original degrowth concept (Martinez-Alier et al, 2010; Kallis, 2011), the second highlights its embeddedness in a broader set of left political values. Critics of the degrowth concept argue that it is politically and socially infeasible, but also environmentally ineffective and economically inefficient (Van den Bergh, 2011). For example, according to the critics, even early indications of degrowth would lead to a stock market crash, a deflation and even economic implosion, followed by a new growth cycle (Tokic, 2012). Moreover, absence of economic growth would likely lead to authoritarianism, unless accompanied by very strong social movements (Kallis et al, 2018: 308).

The boom of degrowth articulations during the early coronavirus crisis

The outbreak of the coronavirus pandemic strengthened many proponents of an ecocentric perspective in their assumption that we need to stop our current way of organizing the economy and have to turn away from economic growth. From this perspective, the corona crisis has demonstrated the unsustainability of our current economic system; for example, with regard to the expansion of zoonotic diseases, the disadvantages of dense city life and the vulnerability of transborder economic processes as well as of our hypermobile lifestyle (Barlow et al, 2020: 3–6). The crisis has also highlighted the importance of public health, a motivation very close to the degrowth agenda (Ouimet et al, 2021). Degrowth activists see in the coronavirus crisis support to their claim that degrowth measures – an intentional suspension of economic activity for the sake the public interest – is possible and that it can lead to environmental improvements. If it is done in a more organized way, they argue, the socio-economic costs would be lower than those associated with the corona closures would.

Actually, activists argue that the coronavirus crisis is not degrowth, because the latter would be democratically planned and would not be based on top-down policies. It also would be a long-term and permanent process, not a temporary emergency measure. Degrowth does also not indiscriminately reduce all economic activities, but only those that are ecologically destructive and socially less than necessary, while other activities would be increased (such as care, education and healthcare). It would also avoid unemployment, by redistributing work time. Finally, a degrowth transformation would have a strong focus on justice and equality (Barlow et al, 2020: 2–3; Hickel, 2020: 4) whereas the coronavirus pandemic just deepened inequalities (see Chapter 7). Moreover, the coronavirus crisis has demonstrated some non-material gains from decreased economic activity (such as much cleaner air or the spotting of fish in the polluted lagoons of Venice). Also, the coronavirus crisis has demonstrated that economic growth and pollution still are closely coupled (see Chapter 24), against the hope of reformist technocentric approaches that the latter can be decoupled. Finally, from a degrowth perspective, economic reconstruction after the coronavirus pandemic is a unique chance to further this project. During the crisis, individuals have changed their lifestyles towards a more sustainable manner, communities have developed networks for mutual support and the state has been involved in economic planning to a degree that has not been witnessed for decades (Barlow et al, 2020: 7–8).

Social forces and the debate about degrowth

So far, degrowth in most societies is a marginal movement in terms of its political influence, but it carries increasing weight in the public discourse of the last two decades, as it is supported by well-established environmental activists and academics, with a specific focus on the Mediterranean (Weiss and Cattaneo, 2017: 221). More specifically, the degrowth movement is influential among the better-off social groups in the Global North. It does not surprise that the upper socio-economic deciles are more willing to make material sacrifices for the sake of fighting global warming than the lower deciles. The latter are likely to support approaches that simultaneously protect the environment, increase employment and avoid additional economic burdens, such as Green New Deals. While certainly not denying that a better protection of the environment is important, their central concern usually is upward social mobility, including higher purchasing power (Muradian, 2019: 258).

The degrowth approach, in contrast, 'represents the values, concerns and interests of a particular social class, namely the "green" European middle class' (Muradian, 2019: 257). It fits well with some newly acquired consumption patterns in this class, such as tourism as intercultural learning and exchange, instead of the mass tourism industry (Everingham and Chassagne, 2020). The degrowth movement is part of the 'post-materialist' tradition (Inglehart, 1977), where self-expression is more important than material gain. During the last decade, however, the assumption that Northern societies are irrevocably on their way to a slow but steady deepening of post-material values has been cast into doubt. Where green parties – the typical representation of these values – are doing well in many countries, they have found a powerful opponent in the rise of populist parties that do not share these concerns (Muradian, 2019: 256–7). Relatedly, lower-middle-class social movements such as the 'Gillets Jaunes' in France rather demand more, not less purchasing power (Muradian, 2019: 259).

In spatial terms, much less is known about the preferences of different social groups in the Global South with regard to degrowth. On the one side, they might me keen to maximize economic growth in order to overcome poverty. On the other side, large groups in the Global South may potentially benefit from a shrinking of global production, given that they suffer most severely from the negative environmental and health effects of capitalist growth. So far, however, the degrowth movement is very much 'Eurocentric', as can be seen from the authorship of core publications (Muradian, 2019: 257). It makes a difference whether a frugal lifestyle is imposed (as is the case for many people in the Global South) or is a voluntary choice. Some degrowth representatives therefore argue that degrowth is a concept for high-income economies only, not for the Global South (Hickel, 2020: 5). Finally, the populist 'counter-revolution' has forcefully affected many countries of the Global South as well, such as Brazil, India, the Philippines and Turkey, driving the environmental agenda backwards (Muradian, 2019: 259–60; see Chapter 30).

Given that the pandemic has provided ample evidence for many degrowth arguments and that the degrowth community is tightly knit and well organized, it does not come as a surprise that many activists, academics and practitioners joined forces soon after the outbreak of the crisis, in order to propagate their common cause. This took the form of an open letter, with more than 2,000 signatures (New Roots Collective, 2020). Moreover, members of the degrowth movement published a whole series of academic articles highlighting how the crisis strengthens the case for degrowth (for example, Barlow et al, 2020; Diesendorf, 2020; Everingham and Chassagne, 2020; Lidskog et al, 2020; Spash, 2020; Kish et al, 2021). Similarly, interest in forms of production that are related to the degrowth agenda – such as home-making and small-scale independent manufacturing – and e-commerce platforms focusing on home-made or recycled products – such as Etsy – were triggered very suddenly after the outbreak of the crisis, as indicated by research on internet search traffic (Dartnell and Kish, 2021).

Later in the crisis, however, articulations that the coronavirus pandemic is the perfect opportunity for a permanent shift to degrowth became somewhat less frequent. Although there are no empirical studies on the latter, this may be related to the fact that the economic hardships of the coronavirus recession highlighted the disadvantages of a lack of economic growth, unless accompanied by massive redistribution from the rich to the poor. Moreover, it also became clear that degrowth conceptions have not succeeded in becoming sufficiently hegemonic in order to prevent massive fiscal reconstruction programmes aiming to restore economic growth (Lidskog et al, 2020; see also Chapter 9).

The need for ecocentric and technocentric approaches to join forces during post-coronavirus economic reconstruction

The health crisis has increased the popularity of degrowth concepts in the short run. It has provided ample evidence that modern industrial capitalism is a very fragile system, that degrowth measures are possible and that they lead to an improvement of our natural environments. The recession, however, will likely decrease this popularity; in particular, when coupled with austerity policies and rising unemployment. The long-term perspectives of degrowth concepts are less clear, given their varying spatial and social popularity. If the recessions are short-lived, the concept may expand its appeal in the societies of the Global North, but this does not look likely in the Global South, due to low material standards of living and the importance of economic growth for improving the latter.

Based on this assessment, we may wonder whether the ecocentric and technocentric should not bury their controversies for the time being and join forces in order to make sure that post-coronavirus economic reconstruction programmes – such as the 'Next Generation EU' plan (see Chapter 28) – maximize their impact in terms of environmental protection and democratic embeddedness. Degrowth ideas will take a long time to become socially hegemonic – if at all – but the next years will see very important decisions about public investments that may well make a difference in terms of carbon dioxide emissions (see Chapter 24) and biodiversity (see Chapter 26). A closer interaction between the highly educated and usually middle-class degrowth community and the often working-class-affiliated supporters of technocentric Green New Deal projects might also assist in finding common ground for long-term strategies for sustainable living.

26

Agriculture: Global Supply Chains or Local Community Support?

The likely origin of the coronavirus in a Chinese wet market, but also food shortages during the crisis have led to additional attention to the global food system. Many observers criticize the latter severely, because its expansion has led to a loss in biological diversity and has brought people too close to wildlife, thereby increasing the risk for zoonotic diseases in the future. Were the developments in Wuhan an isolated accident or is the systemic criticism of the international agricultural and food system warranted? At stake is not only the increased risk of zoonotic diseases, but also widespread hunger. According to the World Food Programme, the pandemic has increased the number of people with acute hunger by more than 80 per cent, towards 270 million people (WFP, 2020: 6). Should we take this observation as an indication to focus agriculture upon local community support or should we further its integration into global supply chains?

Political Economy scholarship on agriculture and the food system

Political economy scholarship can assist us in dealing with these questions by highlighting a number of structural features of contemporary agriculture and food production. Put very simply, scholars working on the 'international political economy of food and hunger' (Balaam and Dillman, 2014: 460) distinguish between transnational agribusiness and its global supply chains on the one hand and local agricultural production for local needs on the other. Which of the two fundamental alternatives gains support through the coronavirus pandemic?

Issues of agriculture and food are not only important to Political Economy because of continued hunger crises and the role of agricultural exports as major problem for the conclusion of global trade negotiations, but also because the economic features of food production changed very dynamically during the last decades. During the last 70 years, we have seen a continuous process of moving global agriculture towards 'the rise of a global food system based on principles of industrial production, specialization and global trade that is progressively taking place via complex global food supply chains dominated by large private sector corporations' (Clapp and Moseley, 2020: 1395). Jennifer Clapp and William Moseley (2020: 1395–9) distinguish between three main phases in the development of the global food system, all driven by the attempt to prevent food crisis via increased efficiency. During the 1960s and 1970s, the focus was on the spreading of industrial agricultural production globally, particularly via development assistance. The background were Green Revolution techniques that had boosted production in some regions since the 1950s, based on consolidation of farms to big units and the sale of fertilizer, seeds and pesticides by Northern agribusiness companies. During the 1980s and 1990s, the focus rather was on global food trade. In particular, the context of the structural adjustment programmes of the WB and the IMF forced many Southern countries to liberalize their agricultural production systems. They had to abolish subsidies for the agricultural sector as well as tariffs for imported food. In effect, these decades ended decades of food self-sufficiency in many countries of the Global South and turned these economies into food importers, often buying from farmers in the Global North. The 2007/08 food price crisis – with price increases of 50 per cent on average and even 100 per cent for some core staples like rice – finally pushed small producers in the Global South into the integration in global agricultural value chains. Now, not only large industrial producers participated in the latter, but also smallholders increasingly focused on exports instead of subsistence production. At the same time, rising and very volatile food prices led to a strong increase in financial investments into the agricultural systems of the Global South; for example, by buying up farmland and speculating on agricultural production. Correspondingly, the most prominent feature of the last decade was the financialization of the global agrifood supply chain (see also Ploeg, 2020).

Global food supply chains during the coronavirus crisis

How does the coronavirus crisis fit into this account – does it provide arguments for a further intensification of industrial food production traded on global markets or does it call for a return to local smallholder agriculture? A particular challenge of the coronavirus crisis for agriculture was the partial breakdown of global food supply chains; for example, because of protectionism and export restrictions (see Chapter 20), lockdowns and border closures as well as the absence or illness of migrant workers (see Chapter 6). While some observers still praise the general resilience of global food system (for example, by pointing to near record-high levels of global food production), others, however, highlight its vulnerability during the crisis (Clapp and Moseley, 2020: 1393–5, 1399–1408). Next to the breakdown of global food supply chains, the pandemic also led to rising hunger because the subsequent recession caused mass unemployment. Thus, while the overall volume of global production of food was sufficient, it did not always reach those in need, either because it could not be harvested and transported to the relevant markets, or because the potential buyers did not have enough money to afford food (Béné, 2020). The latter often was the case either because of lay-offs or because agricultural export revenues were not sufficient for purchasing food for consumption. According to the United Nations (2020b: 11), about 1.1 billion of the 3.2 billion livelihoods globally that depend on work in food systems are at risk, including 60 per cent of jobs in food processing, food services and distribution services, but only 20 per cent of jobs in primary production.

Moreover, the pandemic has also led to massive price fluctuations, with major effects on both producers (who may face insufficient revenues when prices are very low) and consumers (who may be unable to buy sufficient food when prices are very high). Price fluctuations often were an effect of the combination of overspecialized food systems and the pandemic. Specialization has turned even major agricultural exporters (of certain products) into food importers (of other products). While this may be very efficient from a global perspective, it poses particular dangers during a pandemic (Clapp and Moseley, 2020: 1405–8). For example, many countries imposed export restrictions during the crisis, in order to safeguard the food supply of their domestic population. This has led to considerable increases in the prices of core food staples that have to be imported by other countries. Moreover, specialization within the global food system also has led to an increasing concentration of stockholdings of essential staples – such as cereals – in a few countries. Pandemic-related disruptions in these countries can have deep repercussions in importing countries.

Arguably, the pandemic has demonstrated that a system of agriculture where many farmers in the Global South focus on a highly specialized production for long global food supply chains (as well as horticulture and commodities such as cotton and cocoa), while importing a growing share of their daily staple, has become overly fragile. In contrast, local smallholder agriculture has hardly been affected by the crisis; in particular, 'many forms of non-commercial food production that are also labor-intensive, including many cases of subsistence agriculture. These systems are not as vulnerable to COVID-19 outbreaks as commercial, industrial systems because they often involve family labor (as opposed to dormitories of unrelated workers) on small farms in relatively isolated rural areas' (Clapp and Moseley, 2020: 1403).

Finally, the effects of the coronavirus pandemic on extremely extended agricultural supply chains do not only cause crises in the Global South, but also major problems in the North, due to the increasing focus of these chains on 'just-in-time'-production without any leeway for delays. Meat production is a case in point. For example, coronavirus infections in slaughterhouses have led to massive overcrowding in pig farms in Germany. Moreover, the closure of restaurants in Italy – and the related decrease in demand for calve dishes such as *Saltimbocca* or *vitello al tonno* – had major effects on specialized Dutch slaughterhouses and calve-fattening farms, as well as calve farms in Germany, Eastern Europe and Ireland (Ploeg, 2020: 948).

Global agribusiness and zoonotic diseases

However, there is also another issue that links the coronavirus crisis to the alternatives of transnational agribusiness and local production for local nutrition needs. Students of global agribusiness highlight the increased risk for zoonotic diseases (such as the coronavirus) and vector-borne diseases (infections transmitted to humans by blood-feeding arthropods such as fleas and mosquitoes) that goes hand in hand with the intensification of global agricultural production in the last decades; in particular, in countries of the intertropical zone with high forest cover (Morand and Lajaunie, 2021). Large agribusiness companies have now gained access to many of the last virgin forests and farmlands previously held by smallholders. These resources have been replaced by large-scale industrial agriculture, leading to a loss of ecological diversity and complexity on the affected stretches of land. This, in turn, increasingly forced wild hunters to move to untouched parts of the forest. This extension of hunting increases the likelihood of interaction with previously boxed-in pathogens, leading to events such as the coronavirus outbreak that with all likelihoods was transmitted by animals from their emergence with wild bats. As vividly described by Rob Wallace (2016, 2020), COVID-19 was only one in a long series of related diseases. From this perspective, the coronavirus crisis is not an unfortunate coincidence but rather a structural consequence of the extension of the capitalist food production to remote areas.

In this case, the alternative to large-scale transnational agribusiness would not only be a shift back to more varied food production by smallholders, but also an end to the process of global deforestation which not only poses health risks, but also is a major danger with regard to climate change (see Chapter 24). Still, this alternative would encounter massive political opposition by those using deforestation for their livelihood. Moreover, reforestation is also not without dangers and can lead to a degradation of biodiversity, if it is at the expense of grasslands, savannas and open-canopy woodlands, and takes place outside the tropical zone (Morand and Lajaunie, 2021: 3–4). However, the design of recovery packages by governments in order to counter the coronavirus recession offers ample space for incentives to preserve biodiversity. For example, governments can shift subsidies from environmentally harmful ones (for example, fossil fuel subsidies) to beneficial ones (for example, to encourage environmental-friendly farming), can link bailout funds to biodiversity-risk mitigation, can fund ecosystem-related public work programmes or can use public procurement in order to purchase food produced in a sustainable manner. Similarly, they can use taxation for this purpose; for example, via resource-extraction taxes or pesticide taxes (McElwee et al, 2020: 450–2).

Obstacles on the way towards improved food sovereignty

The coronavirus pandemic has vividly demonstrated the dangers of the modern system of global agricultural value chains, both with regard to the spread of zoonotic diseases and the insufficient provision of food for those with limited financial means. While a return to domestic smallholder agriculture may not always be the solution to this problem, there are convincing arguments for a shortening of very long agricultural supply chains and a reduction of hyper-specialization in agricultural production, moving back a lot of food production to peasant agriculture and peasant markets (Ploeg, 2020). A reduced degree of specialization in global agricultural production would also help with the second major problem raised by the pandemic; namely, the potential spread of zoonotic diseases. Specialized production with large monocultures are more prone to the latter than production for local consumption, which often is focused on a variety of products and ecology-friendly inter-cropping.

However, while a move towards increased local and national food sovereignty would be desirable for many economies of the Global South, it does not necessarily seem likely. On the one hand, the highly concentrated sector of transnational agribusiness is politically much easier to organize than the millions of local small-scale producers that would benefit from the reversal of the direction of our agricultural production system. On the other hand, rising food prices or even food shortages during the post-corona era may even assist the food industry in making its claim to be a guarantee against future crises. Finally, important multilateral agencies such as the Food and Agriculture Organization of the United Nations (FAO), as well as most agricultural research institutions remain wedded to the established paradigm of global industrial agriculture (Newell and Taylor, 2018; Bello, 2020: 4–5). Ironically, one glimpse of hope may stem from decreasing interest into industrialized agriculture, be it because of a lower increase of land prices in the Global South, an increasing focus on community-supported agriculture or a decreasing ability of Northern-dominated global institutions to impose their will upon Southern agricultural producers (Clapp and Moseley, 2020: 1409). Finally, we should not underestimate the room for manoeuvre for national governments with regard to a different form of agriculture; for example, with regard to shifting procurement, subsidies or taxation. Correspondingly, governments should utilize these instruments in order to reorient agriculture to local consumption instead of further deepening global industrial agriculture.

PART VI

Geo-economic Shifts in Global Capitalism

So far, we have studied the impact of the coronavirus crisis with regard to general issues that potentially can affect every economy – although we often have distinguished between the different challenges in the Global North and the Global South. However, the discipline of International Political Economy also studies the shifts in global economic power relations between (groups of) countries (Balaam and Dillman, 2014: 266–377; Shaw et al, 2019: 153–262). Among the most prominent topics are the historical effects of imperialism and colonialism and the related North–South dependencies, increasingly complemented by the rise of mid-income economies such as BRICS.

While we cannot do justice to all potential geo-economic shifts caused by the coronavirus crisis, three aspects are particularly important. Obviously, this prominently includes the impact of the crisis on the China–US struggle for global economic hegemony (Chapter 27). However, it is equally important to study the impact of the crisis on EU economic governance: does it lead to further integration or rather to increasing disintegration (Chapter 28)? Finally, the pandemic went hand in hand with a massive increase in individual surveillance in many countries. This leads us to the question how the pandemic impinged onto the political economy of security relations within and between states (Chapter 29).

27

China–US Struggle for Global Economic Hegemony: Contender or Incumbent?

The coronavirus pandemic emerged in a historical situation where the political relations between China and the US, not only the two largest economies, but also the contenders for global economic hegemony, grew increasingly tense. The pandemic has put fuel onto the fire of this rivalry. While the US blamed China to be responsible for the emergence of the pandemic and for undue influence in the WHO, China used its early economic recovery to strengthen its ties to countries globally. How will the pandemic influence the balance of power between these two economies?

The struggle for global order and International Political Economy scholarship

During the last two decades, much International Political Economy scholarship has studied the emerging economic rivalry between China and the US, even if it did not yet find much reflection in the major textbooks. While the discussion during the 2000s mainly focused on the question whether the rise of China would be aggressive or peaceful, it increasingly turns to the question of the stability of the US-led liberal global order during the 2010s. During the first debate, the core contenders were 'power transition theory' and 'offensive realism' on the one side, arguing that the rise of China would lead to military conflicts, and liberal as well as constructivist scholarship on the other side, predicting that this conflict can be avoided, due to economic interdependencies and the socialization of China into a cooperative behaviour (Nölke, 2015: 657–8). The second debates focused on the challenges that China poses for the US-led 'Liberal International Order' (LIO). The latter order has been created by the West under US leadership after the Second World War, in order to contain the expanding

Soviet Union. Core pillars were the support of free trade and of transnational capital mobility, as well as international organizations such as the WB and the IMF (and the more general principle of multilateralism); it also contained more political aspects such as the spreading of democracy and the support of human rights. Over time, it has increased its intrusiveness; for example, with regard to the promotion of human rights, the supranational order of the International Criminal Court or the structural adjustment programmes of the WB and the IMF (Kreuder-Sonnen and Rittberger, 2020: 5–8; Lake et al, 2021: 226–34). Before the coronavirus pandemic, many authors identified an increasing number of challenges for the LIO. A part of these challenges was internal; for example, based on growing opposition to always more intrusive economic and political liberalism (particularly via technocratic international institutions), the economic delegitimation of the GFC or the rise of authoritarianism and right-wing populism in core Western countries. Other challenges stem from outside the LIO; most notably, the rise of China and China-led international institutions (Kreuder-Sonnen and Rittberger, 2020: 8–13; Lake et al, 2021: 234–46).

The coronavirus crisis as a challenge to the liberal global order

Very early in the pandemic, the crisis was seen as a problem for the liberal economic order (Norrlöf, 2020a). Next to the challenges of democratic and liberal capitalism on the domestic level (see Chapters 30 and 31), it also affected some of the core pillars of the LIO in the international economic realm; for example, the freedom of individual movement (see Chapter 6), the transnational openness for the movement of goods (see Chapters 17 and 20) and the transnational openness of financial markets (see Chapter 18). Importantly, these are challenges to the specific LIO, not to intergovernmental cooperation or international organizations per se; the latter often were even able to expand their scope and policy instruments during the crisis (Debre and Dijkstra, 2020), although they were unable to ensure comprehensive international cooperation on core issues such as the prevention of 'vaccine nationalism' (Abbas, 2020).

Similarly, the core Western institutions of the liberal global order – in particular, the G7 and the OECD – did not play a leading role during the crisis. In general, the latter was fought individually on the domestic level, with very little multilateral coordination (Levy, 2021: 562–3). Obligations to international institutions, from the WTO to the Paris Agreement on climate change targets, took a back seat. As far as multilateral economic coordination took place, it involved the G20, an international institution much less dominated by the West and quite neutral to the core normative principles of the LIO. Opportunities for the creation of powerful international institutions were also limited by the rise of nationalism triggered by the pandemic. The latter had a 'rally-around-the-flag' effect, which also has led to a more confrontational climate in foreign policy between China and Western countries, as for example witnessed in the case of Australia's China policy (Pan and Korolev, 2021: 127–33). China-based observers applaud the weakening of the LIO during the pandemic – inter alia, due to the entrenchment of authoritarianism, the increasing nationalism and the return of big power rivalry – and assume that it provides China with many options to increase its options globally. They also argue that China has weathered the storm of the pandemic better than the US (Dunford and Qi, 2020; Huang, 2021).

The further rise of China during the coronavirus crisis

Is China prepared for global leadership? A core requirement for this leadership role would be political and economic stability. These two aspects are interrelated, as political stability in an authoritarian regime such as China depends primarily on the ability to guarantee a constantly improving standard of living. In comparative political economy research on the Chinese economy, we can identify two perspectives on the likeliness of this stability. On the one hand, there are mainly Western observers with a background in liberal economics (for example, Economy, 2007). These observers of China predict that China will be not be able to continue its economic rise, due to the lack of sustainability of its state-centred economy – but they have been articulating this negative prediction for many years already, to no avail. The alternative perspective, more often articulated by political economists and non-Western observers, is that China's economic rise will continue, since it is based on a coherent non-liberal model of capitalism (Nölke et al, 2020). What does the evidence of the coronavirus crisis tell us with regard to these two competing perspectives? Several issues are at stake. China may suffer from a decoupling of global production networks (see Chapter 17). It also encounters backlashes with regard to the acquisition of foreign companies and technologies (see Chapter 18). The Chinese economy, however, has weathered the pandemic well so far. Based on draconian health measures and substantial fiscal as well as monetary policy interventions, China recovered quickly (Tian, 2020), particularly in international comparison.

With regard to its international leadership role, China has suffered some setbacks, such as a bad image as country of origin of the virus. However, China has tried to overcome these setbacks by its concerted diplomatic efforts in terms of health assistance, including emergency supplies to EU member states: 'China's public diplomacy has gone into overdrive' (Seaman, 2020: 8). In contrast to the EU and the US, China has used its health diplomacy successfully as a soft-power weapon in order to further its geo-economic influence (Gauttam et al, 2020). Moreover, China has used the crisis to promote its pre-existing 'techno-authoritarian project' that fuses technological surveillance, a strong focus on public security and public health, although it is yet unclear whether this approach will diffuse globally (Greitens, 2020).

To sum up, it is possible that the rise of China may temporarily slow down due to the pandemic, but there are no indications that it will not continue in the long run. This tendency is also supported by the erosion of the US leadership role with regard to the global institutions of liberal capitalism. While the US is still in a more powerful position than China, due to its control of important economic networks and over the global reserve currency (Drezner, 2020: E28), the slow erosion of its dominant role will continue.

The coronavirus crisis and the weakness of the US-centred global order

Before the coronavirus pandemic, the Trump administration (2016–20) was in the process of weakening – if not even destroying – the global trade regime. Arguably, this was the case because the regime provided more advantages to its rival China than to the US itself, similar as the Bretton Woods regime in its final stages was more helpful to US rivals in Europe than to the US (Stokes and Williamson, 2021). In contrast to the situation after the end of the Bretton Woods system, however, the US looks much less likely to be able to replace the WTO regime with a new global trade regime. Although the Biden administration is less aggressively communicating the need for trade to benefit the US than the predecessor administration, it nevertheless uses its foreign policy for a similar attempt to stop the further rise of China as global hegemon. Furthermore, the US–China confrontation does not limit itself to a 'simple' trade war, but also affects global production networks (see Chapter 17); for example, with regard to a decoupling in the digital sphere following security concerns about Huawei, among others.

The coronavirus pandemic has further increased distrust between the US and China. This also causes major problems for countries traditionally trading with both sides, such as South Korea (Kimura, 2021: 33–5). Correspondingly, it looks more likely that future economic institutions rather will assemble the attempts to contain the extension of China's power globally, similar to the containment of the Soviet Union after the Second World War. This will not lead to rejuvenation of the global liberal order, but rather to the emergence of two regional production and trading blocks, as during the Cold War (Stokes and Williamson, 2021: 48). Correspondingly, it does not surprise that former US champions of the liberal world order now contemplate about a new order that intensifies cooperation among liberal democracies, but gives up any claim to become a global order (Ikenberry,

2020). The US Federal Reserve provided a taste for this new US-led partial global order by selectively offering swap lines – the exchange of much-sought US dollar liquidity against foreign currencies – to US allies such as the EU, Canada, Japan, the UK and Switzerland, but not to China, Iran and Russia (Norrlöf, 2020b: 1299–302).

However, the most severe challenge to the US-centred liberal global order may not even stem from the international level where the US has lost the ability to act as benevolent economic and political hegemon. Even graver are the challenges to the liberal global order that arise on the societal level. Here, widening social inequalities increasingly challenge the legitimacy of this order (Babic, 2021).

Towards a less intrusive liberal global economic order after the coronavirus crisis

Cross-border crises usually benefit international organizations, since they highlight the importance of international cooperation. A first survey indicates that this mechanism seems to be working in the case of the coronavirus as well (Debre and Dijkstra, 2020). Still, the coronavirus pandemic has contributed to the erosion of some core institutions of the liberal economic order, such as the freedom of individual movement across borders and the transnational openness for the movements of goods. So far, the pandemic has assisted the rise of China and weakened the global leadership role of the US, although the Biden administration is working towards stabilizing the latter. However, it looks much more likely that we are witnessing the (re-) emergence of two rival economic orders, this time one China-led and the other US-led.

The emergence of a second Cold War with two rival blocs is an unwelcome development for the global economy and should be avoided. It is very important to retain a stable economic order based on multilateral cooperation in order to solve global problems in fields such as climate change and health. However, the future global economic order cannot be based anymore on an intrusive liberal order, nor on a dominance by the US. It should allow individual states to pursue their own economic and political models. Moreover, it should give more countries a say in the design of international norms.

28

EU Economic Governance:
Erosion or Integration?

The coronavirus pandemic was a novel challenge for the EU. The purpose of combatting a pandemic was not part of its process of evolution. Still, many observers – both inside and outside the EU – assume that it should be able to play a major role in fighting the pandemic and the subsequent recession. The core question with regard to the EU – as always – is whether it leads to more European integration or rather to an erosion of the Union.

EU economic integration and International Political Economy scholarship

Over the decades, European Union Studies has emerged as a major research field of its own, with a multitude of specialized journals and academic associations. Still, from an International Political Economy perspective the core question still is to explain why countries are willing to pool a substantial amount of sovereignty in order to tackle common challenges (Balaam and Dillman, 2014: 295–7; Ravenhill, 2020: 159–61). The EU is by far the most impressive case of sovereignty pooling in the global political economy. Whereas the European Community during the 1950s was a group of completely sovereign states with limited cooperation in selected issue areas, the EU during the 2020s not only encompasses nearly all issue areas, but also holds supranational competences over many fields of economic policymaking.

To explain this development is the task of the classical theories of European integration, although the latter are only a small part of EU scholarship. Again, there is a whole range of theories that seek to explain why EU sometimes moved on with allocating new powers to Brussels and why they sometimes failed to do so, notably including theories of Critical Political Economy (van Apeldoorn and Horn, 2018). Still, the most widely used distinction still is between intergovernmental and neo-functionalist theories of European integration. Whereas the former highlights the importance of the preferences of the (powerful) EU member states, the latter argue in favour of the independent agency of European-level actors such as the Commission (or the ECB) and the driving force of transnational societal actors (mainly business), triggered by the need to solve cross-border problems.

How did the EU do during the coronavirus crisis – did it further the integration process? Or are we witnessing an increasing process of EU erosion? While the latter has been unthinkable for decades, Brexit has demonstrated that it is possible, if we do not watch for growing EU opposition in European societies and growing divergences between these societies (Nölke, 2017). In order to answer these questions, we need to look at several phases of the coronavirus crisis, including the original health crisis, the short-term monetary stabilization, the mid-term fiscal stabilization and the long-term reconstruction, to put it simply (in practice, phases overlap). In contrast to classical European integration scholarship, we should not only look at the transfer (or not) of new competences and resources to the European level, but also at the socio-economic coherence between the European societies.

Health crisis: national action and lack of solidarity

When the pandemic spread to Europe in early 2020, the focus of EU member states clearly was on individual action, not on European unity. Each government sought to maximize health protection for its own population. While this is legitimate and understandable in principle, it did not speak in favour of European integration or at least European solidarity. Even worse, governments sometimes worked against each other, by interdicting the export of medical goods to other European economies, even if the latter were affected by the pandemic in particularly strong ways: 'The belated – or lack of – reaction by the EU during the crisis has reinforced the national sovereignty of the member states and the dominance of the intergovernmental method in moments of crisis' (Lang and Ondarza, 2020: 1).

A striking incident was the reaction of EU member states to the Italian request for assistance with regard to additional protective equipment through the EU Civil Protection Mechanism in February 2020 (Italy was the most strongly affected country during this period): the member states provided no support at all, in contrast to a well-published support action to China just a few days before (De Pooter, 2020). Moreover, even core achievements of European integration such as the abolition of border controls in the Schengen Area were put aside without much concern. In order to prevent intra-European mobility, almost all countries closed their borders, without European coordination.

As a result of the high degree of unilateral action, the health crisis further deepened economic and social differences within the Union. Germany, for example, was affected in much more limited ways in the first phase of the pandemic, but still could bear a very well-funded health system upon the pandemic, whereas countries such as Italy and Spain were hit far more severely and had more limited health resources to combat the crisis. As a result, the economic inequalities between EU member states have deepened further. In the decade before the outbreak of the crisis, the economic gaps between, for example, Germany on the one side and Italy and Spain on the other had widened substantially, in comparison with the first decade of the 2000s (Camous and Claeys, 2020: 330–1).

Also later during the crisis, the very low degree of European integration in the field of pandemic preparedness and intervention has not been corrected (yet). Although the European Commission was able to announce the launching of a European Health Emergency Response and Preparedness Authority (HERA) in late 2020 and the first work plan of the EU4 Health programme in early 2021, national governments still decide all important health-related issues on their own, even if decisions have massive repercussions on other member states (for example, with regard to border closures or export restrictions). Further integration in this field will be incremental at best, strongly circumscribed by national concerns (Brooks and Geyer, 2020).

Short-term macroeconomic stabilization: powerful ECB technocratic action – but increasing controversies

During its early phase, the coronavirus pandemic quickly mutated from a health crisis into an economic crisis, with a substantial reduction of GDPs caused by border closures and lockdowns. Although governments soon reacted with fiscal support packages for their national companies (to be discussed later), the crisis also affected equity markets in a severe way. March 2020 saw a record collapse of stock market valuations. Not only the US Federal Reserve, but also the ECB intervened against these and other problematic economic developments in a very powerful way; in particular, with the announcement of the 'Pandemic Emergency Purchase Programme' (PEPP) in mid-March 2020 and a further extension of the programme in June 2020 (see also Chapter 8). This proved to be a very effective intervention in terms of countercyclical economic stimulus, thereby demonstrating European capacity for joint action (Camous and Claeys, 2020: 335).

With regard to European integration, the decisive action by the ECB is remarkable. The very quick and comprehensive interventions stood in marked contrast to the behaviour of the ECB in the Eurozone crisis during the early 2010s, where the central bank allowed speculative attacks and extremely high spreads between national government bonds without intervention. It only solved the crisis via the announcement of the potential of massive interventions (including the 'Outright Monetary Transactions' programme) in 2012, after the establishment of the European Stability Mechanism (ESM) and the integration of debt brakes into national constitutions.

However, the aggressive monetary policy of the ECB becomes increasingly controversial within the EU, due to its substantial distributive consequences. Extremely low interest rates favour the (usually better-off) owners of real estate and equities, whereas (often small) savers who invest in government bonds and other very safe assets are disadvantaged. Given these effects, it becomes increasingly difficult to defend the technocratic nature of the ECB, the reason for its very high degree of independence. Although the highly independent ECB can ignore societal protest in principle, it has repeatedly become the focus of legal action before the German Federal Constitutional Court (Camous and Claeys, 2020: 335–6). Subsequently, the German court has openly challenged the authority of the Court of Justice of the European Union and the European Commission has opened infringement proceedings against Germany in June 2021. While the judicial system still was 'enabling' with regard to the role of the ECB during the Eurozone crisis, it has become 'constraining' during the coronavirus crisis (Saurugger and Terpan, 2020: 1167).

Mid-term fiscal stabilization: further increasing divergence between national economies

Next to monetary policy, the EU member states also used various instruments of fiscal policy (see Chapter 9) in order to stabilize their economies. Again, achievements of European integration were quickly discarded, such as the fiscal rules of the Stability and Growth Pact, although it is controversial whether the latter really were a positive achievement (see Chapter 8). In contrast to monetary policy (and to long-term economic reconstruction, to be discussed later), these measures were implemented in a strictly national and uncoordinated way. Correspondingly, governments differed very substantially with regard to the volume of support for domestic business, with Germany mobilizing the highest volume of support to domestic business by far. While Germany was able to provide 8.3 per cent of GDP in immediate fiscal impulse in 2020 (similar to the UK with 8.3 per cent and the US with 9.1 per cent), this was limited to 5.1 per cent in France, 3.1 per cent in Greece, 3.4 per cent in Italy, 2.5 per cent in Portugal and 4.3 per cent in Spain (Bruegel, 2020). This came on top of an existing macroeconomic divergence that was already very disadvantageous to the Southern European economies (Gräbner et al, 2020).

In principle, it would have been necessary (and legitimate) to harmonize fiscal stabilization measures at the European level, given that different degrees of state support to national economies contradict the idea of a level playing field within the Common Market, one of the core pillars of the EU. Still, the European Commission did not intervene and also was very lenient with regard to allowing state subsidies in the early phase of the crisis. It simply suspended its usual framework for state aid rules for most types of aid in March 2020 (Meunier and Mickus, 2020) and only much later reimposed stricter limits upon the ability of member states to support domestic business (see Chapter 16).

Given the limited fiscal means of some member economies that were particularly hard hit during the crisis, the Eurozone finance ministers established two EU loan facilities early in the crisis. One is a specific 'Pandemic Crisis Support' credit facility within the ESM (but with a more lenient conditionality than usual ESM support) and the other the new instrument 'Support to mitigate Unemployment Risks in an Emergency' (SURE) for the financing of short-term work schemes. However, these schemes did not address the most important needs of the member states (that is, grants instead of credit) and the ESM credit line carries the stigma of the earlier Eurozone crisis (Camous and Claeys, 2020: 333–4). Correspondingly, they achieved very little in reducing the growing socio-economic divergence in the Union.

Long-term economic reconstruction: limited solidarity at last

Due to these socio-economic divergences, the coronavirus crisis has been leading to increasing political tensions within the EU. The particularly hard-hit Southern European countries, most notably Italy and Spain, had asked for common financial resources in order to combat the crisis. Northern European countries, led by the Netherlands, Germany, Austria and the Scandinavians were unwilling to provide the latter. This has further increased societal tensions within the EU – and the Eurozone in particular – given that Germany and its allies were the core driving forces behind the austerity policies in Southern Europe during the early 2010s. These austerity policies also depleted resources for public health systems, thereby contributing to the severity of the health crisis in the Southern European economies (Moreira et al, 2020). Correspondingly, 'the coronavirus pandemic has deepened the North–South divide in the EU and the Eurozone' (Lang and Ondarza, 2020: 2).

In contrast to previous times, however, the German government partially switched sides and agreed to a measure of European fiscal solidarity in May 2020. Arguably, Germany has chosen 'polity maintenance'; that is, 'keeping the EU polity together, regardless of deep interest-based divisions' (Ferrera et al, 2021: 19). The accumulation of the ongoing social and economic crisis in Southern Europe together with the coronavirus crisis constituted an 'existential threat to the European integration process' (Landesmann, 2020: 449), thereby provoking a counter-reaction (although the EU already is in 'permanent emergency' for more than a decade, Wolff and Ladi, 2020). Arguably, the German strategic adjustment was less based upon genuine concerns over the future of the European integration project, but rather motivated by worries about the loss of important German export markets (Schoeller and Karlsson, 2021: 201). Indeed, core German exports were shrinking substantially in the early coronavirus crisis (Ban, 2020: 20–1). Correspondingly, the German move was not based on genuine European solidarity, but rather on cost–benefit calculations. The latter seem to be highly relevant in general, as demonstrated by related surveys in Austria (Bobzien and Kalleitner, 2021).

In order to support post-coronavirus reconstruction, the EU was allowed to raise debt for fiscal support via the new the 'Next Generation EU' recovery fund which is able to disburse €390 billion in grants and €360 billion in loans. Due to the adoption of this programme in July 2020, the EU budget de facto has been doubled for three years after the crisis, with an over-proportional share of expenditures going to those member states that are less well off. In order to refinance the grant share of the programme, the EU is authorized to raise debt, to be refinanced by new pan-European taxes (and guaranteed by the member states via the general EU budget, should taxes not arise sufficient resources in time). Although the size of the stimulus programme is substantial, if compared with the size of the 2020 recession, it is by no means able to equalize the deep economic divergences that have emerged in Europe during the previous decade (Camous and Claeys, 2020: 337). The core question with regard to this move thus is whether it is a unique measure during a unique situation of crisis – or whether this indicates a permanent increase of fiscal solidarity within the Union. The strong opposition against debt-finance transfers by the 'frugal four', that is the governments of Austria, Denmark, the Netherlands and Sweden (with sympathy from Finland), so far indicates that the former may be a more realistic assumption. Moreover, 'the German government conceives of its own and the EU's response as being a temporary fix to deal with rapidly increasing functional pressures to act, in the context of the most severe recession and economic crisis since the Second World War and the most serious risk of European disintegration' (Howarth and Schild, 2021: 220). Thus, the response is temporary – and also very limited, since it does not include any direct transfers of grants between the budgets of the EU member states. This is in line with a survey of the German residential population that shows strong support for medical solidarity, but very limited support for financial redistribution, including a clear broad aversion to Eurobonds (Koos and Leuffen, 2020). Generally, surveys of public opinion indicate that European solidarity is a scarce good, in very short supply if compared with demands – and that it can best be mobilized in a specific situation of exogenously caused crisis, not with regard to more permanent and endogenously caused problems (Cicchi et al, 2020: 435–6).

Instead of focusing on unpopular fiscal transfers, it thus might be a better idea that Germany balances its extremely export-oriented economy via a stimulation of domestic consumption and investment, in order to provide Southern European companies with additional demand and improved competitiveness (Nölke, 2021). However, this looks equally unlikely, given that the leading representatives of German politics strive to return to pre-coronavirus rules of budget retrenchment and fiscal prudence (Donnelly, 2021: 237). Again, this is based on broad support of public opinion, with Germans showing the lowest share of population in the whole EU with regard to the loosening of EU budgetary rules as important priority (Schoeller and Karlsson, 2021: 202).

The EU in post-coronavirus capitalism: a mixed bag

The balance with regard to European integration during the coronavirus pandemic is mixed. European integration was particularly limited in the original phase of the crisis when each member state only looked after the health protection of its own citizens. European integration worked much better during the second phase – short-term macroeconomic stabilization – when the ECB prevented a major economic crisis without much delay. This is a marked improvement with regard to the Eurozone crisis in the early 2010s – but it is also an increasingly politically contested improvement, given the redistributive consequences of ECB policies and its lack of democratic legitimacy. The third phase of the pandemic, with a focus on the compensation of companies and workers for lockdown policies, rather speaks in favour of disintegration, given the extremely different abilities of EU member states to support national companies. Finally, during the fourth phase, we are witnessing a clear measure of integration, with the temporary doubling of the EU level budget via Next Generation EU. Given this wild ride, it is difficult to say whether post-coronavirus capitalism will see a more or less integrated EU. It very much depends on the measure applied: if the focus is on institutional change, the creation of new agencies and budgets speaks in favour of integration (for example, V. Schmidt, 2020: 1191). If the focus is on an equitable development throughout Europe and on harmonious relations between European societies, the assessment is negative. From the latter perspective, the EU has barely avoided further disintegration (for example, Howarth and Schild, 2021: 220).

In any case, the coronavirus has exposed some tensions that need to be addressed in order to prevent further disintegration after Brexit. The European economy needs to become more equilibrated, particularly in a North–South perspective. Given the unsurmountable impediments to a transfer union, this has to take place via a rebalancing of the German economy. Since the technocratic reasoning for the independent status of the ECB does not apply anymore (due to the extremely far-reaching political decisions in an era of unorthodox monetary policy), it should be put under parliamentary control (see Chapter 8). Finally, the EU should terminate its counterproductive fiscal constraints (see Chapter 9) and very strict rules on state support for the economy, in order to allow a rejuvenating of the Southern European economies via well-funded industrial policies (see Chapter 11). There is a strong likelihood that we are moving away from liberal and towards organized capitalism (see Chapter 31). The EU should avoid being trapped by its traditional focus on economic liberalization and rather should manage the shift towards a more interventionist economic model (Bergsen et al, 2020).

29

The Political Economy of Security: Less or More Protection?

The coronavirus pandemic very often has been framed as an economic security problem. For example, lack of access to medical equipment (see Chapter 20) or the disruption of supply networks (see Chapter 17) have been issues of major concern. However, the pandemic also raises further security issues, with regard to the conventional military, to armed domestic groups and to domestic surveillance. The core question then is whether post-coronavirus capitalism will provide more or less protection from security threats. Given that contagious diseases have spread more easily with the development of economic globalization, the security dimensions of pandemics are becoming more and more prominent over the years, from HIV/AIDS via SARS to Ebola (O'Brien and Williams, 2016: 296–8).

Security issues in International Political Economy

Security Studies and International Political Economy developed as institutionally separate fields in International Relations/Political Science. Still, there are important fields where economy and security intersect. Simplified, we can distinguish between the classical discussion on military aspects of interstate security (particularly important during the Cold War), a modernized version of this discussion ('new security studies') that also takes non-military threats to state security (such as environmental issues or digital disinformation) into account and a fairly radical departure from traditional security concerns that focus on the security of the individual (human security), pointing to the fact that starvation is killing more people than war (O'Brien and Williams, 2016: 279–82).

All three understandings of security share an important role for economic factors. The latter may be least relevant for traditional interstate security, but even here a powerful economy is precondition for a powerful military, at least in a long-term perspective. Economic issues become even more important within the new security studies, where threats may stem from economic dependencies; for example, upon cross-border infrastructures such as the SWIFT payment system (where Iran has been excluded). Arguably, the growing complexity of the financial sector makes it particularly vulnerable to security threats (LeBaron et al, 2021: 289). Economic dimensions even move centre stage in discussions about human security. Civil wars or ethnic disputes often focus on the control over economic resources and they very often are connected to transnational organized crime, as armed groups smuggle drugs, natural resources, people or weapons in order to finance their operations. However, given the particularly difficult data situation with regard to transnational organized crime, it does not yet make sense to draw conclusions on the effects of the pandemic (Giommoni, 2020).

Among the most important elements of the new security studies is the concept of 'securitization'. The concept (coined by Buzan et al, 1998)

> describes a process when an issue becomes so 'hot' that it is lifted out of regular political decision making and made into an existential question. As a result, extraordinary counter-measures are warranted in the name of security. ... The point is that it is not objectively given what can be regarded as a threat and how states respond to them. (Friis, 2020: 4)

Securitizing an issue – such as a virus – legitimizes agents to use wide-ranging powers and often leads to the application of harsh security measures, instead of economic and social reforms.

The pandemic and the economic dimensions of conventional interstate security

The most obvious implication of the pandemic for the military worldwide was fairly unusual: military personnel has been deployed in order to support the crisis response; in particular, with regard to medical resources. The latter were needed and the military had spare capacities. Issues of legitimacy also were hardly raised, given the high degree of securitization of the pandemic (to be discussed later), although there were concerns about civilian control over the military and excessive violence in enforcing curfews. The military itself has a keen interest into its deployment during the pandemic, not only to test operational readiness and prevent infections in the forces, but also in order to have a strong position in post-pandemic discussions on public budget cuts (Friis, 2020; Kalkman, 2020; Wilén, 2021).

More important for post-coronavirus capitalism, however, is what the pandemic has taught us with regard how states use economic statecraft for their strategic gain. States have developed new strategies during the pandemic. They 'manipulate medical supply chains for their own self-interest, use cyberattacks to obtain sensitive vaccine research, and engage in pandemic disinformation campaigns' (McNamara and Newman, 2020: E69). This has also affected the most powerful state – the US. Some observers even go as far as to claim that the coronavirus pandemic is the tipping point where the US turns from a 'provider' of security (for the world, the Western alliance or only Americans) to a 'consumer' of security, and from 'interdependence' to 'dependence' (Reich and Dombrowski, 2020). The pandemic has demonstrated that the US national defence establishment puts too much focus on 'kinetic' threats such as projective weapons and explosives, thereby ignoring 'anthropogenic' threats (such as climate change), 'naturogenic' threats (such as the coronavirus) and 'economic' threats (such as poverty, but also non-military technology). This is even more problematic if we take into account that by 2020 the coronavirus had already 'killed more Americans than died in the Korean, Vietnam or First World Wars' (Reich and Dombrowski, 2020: 1261). Correspondingly, future US interstate security policy should also comprise a 'national medical–industrial complex' and the avoidance of too tightly coupled global supply chains.

The pandemic and the economic dimensions of domestic conflicts

The effects of the first phases of the pandemic on intergroup armed conflicts are mixed. Generally, both the coronavirus threat and the typical responses to the threat (such as national shutdowns) have led to a short-term temporary reduction in the number of conflict events, particularly via a declining number of protests (Bloem and Salemi, 2021: 8). Both the danger of infection and the threat of violence by police forces seem to play a role here. With regard to armed conflict, a number of groups have announced ceasefires in order to assist rescue operations – for humanitarian reasons, but also because of logistical problems (Ide, 2021: 2). In other cases, however, armed conflicts have been on the increase, either because the pandemic has weakened the state or because international attention was detracted via the pandemic (Ide, 2021: 8). While the early phase of the pandemic has led to a 9-percentage point reduction in the likelihood of daily conflict globally, this reduction has not been encountered in low-income countries and in countries torn apart by ethnic or religious conflict (Berman et al, 2020).

Longer-term effects, however, are still unclear. On the one side, the recession could lead to a reduction in the price of natural resources – and of the benefits to get access to these resources via violent means. Military offensives may become more difficult to implement during the pandemic or may become unpopular, particularly if hospitals are attacked (Ide, 2021: 3).

On the other side, the pandemic and the subsequent recession 'may lead to a reduction in local income levels and, in turn, a reduction of the opportunity cost of violence – thereby increasing violence' (Bloem and Salemi, 2021: 1). In a related vain, the pandemic may substantially reduce life expectancy and thereby reduce the threshold for a participation in dangerous activities (Ide, 2021: 2). Moreover, the pandemic also leads to the disruption of global food chains and higher food prices (see Chapter 26), which could increase the frequency of conflicts. Similarly, the pandemic and recession make it more difficult to appease grievances, due to depleted budgets and increased financial demands (Ide, 2021: 2). Another factor that could well lead to an increasing number of violent domestic conflicts after the pandemic is the combination of an economic downturn with ethnic or religious cleavages (Ide, 2021: 8).

Country case studies also show inconclusive patterns so far and the attribution of causality to the coronavirus pandemic often is difficult. For example, Syria has seen a clear downward trend with regard to violent conflict in 2020, but the share of the coronavirus is unclear, compared with the ceasefire in the Idlib region (Bloem and Salemi, 2021: 5–6). In Lebanon, in contrast, protests and rioting continued in spite of the lockdown, apparently, because the coronavirus recession has further increased desperation about economic developments; only the Beirut harbour explosion has led to decreasing protest activity which might be related to the increasing importance of survival needs (Bloem and Salemi, 2021: 7).

The securitization of the pandemic: a danger for human security?

In Northern societies, however, the most prominent security dimension of the pandemic is its 'securitization'; that is, the practice to 'declare war' upon a health problem. The strong degree of securitization of the coronavirus is remarkable if we compare it with other communicable diseases that could be prevented by vaccines; for example, the measles that has led to 140,000 deaths in 2018 alone (Daoudi, 2020: 12). Governments (and experts) have securitized the coronavirus pandemic to different degrees, leading to very different responses, ranging from strict curfews to business as usual. In most cases, the securitization of the virus was very strong, thereby also legitimizing very powerful responses; for example, with regard to the temporary cancellation of civil liberties (see Chapter 30). Moreover, the securitization of the pandemic has led to the usual effect 'of creating enemies from categories of people that are framed as threatening' (Baele, 2020: 2). Next to the categorization as a 'Chinese virus' by the Trump administration (see Chapter 27), this also has affected Asian minorities in some countries of the Global North.

Maybe even more importantly, a strong securitization of the pandemic may lead to the wrong counter-measures. Securitization usually results in short-term security measures, instead of long-term social reforms (Baele, 2020: 3); it leads to a 'logic of exceptionalism' instead of a 'logic of solidarity' (Sondermann and Ulbert, 2020: 318). In the case of the pandemic, this for example translates into comprehensive lockdowns and digital surveillance (for contact tracing), instead of higher investments in the health sector or more generous regulations for working from home. Finally, it is also very difficult to de-securitize a topic once it is securitized (Baele, 2020: 3). Strict measures that have been introduced to counter a (perceived) security threat may stay in place longer than necessary – or even permanently – after the real health challenge has receded. Correspondingly, new techniques of digital surveillance may be with us long after the pandemic has receded.

Balancing security concerns in post-corona capitalism

The coronavirus pandemic very often is perceived as a major security threat. Although it is a health problem, it has found its way in discussions on interstate security policies. Even more substantial are the impacts of the pandemic on domestic conflicts in the Global South, the most prevalent contemporary security challenge. However, pandemic-related security threats (and counter-measures) do not only evolve from international and domestic use of the military, but also in the field of human security. One could even argue that the tendency to securitize the pandemic may lead to the comparatively gravest security threats in countries of the Global North, if measures for digital surveillance that have been introduced during the pandemic stay in place indefinitely.

Treating the pandemic primarily as a security threat can have unwelcome consequences. It may lead to more forceful reactions than strictly necessary; in particular, with regard to digital surveillance and the suspension of civil liberties. While popular concerns about the security challenges going hand in hand with the pandemic need to be taken serious, we should rather ameliorate these challenges with well-funded economic and social policies in the future, instead of short-term security measures and increased military budgets. In a more positive vein, the pandemic could also contribute to a broader understanding of security and therefore reduce the traditional focus on kinetic threats.

PART VII

Ideologies in Contemporary Capitalism

The study of broadly encompassing ideas on the changing nature of capitalism is not part of Political Economy textbooks, neither in its Comparative, nor in its International variety (although the latter always contain applications of theories from International Relations, such as Realism, Liberalism and Marxism). Still, these ideologies on the normatively preferred nature of capitalism allow us to create some order in the long list of individual observations assembled in the book, as an 'early conclusion'. Three broad juxtapositions seem particularly useful to make sense of the changes triggered by the coronavirus crisis. The most obvious choice is between authoritarian and democratic capitalism – which model gains, which loses (Chapter 30)? Some three decades ago, most people shared the assumption that (successful) capitalism can only go together with democracy, but the rise of China and authoritarian tendencies in previously capitalist-democratic countries have cast this assumption into doubt. Moreover, a historical perspective demonstrates that capitalist systems not only differ with regard to their system of government, but also with regard to more liberal and more organized systems of capitalism. Again, the question is how does the coronavirus crisis affect these tendencies (Chapter 31)? During the last decades, finally, the rise of populism has pointed to another increasingly important juxtaposition in contemporary capitalism; namely, the one between communitarians and cosmopolitans. Here, the focus is not on the nature of the domestic system of government, but on the degree of openness to outside influences, with communitarians sceptical and cosmopolitans open. Does the pandemic lead to more international openness or rather to closures (Chapter 32)?

Authoritarian or Democratic Capitalism?

From the start, the coronavirus crisis was a propaganda contest between democratic and authoritarian capitalist regimes: who is better equipped to fight against the crisis? Authoritarian countries such as China and Singapore were lauded for their draconian and successful measures against the spreading of the crisis, but also detested for their lack of transparency. Later in the crisis, other authoritarian countries such as Russia, in contrast, suffered more from infections than democratic ones. Which type of capitalism will win the propaganda contest?

Regime types in Comparative Political Economy

Whereas regime types do not matter much in International Political Economy, they are a very established topic in Comparative Political Economy. A core question is whether capitalism and democracy are closely connected. Among the most well-known claims is that liberal capitalism and democracy are the 'end of history' (Fukuyama, 1992). While this claim has been cast into doubt via the rise of China, important recent scholarship still claims that capitalism and democracy mutually support each other, particularly during turbulent times (Iversen and Soskice, 2019). Even during a situation of crisis, democracy reinforces capitalism and capitalist economies remain democratic, the argument goes. While it is based on comprehensive historical evidence on developments in the OECD, it may be less convincing with regard to the current populist backlash. Other perspectives in Comparative Political Economy rather assume that the marriage between capitalism and democracy is nearing its end (Streeck, 2016). Moreover, all of these works focus on the OECD. Given that the centre of capitalism increasingly moves to East and South Asia and that these regions are not known for a prominent role in liberal democracy, we may wonder whether the assumption of a close connection between capitalism and democracy holds globally and in the near future.

Comparisons of authoritarian and democratic handling of the crisis

During the last decades, authoritarian capitalism increasingly has contested the superiority of democratic capitalism that had been claimed, for instance, by Francis Fukuyama after the end of the Cold War. First, China and Singapore, but later also countries such as Hungary, Russia and Turkey at least temporarily argue to be able to provide a superior alternative to democratic capitalism. Correspondingly, it does not surprise that some authors have tried to quantitatively establish whether authoritarian or democratic systems have fared better throughout the crisis. The outcome is mixed – and a moving target (even if we disregard studies linking regime types to COVID-19 death numbers, such as Cepaluni et al, 2021, for methodological reasons). Accounts highlight the lack of transparency and government communication in authoritarian regimes such as China and the related delay in response (Alon et al, 2020; Greer et al, 2021a: 11–13). With regard to the health directives actually implemented, however, authoritarian regimes such as China were ranked quite highly (Bunyavejchewin and Sirichuanjun, 2021: 4). They are able to implement their most stringent public health policy measures in a shorter period of time (Senters Piazza and Stronko, 2020). Moreover, country authoritarian regimes such as China, Hong Kong, Singapore and Vietnam were very quick and heavy handed with their health measures – but the same applies to New Zealand, Norway, South Korea and Taiwan (Greer et al, 2021a: 12–14). Similarly, during the early phase of the pandemic, lockdowns in authoritarian regimes were more stringent and relied more on contact tracing; however, they were less effective in terms of reducing mobility, as measured by 'Google Mobility Reports' data (Frey et al, 2020). Furthermore, regime-related results with regard to the amount of testing during this phase were also not conclusive (Petersen, 2020).

To wrap up, democratic capitalism appears to be better with regard to transparency, but authoritarian capitalism often implements more striding measures (more quickly). After all, authoritarian regimes have to deliver in terms of coronavirus, since their legitimacy in large parts is based on performance. While it is yet impossible to comprehensively determine which regime type fares better with regard to the fight against the pandemic in the end, we can nevertheless study how the pandemic affected each of the two types. This provides us with a clearer picture: democratic capitalism has become more authoritarian during the crisis; authoritarian capitalism even more authoritarian.

Deepening of authoritarian capitalism during the crisis

It is too early to tell which of the two rival ideologies will carry the day in post-corona capitalism, but one tendency has been striking during the crisis: the latter has provided rulers in (semi-)authoritarian capitalist countries an opportunity to strengthen the authoritarian character of their rule. In these countries, the crisis has been used in order to limit fundamental rights, strengthen the position of the executive and to erode the rule of law. While 2019 was a year of global protest – in Algeria, Bolivia, Chile, Hong Kong, India, Iraq, Iran or the Lebanon – protest movements have lost their ability to put pressure on governments nearly completely in 2020 (Sydiq, 2020). Globally, governments have imposed severe limitations on the freedom of assembly, thereby boosting the process of shrinking of civic spaces since the early 2000s, after 9/11 (Bethke and Wolff, 2020). Moreover, 'governments that have recently engaged in state violence against civilians have been more likely to enact lockdown and curfew policies, have done so earlier in the pandemic, and have implemented these policies over a longer period' (Barceló et al, 2021: 1). These general observations can be complemented by numerous country-specific ones. For example, the new 'TraceTogether' app released by the government of Singapore increases government power and control, by centrally collecting contact and movement data of citizens (Stevens and Haines, 2020). In China, the pandemic enabled the government to expand its 'digital authoritarianism', by increasing censorship, enlarging citizen surveillance and including new point-scoring options in its Social Credit System (Khalil, 2020).

Possibly even more worrying than the deepening of authoritarian rule during the crisis, however, is the deepening of authoritarian tendencies in formally democratic countries with 'pre-existing conditions' (Croissant, 2020) for a weakened democracy. In Egypt and Turkey, the governments reacted to the coronavirus crisis – a threat to their survival, given the economic impact of the pandemic and the importance of economic performance for their legitimacy – by increasing control over national media and monopolizing crisis management (Grancayova, 2021). In Hungary, the government curtailed civil liberties and relocated property rights from opposition-controlled to government-controlled entities (Ádám, 2020). In Poland and the Czech Republic, governments also intended to use the emergency to increase the power of the government, but were largely refuted during the first wave of the pandemic (Guasti, 2020). Also in India, Prime Minister Modi has used the opportunity of the pandemic to centralize crisis management, thereby weakening parliament, federal states, judicial review and the media (Mukherji, 2020). This is mirrored by authoritarian developments elsewhere in the Indo-Pacific; for example, the militarization of public life in countries such as Bangladesh, Indonesia, Pakistan and the

Philippines, the centralization of executive powers in the Philippines and Cambodia and the activation of laws to arrest government critics in Malaysia and Thailand (Croissant, 2020: 11–13).

Challenges to democratic capitalism during the pandemic

Still, not all countries have moved in the direction of authoritarian capitalism during the pandemic. For example, other countries of the Indo-Pacific such as Japan, Taiwan and South Korea have managed the health crisis without compromising democracy (Greitens, 2020). Moreover, most countries found solutions to the substantial challenges for the electoral cycles posed by the coronavirus crisis (Landman and Di Gennaro Splendore, 2020). Generally, those countries that show a particularly strong protection of democratic principles in 'normal times' also tend to avoid an erosion of democracy during the pandemic (Engler et al, 2021). Still, even well-established democracies are witnessing subtle challenges, in addition to social changes that are indicating an increasing support for authoritarian government caused by the pandemic (Amat et al, 2020).

One of the core challenges is the shift in power from legislatives to governments during the coronavirus crisis. Typically, the pandemic has supported voting intentions for the incumbent prime minister or president (Bol et al, 2020). Parliaments have clearly taken a back seat in decision-making with regard to the pandemic; for example, in Germany (Merkel, 2020). Next to executive dominance, problems also include lack of parliamentary oversight and 'a general disregard for the proper constitutional order' (Comarcain and Bar-Siman-Tov, 2020: 8). In part, the weakness of parliaments during the pandemic has to do with institutional features such as the size of the parliamentary building or the demographic features of parliamentarians (Bar-Siman-Tov, 2020: 4–10). While these are general problems, they become particularly acute if combined with a political crisis, as in the case of Israel where the pandemic was used to reduce parliamentary oversight and effective oversight of the executive (Bar-Siman-Tov, 2020: 20–33).

Related to this neglect of parliaments is another subtle development that may undermine democratic capitalism; namely, the confrontation between technocracy and populism. During the early phase of the coronavirus crisis, the world has witnessed a tremendous rise of technocratic forms of governance. Some even call this a shift 'from parliamentary sovereignty to autocratic technocracy' (Windholz, 2020). Virologists, epidemiologists and other medical experts played the lead role in combating the crisis. Governments did not always make their own choices for combatting the crisis, but sometimes simply implemented the advice of the medical experts (see Chapter 2), even if these decisions implied a deep recession and massive infringements of civil liberties. The most extreme case of technocratic decision-making during the crisis was Sweden's 'tyranny of experts' (Andersson and Aylott, 2020; Bylund and Packard, 2021). Temporarily, the technocratic course of action was broadly supported by the population, although it limited the reach of democratic decision-making. The longer the crisis continued, however, the more frequent the critique of this form of governance became. Populist politicians – sometimes even the heads of government, as in Brazil, the Philippines and the US (Lasco, 2020) – increasingly contested not only (inter-) governmental decisions, but also the authority of the experts. Inconsistencies between different experts' recommendations – which are normal, since there cannot be perfectly neutral recommendations (Lavazza and Farina, 2020) – have been exploited in great detail. Based on the claim to represent the point of view of 'the people', populists increasingly opposed 'elitist' technocrats. Technocracy often has won the early battle, also given the inability of most populists to come up with a coherent account of the pandemic. However, increasing disaffection with expert rule indicates that populism may win out in the medium or long term. Finally, both technocracy and populism are alien to the pluralist democratic process which should be based on the competition between political proposals with different values and social support groups.

How to strengthen democratic capitalism after the coronavirus crisis

So far, the coronavirus pandemic has weakened democratic capitalism, in favour of authoritarian tendencies. This is particularly worrying because the global state of democracy was already quite problematical before the outbreak of the crisis, as highlighted by all major reviews on the state of democracy in 2019/20 (Flinders, 2021: 485–6). The pandemic has deepened authoritarian tendencies where these were already relevant and has posed new challenges to democratic systems, particularly to parliaments. The pandemic originally had strengthened technocratic authority, but later has cast this authority frequently into doubt and politicized debates about health measures.

Politicization of debates is not necessarily a bad development. Technocratic decision-making often is not democratic. Still, the destruction of expert authority and its replacement by populist misinformation also is not helpful for the democratic political process. Against both perspectives, proponents of democratic politics should highlight the importance of conscious political choices made by the elected representatives of competing political parties.

31

Liberal or Organized Capitalism?

During the coronavirus crisis, we have been witnessing a renewed role for the state. Some observers even claim that these increases mark the beginning of a new era of state capitalism, ending the current era of neoliberalism. Others point towards the very fast development of vaccines by pharmaceutical companies and argue in favour of a rebirth of liberalism. In order to make sense of these competing claims, we put them into the context of Political Economy debates about phases of capitalism; notably, its juxtaposition of liberal and organized ones. Are we moving towards liberal or organized capitalism?

Theories about phases of capitalism

Any observer of the historical development of the economy will notice that capitalism is not a timeless entity. Think, for example, about the changes that neoliberalism and the rise of the financial markets have brought to capitalism since the 1970s. Political Economy scholarship has produced several conceptual frameworks about phases of capitalism. There is a wealth of theories such as world systems, regulation or those named after Kondratieff, Marx or Schumpeter (Nölke, 2012, 2017; Nölke and May, 2019; Kilic, 2020). Arguably, the most widely used frameworks in contemporary research are the 'social structures of accumulation' approach (Kotz et al, 1994) and studies drawing on Polanyi (1944). Polanyi's concept of the double movement arguably has become the most popular mode of thinking about the historical development of the economy since the GFC. The basic idea is that we have a pendulum between liberal and social embedded capitalism. Liberal reformers try to dis-embed the economy by turning everything into a commodity. This gives rise to a countermovement seeking to re-embed the economy in social relations. While Polanyi had developed his ideas as a reaction to the Great Depression of the 1930s, it witnessed a revival after the Great Recession of 2007–09.

The social structures of accumulation (SSA) approach is less popular than Polanyi's idea, but is probably the most widely used one by those scholars systematically working on phases of capitalism today. Its basic idea is quite similar to those of Polanyi, but worked out in much more economic detail (Kotz et al, 1994). SSA scholars assume an alternation between liberal and regulated phases of capitalism. Each of the two types of phases ends in a specific form – liberal in a turbulent crisis and regulated in a long-term stagnation. Turbulent crises are a consequence of the under-consumption inherent in liberal capitalism – a weak role of labour will lead to low wages and, correspondingly, insufficient demand. Stagnation crisis follows from the profit squeeze going hand in hand with regulated capitalism, due to increasing wages and a strong role of the state.

However, we may wonder whether the idea of a powerful global regulation of capitalism still is plausible today, under the conditions of cross-border mobile finance that started with the demise of the Bretton Woods system. It seems more realistic to expect a powerful regulation of capitalism on the national level, at least in some economies (see, for example, Chapter 27). This brings us to theories of organized capitalism, going back to authors such as Hilferding (1910) and Sombart (1932). In a nutshell, the core question about organized capitalism is whether firms are the private business of their owners and insiders (as in liberal capitalism) or quasi-public infrastructures and, therefore, constrained in their economic decisions by institutionally sanctioned collective interests. The latter is called organized capitalism, with the collective interests ranging from sectoral interests over class interests to political interests, such as supporting a war economy (Höpner, 2007). Importantly, organized capitalism can both be a 'friendly', social-democratic capitalism as in the US New Deal, but also a very dangerous and aggressive form of capitalism, as in Nazi Germany.

Subsequently, we will discuss early evidence about the coronavirus crisis in the context of a framework that combines the two pendulum theories with theories about organized capitalism. This framework assumes an alternation between liberal and organized phases of capitalism. Both types of phases endure a couple of decades, but are inherently unstable. Given the historically liberal character of capitalism since the 1980s, we may wonder whether the coronavirus crisis is part of a major crisis of liberal capitalism, leading to a new phase of organized capitalism.

Symptoms for a major crisis of (neo)liberal capitalism

Even during the early stages of the coronavirus crisis, there are considerable indications that we are witnessing a fundamental crisis of liberal capitalism.

These indications include, for example, the failure of privatized health systems (see Chapter 2), the ever deeper inequalities in our societies (see Chapter 7), the growing opposition to liberal concepts of shareholder value (see Chapter 12), the growing concerns about economic concentration through liberal markets (see Chapter 16), the breakdown of GVCs and the related concept of liberal globalization (see Chapters 17–20), the ever louder calls for a waiver on IPR – a core concept of economic liberalism – in the pharmaceutical sector (see Chapter 21), or the erosion of the US-led liberal global order (see Chapter 27). These developments came on top of the GFC, which was before the coronavirus recession the largest economic crisis since the 1930s. From an SSA perspective, the latter began to weaken the current mode of capitalism, whereas the coronavirus is expected to be its 'final blow' (Kilic, 2020: 5).

Correspondingly, claims about a fundamental crisis of the neoliberal social structure of accumulation (Kilic, 2020), or of market fundamentalism (Ötsch, 2020), or of a deepening of the legitimation crisis of the neoliberal order (Condon, 2020) or an 'interregnum' at the end of neoliberalism (Rugitsky, 2020) are not far-fetched. However, symptoms for a crisis of liberal capitalism are not sufficient to indicate that a liberal phase of capitalism ends. We also need indications for the emergence of a new phase of organized capitalism. The 2007/08 GFC, for example, did not directly lead to a phase of organized capitalism (Kilic, 2020). Still, this time it may indeed be different.

Tendencies towards organized capitalism during the coronavirus crisis

We observe strong tendencies towards organized capitalism during the coronavirus crisis. These tendencies include, among others, a huge increase of public expenditures (see Part II Domestic Institutions of Capitalism on the Demand Side), a stronger role for the state in the financing of companies (see Chapter 12), more protectionist policies (see Chapter 20) and a triumph of state capitalist economic systems (see Chapter 27). These tendencies strengthen developments that have started in the years before the crisis (Nölke, 2017). The Brexit decision, for example, was taken against the clear advice of the proponents of liberal capitalism, particularly with regard to the freedom of capital flows and the freedom of human movement. The latter also played a prominent role in the election of Donald Trump, together with his stance against trade liberalization. The liberal mode of capitalism also was weakened on the international level; for example, with regard to the ongoing blockade of the WTO or the turning away of the IMF from core liberal tenets such as the demand for the abolition of all capital controls.

Correspondingly, there are indications for a more general move towards organized capitalism. Observers from the political left appeal to use the situation for a final assault on neoliberalism (Saad-Filho, 2020). However, there are also voices arguing that neoliberalism is too deeply entrenched in order to be seriously affected even by the very deep coronavirus recession (Guillén, 2020). Others argue that we should not confuse the 'emergency Keynesianism' of the state with a turn away from neoliberalism; the latter, however, is understood as a political ideology, not as a phase of capitalism (Sumonja, 2020).

Finally, some observers claim that there are also indications for a rejuvenation of liberal capitalism during the coronavirus crisis. They point, for example, towards the fast production of vaccines during the coronavirus crisis that can be understood as a triumph of liberal capitalism. Correspondingly, they rather expect a rejuvenation of liberal capitalism instead of a turn towards organized capitalism. However, closer inspection demonstrates that both the limited research on vaccination before the crisis and the slow vaccination in the Global South due to the unwillingness of pharmaceutical companies to give away IPR casts doubt on this triumph. A more convincing argument in favour of a stabilization of liberal capitalism could be that the state may have won a pyrrhic victory during the coronavirus pandemic. This argument would grant that the state has tremendously gained importance during the crisis. But with great power comes great responsibility. If the state does not manage the crisis well (for example, by botched vaccination campaigns), this could lead to an anti-statist backlash – and a turn towards liberal capitalism. However, it is yet too early to corroborate these assumptions.

How to avoid the dark features of organized capitalism in the future

When we understand the recent history of capitalism as a pendulum movement between liberal and organized phases of capitalism, a new phase of organized capitalism currently looks far more likely than a stabilization of liberal capitalism. Correspondingly, we may assume a more prominent economic role for the state in many economies in the next years. This entails a larger role for the state not only in terms of spending, but also in the control of companies and the steering of markets.

The core question will be whether these tendencies can be harnessed as a progressive force (as during the New Deal) or not (as under Fascism). This depends on the actors and social groups that make these changes politically viable by creating a new social bloc in favour of organized capitalism. From an SSA perspective, the transition phase between one SSA to the other goes hand in hand with particularly intense class struggle (Kilic, 2020: 8).

Moreover, the result of this struggle is open. If, for example, labour unions play an important role in the creation of this social bloc, a progressive outlook looks more likely. If it is based on exclusionary populist movements, the outlook is much bleaker, pointing towards a racist and reactionary form of organized capitalism (see also Chapter 30).

32

Communitarian or Cosmopolitan Capitalism?

Within days after the first victims of the coronavirus were identified, governments took decisions on a comprehensive closure of national borders and restricted flights. Particularly striking was the closure of borders within the Schengen Area of the EU, within which people were used to move freely on a daily basis for work and leisure. Accordingly, the ban on travelling freely within the Schengen Area had a radical impact not only on the EU economy but also on its identity. It was as if the pandemic pushed Europe back to its past: an area constructed of small nation states divided by real geographical borders (see Chapter 6 and Chapter 28). The ban on the freedom of movement of people within the EU was only the most extreme measure taken by governments that reminded us that the world is still made of territorial states and that the primary responsibility of governments usually is perceived to be towards the domestic population. Related measures included the ban on exports of coronavirus-related health products (see Chapter 2) or the focus on the rescue of national enterprises (see Chapter 12). We can order all of these observations by locating them in the struggle between communitarian and cosmopolitan ideologies of capitalism. Which of the two conceptions will have the upper hand in post-corona capitalism?

Communitarian and cosmopolitan models of capitalism

Like the immigration crisis in Europe and the US beforehand, the pandemic deepened the tensions between two sets of modern values. On the one side, we can find the cosmopolitan set of values, which is based on universal human rights, supranational integration and open borders. On the other side, we find the communitarian set of values, which perceives human beings as social animals and embedded in their local community, with a strong focus on the nation state as protector of the latter. In recent years, amid an acceleration of globalization, the cosmopolitan/communitarian divide cut through traditional cleavages, between conservatives and liberals on the one side and social democrats and socialists on the other. Correspondingly, the new divide transformed the ideological map in many societies.

The communitarian/cosmopolitan divide stems from Political Theory and later was applied to diverse (sub-) disciplines such as Party Politics and International Relations (Zürn and de Wilde, 2016; de Wilde et al, 2019). Still, it also has a strong significance for Political Economy. Economic globalization is a core topic for the latter, with cosmopolitans very positive about the various aspects of globalization and communitarians more negative. Before the coronavirus crisis, the cosmopolitan-communitarian division took place mainly in relation to cross-border migration, with the cosmopolitans being in favour and communitarians more reluctant. In some regions, additional issues were at stake, such as supporting or rejecting the supranational aspects of the EU (including increased transnational fiscal solidarity) or NAFTA. Most likely, the coronavirus crisis will not only intensify this cleavage, but will also often shift popular support towards communitarianism, at least for the short- and medium term.

The turn towards communitarianism during the post-coronavirus era

The coronavirus crisis, and the response to it, is highly likely to deepen the tension between the cosmopolitan and the communitarian sets of values. Some would argue that the crisis is a global one, and therefore a powerful role for international (or even supranational) organizations is essential; others would see in the crisis more evidence for the necessity of the nation state and the importance of a robust local community characterized by solidarity. The question arises, therefore, whether capitalism is likely to become, once again, more 'national', or that powerful global governance is a necessity. Judging from the development of the crisis so far, the coronavirus crisis will not only intensify this cleavage, but may also shift support towards communitarianism, at least for the short- and medium term. This shift has three dimensions: governments' decisions and policies, the structure of global capitalism and the public discourse.

Although there is no shortage in the declarations of global openness and solidarity by politicians, the actual measures implemented by the latter seem to favour communitarian positions. In terms of political measures implemented during the coronavirus crisis, border closures stand out as one of the first and most comprehensively adopted measures by governments across the world. Moreover, many governments have implemented increasingly restrictive regulations on immigration (see Chapter 6). Countries also limited the export of medical products relevant for combatting the health crisis, even if these products were in very short supply in other economies (see Chapter 2). More generally, decisions made during the crisis underlined the critical role of the nation state. National governments made the most important political decisions in order to combat the virus. This concerns decisions on public health, but also on economic measures to combat the recession. Instead of a common global economic strategy, each government has implemented its individual economic rescue programme (see Part II). Moreover, many countries have implemented measures in order to protect national companies against foreign acquisitions (See Chapter 12). To be sure, most countries followed the same set of policies to combat the health crisis. This was based on an exchange of information and mutual learning. However, formal international coordination to combat the coronavirus crisis during its early phase was extremely limited. It consisted mainly of the efforts of the WHO. The G20 issued some declarations, but without any measurable impact. The G7, the OECD and most central UN institutions were largely sidelined, also in the medium term (see Chapters 22 and 27). In Europe, coordinated economic measures to prevent a deep recession were only taken by the member states of the EU. However, even here, these measures were very limited and most observers agree that they fall well short of what would have been necessary, especially to support the weaker member states. The supranational institutions of the EU hardly played a role during the early phases of the coronavirus crisis; clearly, the focus was on intergovernmental negotiations. Later, however, the crisis has led to a strengthening of fiscal solidarity in the Union, as witnessed by the establishment of the Next Generation EU Recovery Fund (Genschel and Jachtenfuchs, 2021; see also Chapter 28).

Changes in the general structure of global capitalism during the coronavirus crisis also indicate a communitarian direction, at least during the short- to medium term (Legrain, 2020). Not only migration partially came to a standstill during the crisis. Many governments have announced action in order to reduce the dependence of their economies on global production networks, in order to avoid similar problems with production processes as encountered during the crisis; in particular, in the health sector (see Chapter 17). In fact, the coronavirus crisis may prove to be the tipping point with regard to changes in the development of capitalism that were in the making for some time already; for example, with regard to the risks that the complex China-centred global supply chains are facing in the context of the increasing conflict between China and the US.

Not only government actions and changes in the nature of capitalism reflect a strengthening of communitarianism tendencies – at least in the short- to medium term. There are also some early indications that the crisis has strengthened the social support for this position. In theory, governments could realize these developments and political decisions against the will of the population. Accordingly, after the crisis, opposition to the communitarian handling of the crisis could still win the day. However, very early evidence with regard to public opinion on the measures taken by the governments to combat the crisis, including a strong focus on national (instead of international) measures and the closure of borders, shows a broad support for these measures (Amat et al, 2020). One could even argue that the coronavirus crisis has given additional support to long-dormant traditions of thought favouring national self-sufficiency, if not even autarchy (Helleiner, 2021). Still, these surveys are in a very early stage and have to be supported by much more comprehensive research. Hypothetically, public opinion could also shift to cosmopolitanism values in the long run.

The need for international cooperation – even in communitarian capitalism

Both the direction of political measures and of the working of capitalism during the coronavirus crisis so far favour communitarian positions. If early developments in public opinion are confirmed, it is likely that communitarian ideology plays a much more prominent role in post-coronavirus capitalism. Accordingly, the prospects for powerful forms of global governance are bleak. Nor will the supranational elements of the EU be strengthened in the coming years. Governments will probably control migration more strictly than before, and many economic processes will be reshored.

For some observers, not only for fervent advocates of cosmopolitanism, these developments point in a problematic direction. They would become particularly dangerous, if an increasing importance of communitarian motivations in the design of capitalism also leads to a breakdown of international cooperation. This would not only considerably weaken institutions such as the EU, but also most likely aggravate the situation with regard to global problems such as climate change and migration. However, an increasing importance of communitarian perspectives does not necessarily lead to a breakdown of international cooperation. The latter could also take a somewhat different institutional form, by focusing on international regimes (intergovernmental cooperation in specific issue areas) instead of powerful international or even supranational organizations. After all, there is a great variety of (institutional) solutions for international cooperation (Aggarwal and Dupont, 2020).

33

Conclusion: Competing Visions of Capitalism and their Perspectives

What will post-corona capitalism look like? We don't know. It is the core contention of this book that important political choices about the future of capitalism lie ahead. It has described some 30 of these choices and the alternatives available. The next years will demonstrate which of the alternatives will be realized and which not. This will be the outcome of political struggles and the book hopefully can contribute towards making these struggles more democratic, by highlighting the alternatives at hand. Still, this book has also assembled empirical evidence with regard to the likelihood of these alternatives, based on developments during the first two years of the crisis. While this is still very early in the process, we can nevertheless summarize broad tendencies.

Competing visions of post-coronavirus capitalism

In order to reduce the complexity of a long list of individual observations, this chapter will allocate the latter to a small number of alternative visions of future capitalism (see also Dummer and Neuhäuser, 2020). The identification of these visions follows the alternative options discussed in some individual chapters. The book distinguishes five different options for the near future of capitalism. Since space does not permit for a long description of these models, we can link the latter to recent governments that have pursued related policies (where available):

- *Classical liberal capitalism*: The focus is on a central role for private business, the preponderance of shareholder value and unregulated markets (laissez-faire), in order to maximize the productive potential of capitalism. Traditionally, this vision of capitalism has been pursued in the US (Republicans before Trump) and the UK (particularly by Tory governments under Thatcher).

- *Cosmopolitan technocratic capitalism:* While sharing some concerns with classical liberal capitalism, the focus here is on managing global capitalism in a frictionless way, which includes some form of regulation and often the delegation of authority to non-majoritarian institutions, both domestically (for example, central banks) and internationally (for example, the IMF). This is a vision of capitalism that can be found with many global organizations, but also within EU institutions and the German government (during the Merkel chancellorship).

- *National social-democratic capitalism:* Departing from a vision of Northern capitalism after World War II, the emphasis is on social equality and parliamentary democracy, with an important role for the welfare state. Both parliamentary democracy and the welfare state still work best on the national level and supranational institutions are seen with a certain degree of suspicion, as is unlimited migration. Geographically, this vision of capitalism is typically to be found in Scandinavia. It should not be confused with the line of contemporary social democratic parties, because some of the latter lean strongly towards cosmopolitan technocratic capitalism (for example, the Blair government in the UK, the Schroeder government in Germany or the Obama government in the US).

- *Authoritarian capitalism:* This is a vision of capitalism that has gained much popularity during the last decade, usually under the heading of 'populism'. The preference is for a strong national leadership, with very limited restraints via democratic process or supranational authorities and a distrust of migration as well as gender policies and climate concerns. While this model of capitalism is particularly popular in emerging economies such as Brazil, China, India, Russia or Turkey, it has also made inroads into some economies of the North, such as Hungary, Poland and the US (during Trump).

- *Alternative capitalism:* This could also be called 'alternatives to capitalism', with its opposition to economic growth, inequalities of all kinds and top-down policies. In contrast to the other four models, it has not (yet) become hegemonic in any country or under a specific government, but it is particularly prominent in parts of the Mediterranean societies (France, Spain).

In refraining from imposing one single vision of post-coronavirus capitalism, this chapter is sticking to the importance of political alternatives. Subsequently, the chapter highlights how the empirical developments during the early phases of the coronavirus crisis discussed in the book speak in favour of the various alternative vision of capitalisms. Finally, the chapter summarizes some of the policy suggestions contained at the end of each chapter, in order to sketch how empirically the most likely among the normatively preferable visions of capitalism can be realized.

Which vision of capitalism will have the upper hand after the coronavirus pandemic?

The five alternative projects are phrased in normative ways. Still, we should not only choose projects with regard to their proximity to our normative obligations, but also with regard to the likelihood whether they can find social and political support. If we disregard the latter, we may find ourselves in a situation where we have to live under the least-preferred model, because our favourite one was too unpopular with the overwhelming majority of the population. Each of the 31 chapters on the political alternatives for post-coronavirus capitalism has summarized empirical developments during the first two years of the crisis. What do they tell us about the future popularity of the five options?

- *Classical liberal capitalism* will be weakened by the coronavirus crisis. Private health systems have often proven to be not reliable during the pandemic (Chapter 2). Many people also were very grateful for a comprehensive coverage via the welfare state (Chapter 3), an institution that classical liberal capitalism always wants to trim. The inequalities going hand in hand with this model of capitalism have become more glaring than ever (Chapter 7), thereby weakening its promise of 'wealth for everybody'. Moreover, classical liberal capitalism also has lost appeal in the eyes of many policymakers, as the comprehensive turn away from conservative central banking indicates (Chapter 8). Similarly, the revival of industrial policy (Chapter 11) speaks against core tenets of classical liberal capitalism, as does the turn against shareholder value (Chapter 12) and against a strict competition policy (Chapter 16). The belief in a smooth functioning of market forces also has been shattered by the proven vulnerability of GVCs (Chapter 17). Increasing restrictions on FDIs (Chapter 18) and growing protectionism (Chapter 20) also speak against a growing role for classical liberal capitalism, as does the rising popularity of organized capitalism (Chapter 31).
- *Cosmopolitan technocratic capitalism* suffers from the malfunctioning of some of its institutions, such as autonomous science-focused health agencies during the pandemic. Moreover, international institutions close to this model, such as the IMF and the WB have to accept responsibility for a deepening of the crisis, since their austerity policies led to a reduction of funding of health systems in many countries of the Global South (Chapter 2). During the crisis, easy trans-border migration – a core pillar of cosmopolitan convictions – has been stopped completely and the

harsh treatment of many migrant workers does not bode well for future migration-friendly policies (Chapter 6). More generally, increasing social inequality will undermine the satisfaction with this vision of capitalism. This also pertains to its core institutions, such as central banks, given that the latter become more and more politicized, thereby eroding their technocratic appeal (Chapters 8 and 28). Similarly, transnational capitalism becomes more and more politicized, by restrictions against the foreign acquisition of domestic companies (Chapter 18), increasing opposition against the current system of ISDS (Chapter 19) and more protectionist trade policies (Chapter 20). The image of cosmopolitan technocratic capitalism will also suffer from its inability to safeguard a fair global distribution of vaccines (Chapters 21 and 22) and by the too limited relief for debt-ridden low-income economies (Chapter 23). Given that the fight against global warming via carbon dioxide emission prices is a core tenet of this vision of capitalism, it will also become unpopular with low-income groups that are worried that these prices inhibit core practices of their established lifestyle (Chapter 24). The coronavirus crisis has further undermined the liberal economic order, a core pillar of cosmopolitan technocratic capitalism (Chapter 27) and has led to eroding tendencies in the EU, its poster child (Chapter 28). Correspondingly, it does not surprise that we can identify a general tendency away from cosmopolitan capitalism during the post-coronavirus pandemic (Chapter 32).

- *National social-democratic capitalism* will be somewhat strengthened ideologically. Well-funded public health systems have proven to be a crucial resource in order to ameliorate the effects of the pandemic (Chapter 2). While comprehensive welfare states of the Scandinavian kind have proven to be stable, the future fate of Continental European welfare states depends on whether the process of dualization will be continued (Chapter 3). If the latter is the case, social-democratic capitalism may lose its popularity and more people will favour a universal basic income, a model of welfare state more in line with alternative capitalism (and, ironically, with classical liberal capitalism). Generally, the fate of this vision of capitalism will depend on the ability to reverse the process of increasing inequality triggered by the crisis (Chapter 7) – and to implement its core promise; namely, social mobility. In terms of welfare state funding, the 'Zeitgeist' may be on the side of national social-democratic capitalism, given that wealth taxes and company minimum taxation are becoming popular (Chapter 10). The revival of industrial policy (Chapter 11 and Chapter 17) also fits well with this vision of capitalism, as does an important role of the state within systems of innovation (Chapter 15) and the need to set up large public investment programmes to fight climate change without over-burdening population groups that are less well off (Chapter 24). Given its focus on national democracy and welfare state, this model of capitalism also profits from the turns towards communitarian and organized capitalism (Chapters 31 and 32). Finally, the vision of social-democratic capitalism that is mainly organized on the national level also harmonizes better with the erosion of the liberal economic order that had become quite intrusive with regard to the prescription of liberal economic and political models after 1990 (Chapter 27).

- *Authoritarian capitalism* likely will gain popularity after the crisis due to the intensification of inequalities (Chapter 7), given that the latter will undermine the legitimacy of democratic political systems in large groups of the population. Similarly, the weak role of labour unions during the pandemic may play in favour of this type of capitalism (Chapter 14). Generally, authoritarian regimes have strengthened their grip upon the population during the pandemic and authoritarian tendencies have increased in still formally democratic countries (Chapter 30). Authoritarian capitalism already is hegemonic in the most populous emerging economies and in many smaller low-income countries. During the pandemic, the highly problematic treatment of transnational care workers (and other migrant workers) in many countries demonstrated the low social status of migrants in many societies (Chapters 4 and 6), a core topic of contemporary carriers of this vision of capitalism. Similarly, the deepening of gender pay gaps during the pandemic indicates the still prominent role of traditional social norms playing in favour of this vision of capitalism (Chapter 5). Authoritarian leaders in the Global South will also be able to stabilize their rule by pointing at the failure of Western democracies to provide fair systems for the utilization of IPR on vaccine development (Chapter 21) and for the global distribution of vaccines (Chapter 22). Securitizing the pandemic also helps these forces in stabilizing their rule (Chapter 29). Similarly, these leaders will be able to mobilize against cosmopolitan technocratic capitalism by highlighting the repercussions of increased carbon dioxide prices on lower-income groups and low-income economies (Chapter 24). Within the EU, authoritarian (right-wing populist) parties will point towards the lack of solidarity, particularly during the early phase of the pandemic and during mid-term financial stabilization (Chapter 28). Finally, similar to national social-democratic capitalism, authoritarian capitalism benefits from the turns towards organized and communitarian capitalisms (Chapters 31 and 32) and from the weakening of the US-led liberal economic order (Chapter 27) as well as of eroding tendencies in the EU (Chapter 28).
- *Alternative capitalism* has seen a temporary increase of popularity during the early phase of the crisis. This refers to the concept of universal basic income that promises to shield people from stressful labour activation policies in most welfare states (Chapter 3), but also to the concept of degrowth (Chapter 25). However, there are hardly any chances for this

vision to become hegemonic in the short term. In the long term, however, these concepts may become more popular. The same applies to changes with regard to the sharing of reproductive work within families, where the pandemic has started a process of reorientation (Chapter 4). The biggest support for alternative capitalism was seen in the sudden improvement of environmental conditions during the crisis (Chapter 24), the short-term boom of degrowth articulations during the early coronavirus crisis (Chapter 25). Similarly, the disappointment with the global agrifood systems and the re-emergence of the importance of peasant agriculture and peasant markets fit well with a vision of alternative capitalism (or alternatives to capitalism), but they also have proven to be rather short-lived (Chapter 26).

A programme to avoid the (further) descent into authoritarian capitalism

All in all, there is a substantial likelihood that the coronavirus pandemic will further increase the turn towards authoritarian capitalism that we have witnessed during the last decades. Since few readers will share the normative preferences of authoritarian capitalism, this leads to the question how we can use the political decisions that have to be taken after the coronavirus crisis in order to prevent this outcome. Not all of the four alternative visions look equally likely. Neither classical liberal capitalism, nor alternative capitalism seem to command sufficient social support in order to put up a credible counter-project to authoritarian capitalism in the very near future. This leaves us with two alternatives – cosmopolitan technocratic capitalism and national social-democratic capitalism. Cosmopolitan capitalism has been the dominant model in the Global North during the last decades, but has suffered severe setbacks during the crisis. Correspondingly, the conclusion of the book is that we should strengthen the national social-democratic capitalism project as a contemporary antidote to authoritarian capitalism (while not excluding other projects in the more long-term future). However, it is by no means sure that social-democratic capitalism will win the day, in particular if its representatives are unable to reverse the process of increasing inequality. The frequent association between the current situation and the 1930s is not far-fetched – in both cases, the most popular alternatives were national social democracy (US New Deal) and authoritarian capitalism (Fascism).

This account of the pandemic also informs us about the necessary steps to support national social-democratic capitalism against the rise of authoritarian capitalism. It is imperative to invest into well-funded national public health systems (Chapter 2) and to restore welfare states that have been eroded by a process of dualization that excludes substantial parts of the population (Chapter 3), thereby making the latter more open for the siren calls of authoritarian capitalism. Moreover, unions should seize the opportunity and negotiate for better payment in reproductive work sectors such as health (Chapter 4). Instead of focusing on traditional physical infrastructures within reconstruction packages after the crisis, the latter should give a more prominent role to social infrastructures such as childcare and education (Chapter 5).

In order to rob the alternative vision of authoritarian capitalism one of its most powerful political weapons, it is important to conduct open and pragmatic discussions about low-skill labour migration (Chapter 6) which should neither be idealized (as often is the case within concepts of alternative capitalism) nor demonized (by xenophobic undercurrents in authoritarian capitalism). Similarly, it is crucial to reduce the degree of inequality in our societies, in order to weaken the appeal of authoritarian capitalism (Chapter 7). Minimum taxation for companies, more progressive income taxation and wealth taxes can play an important role here (Chapter 10).

This is not only a task for the welfare state. Reversing processes of financialization – for example, via transaction taxes – will also avoid deepening income and wealth inequality (Chapter 13). Also, governments need to develop accountability mechanisms in order to make sure that selective state ownership of companies maximizes benefits for society (Chapter 12). Strengthening the role of labour unions will contribute to the same purpose, also with regard to training systems (Chapter 14). Governments also should take steps to make production less fragile; for example, by using public procurement for ensuring sufficient domestic production in the case of vital goods (Chapter 17).

In terms of political organization, it is important to make sure that the ultimate decision-making competence in important matters rests with the government and not with technocratic bodies. This refers to national health authorities (Chapter 2), central banks (Chapter 8) and the current form of global health governance that gives crucial decision-making authority to private foundations (Chapter 22). Moreover, countries should refrain from imposing spending limits via their own constitutions or via supranational institutions such as the EU, in order to decide about spending decisions in a democratic process (Chapter 9).

While most of the suggestions mentioned earlier relate to the Global North, we also need to enable Southern economies to pursue social-democratic economic policies, based on catch-up industrialization. A strengthening of UNIDO vis-à-vis more liberal or technocratic international institutions such as the WB might be an important first step (Chapter 11). Similarly, countries of the Global South should utilize inward FDI more strongly for the purpose of technology acquisition (Chapter 18). The Global North should support this process by relieving its pressure to include ISDS mechanisms in trade agreements (Chapter 19), refrain from further protectionist moves (Chapter 20) and create a global safety net for future debt crises (Chapter 23). Generally, the international order should be based on the multilateral cooperation between governments, but without the intrusive liberal supranationalism carried by the powerful technocracies of the existing order (Chapter 27).

Post-corona capitalism: a call to arms

This book has demonstrated that the period after the end of the coronavirus pandemic will be the focus of a large number of important economic and political decisions that will shape the face of capitalism during the next decades. Readers will have different normative frames. Correspondingly, their preferences with regard to the alternative options available will differ. Other readers, however, still need to make up their minds with regard to their policy preferences. This book assists them with this task.

However, there is also the bigger picture. According to the assessment of this book, we are witnessing an increasing likelihood of a turn towards authoritarian capitalism in the years to come. If we want to avoid this fate, we need to consolidate the opposition to authoritarian capitalism. Currently, non-authoritarian forces are split between numerous counter projects that can be divided into four main alternatives. Due to this fragmentation, authoritarian capitalism may win the day, even if it is not the preference of societal majorities. Correspondingly, it seems necessary to overcome established controversies in the democratic-progressive camp, in order to avoid a descent into barbarism as witnessed during the 1930s.

Among the four alternatives to authoritarian capitalism, social-democratic national capitalism seems to be the model that has been strengthened substantially during the crisis. Correspondingly, the suggestion of the book is to rally around this flag, even if it is not one's number one preference. But even with combined democratic and progressive forces, national social-democratic capitalism will not come about automatically. It requires the implementation of a comprehensive political agenda, as outlined earlier. Let us hope that many issues of this agenda will be implemented during post-coronavirus capitalism.

References

Aalbers, M. (2016) *The Financialization of Housing: A Political Economy Approach*, London: Routledge.

Abbas, M.Z. (2020) *Practical Implications of 'Vaccine Nationalism': A Short-sighted and Risky Approach in Response to COVID-19* (Research Paper 124), Geneva: South Centre.

Abedi, V., Olulana, O., Avula, V., Chaudhary, D., Khan, A, Shahjouei, S., Li, J. and Zand, R. (2021) 'Racial, economic, and health inequality and COVID-19 infection in the United States', *Journal of Racial and Health Disparities*, 8: 732–42.

Acharya, A. (2020) *Making a COVID-19 Vaccine Globally Available once Developed* (WIDER Background Note 6/2020), Helsinki: United Nations University World Institute for Development Economics Research.

Ádám, Z. (2020) 'Ultra-orthodoxy and selective voluntarism: how did the Orbán regime react to the first wave of the pandemic?', *European Policy Analysis*, online first.

Adams-Prassl, A., Boneva, T., Golin, M. and Rauh, C. (2020) *Inequality in the Impact of the Coronavirus Shock: Evidence from Real Time Surveys* (IZA Discussion Paper No. 13183), Bonn: IZA Institute of Labour Economics.

Aggarwal, V.K. and Dupont, C. (2020) 'Cooperation and conflict in the global political economy', in J. Ravenhill (ed) *Global Political Economy* (6th edn), Oxford: Oxford University Press, pp 52–75.

Aiginger, K. and Rodrik, D. (2020) 'Rebirth of industrial policy and an agenda for the twenty-first century', *Journal of Industry, Competition and Trade*, 20: 189–207.

Albertoni, N. and Wise, C. (2021) 'International trade norms in the age of Covid-19: nationalism on the rise?', *Fudan Journal of the Humanities and Social Sciences*, 14(1): 41–55.

Alon, I., Farrell, M. and Li, S. (2020) 'Regime type and COVID-19 response', *FIIB Business Review*, 9(3): 152–60.

Alon, T., Doepke, M., Olmstead-Rumsey, J. and Tertilt, M. (2020) *The Impact of COVID-19 on Gender Equality* (NBER Working Paper Series No. 26947), Washington, DC: National Bureau for Economic Research.

Amat, F., Falcó-Gimeno, A., Arenas A. and Munoz, J. (2020) 'Pandemics meet democracy: experimental evidence from the COVID-19 crisis in Spain', *SocArXiv paper*, 5 April, Available from: https://osf.io/preprints/socarxiv/dkusw/ [Accessed 2 April 2021].

Anand, P. (2020) 'Covid-19 and ISDS moratorium: an indiscreet proposal', Available from: http://opiniojuris.org/2020/06/15/covid-19-and-isds-moratorium-an-indiscreet-proposal/ [Accessed 16 May 2021].

Anderson, J., Papadia, F. and Véron, N. (2021) *COVID-19 Credit Support Programmes in Europe's Five Largest Economies* (Working Paper 03/2021), Brussels: Bruegel.

Andersson, E. (2020) *Reconstructing the Global Political Economy: An Analytical Guide*, Bristol: Bristol University Press.

Andersson, S. and Aylott, N. (2020) 'Sweden and coronavirus: unexceptional exceptionalism', *Social Sciences*, 9(232): 1–18.

Andreoni, A. and Chang, H.-J. (2019) 'The political economy of industrial policy: structural interdependencies, policy alignments and conflict management', *Structural Change and Economic Dynamics*, 48: 136–50.

Antràs, P. (2020) *De-Globalisation? Global Value Chains in the Post-COVID-19 Age* (NBER Working Paper No. 28115), Cambridge, MA: National Bureau of Economic Research.

Appelbaum, E. and Batt, R. (2020) *Private Equity Buyouts in Healthcare: Who Wins, Who Loses?* (INET Working Paper No. 118), New York, NY: Institute for New Economic Thinking.

Ardanaz, M., Cavallo, E., Izquierdo, A. and Puig, J. (2021) 'Growth-friendly fiscal rules? Safeguarding public investment from budget cuts through fiscal rule design', *Journal of International Money and Finance*, 111, online first.

Arrelano, C., Bai, Y. and Mihalache, G.P. (2020) *Deadly Debt Crises: COVID-19 in Emerging Markets* (NBER Working Paper No. 27275), Cambridge, MA: National Bureau of Economic Research.

Assa, J. (2020) *Privatization and Pandemic: A Cross-Country Analysis of COVID-19 Rates and Health-Care Financing Structures* (Working Paper 08/2020), New York, NY: Department of Economics, The New School for Social Research.

Austin, K.F., Desciscolo, C. and Samuelsen, L. (2016) 'The failures of privatization: a comparative investigation of tuberculosis rates and the structure of healthcare in less-developed nations, 1995–2010', *World Development*, 78: 450–60.

Avis, J., Atkins, L., Esmond, B. und McGrath, S. (2021) 'Re-conceptualising VET: responses to Covid-19', *Journal of Vocational Education & Training*, 73(1): 1–23.

Babic, M. (2021) 'The COVID-19 pandemic and the crisis of the liberal international order: Geopolitical fissures and pathways to change', *Global Perspectives*, 2(1), online first.

Baccaro, L. and Pontusson, J. (2016) 'Rethinking comparative political economy: the growth model perspective', *Politics & Society*, 44(2): 175–207.

Baele, S. (2020) 'On the Securitization of COVID-19', Available from: https://pandemipolitics.net/baele/ [Accessed 27 June 2021].

Bahri, T. and Singh, A. (2021) *COVID-19 and the Impact on Debt: Policy Implications* (Working Paper 07/2021), New York, NY: The New School for Social Research, Department of Economics.

BakerMcKenzie (2020) 'Preserve, Protect and Defend: Global Nationalization Risk – Practical Considerations for Investors', Available from: www.bakermckenzie.com/en/insight/publications/2020/04/global-nationalization-risk [Accessed 27 May 2021].

Balaam, D.N. and Dillman, B. (2014) *Introduction to International Political Economy*, New York, NY: Pearson.

Baldwin, R. and Evenett, S.J. (2020) 'Introduction', in R. Baldwin and S.J. Evenett (eds) *COVID-19 and Trade Policy: Why Turning Inward Won't Work*, London: CEPR Press, pp 1–20.

Ban, C. (2020) 'Emergency Keynesianism 2.0: the political economy of fiscal policy in Europe during the Corona Crisis', *Samfundsökonomen*, (4): 16–26.

Bar-Siman-Tov, I. (2020) 'Covid-19 meets politics: the novel coronavirus as a novel challenge for legislatures', *The Theory and Practices of Legislation*, online first.

Barake, M., Neef, T., Chouc, P. and Zucman, G. (2021) *Collecting the Tax Deficit of Multinational Companies: Simulations for the European Union*, Paris: Eutax Observatory.

Barceló, J., Rahn, T.H., Cheng, C., Kubinec, R. and Messerschmidt, L. (2021) 'Suppression and Timing: Using COVID-19 Policies against Political Dissidents?', Available from: https://osf.io/preprints/socarxiv/yuqw2/ [Accessed 27 June 2021].

Bariola, N. and Collins, C. (2021) 'The gendered politics of pandemic relief: labor and family policies in Denmark, Germany, and the United States during COVID-19', *American Behavioral Scientist*, online first.

Barlow, N., Hepp, C., Herbert, J., Rilovic, A., Saey-Volckrick, J., Smessaert, J. and von Andrian, N. (2020) 'A degrowth perspective on the coronavirus crisis', *Visions for Sustainability*, 14: 1–13.

Beck, M. and Knafo, S. (2020) 'Financialization and the uses of history', in P. Mader, D. Mertens and N. van der Zwan (eds) *The Routledge International Handbook on Financialization*, London: Routledge, pp 125–46.

Béland, D., Cantillon, B., Hick, R. and Moreira, A. (2021) 'Social policy in the face of a global pandemic: policy responses to the COVID-19 crisis', *Social Policy & Administration*, 55: 249–60.

Bello, W. (2020) *'Never Let a Good Crisis go to Waste': The Covid-19 Pandemic and the Opportunity for Food Sovereignty*, Bangkok and Amsterdam: Focus on the Global South and Transnational Institute.

Béné, C. (2020) 'Resilience of local food systems and links to food security: a review of some important concepts in the context of COVID-19 and other shocks', *Food Security*, 12: 805–22.

Benmelech, E. and Tzur-Han, N. (2020) *The Determinants of Fiscal and Monetary Policies during the COVID-19 Crisis* (NBER Working Paper No. 27461), Cambridge, MA: National Bureau of Economic Research.

Bergsen, P., Billon-Galland, A., Kundnani, H., Ntousas, V. and Raines, T. (2020) *Europe after Coronavirus: The EU and a New Political Economy* (Research Paper), London: Chatham House.

Berman, N., Couttenier, M., Monnet, N. and Ticku, R. (2020) *Shutdown Policies and Worldwide Conflict* (ESI-Working Paper 20/16), Orange, CA: Economic and Society Institute, Chapman University, Available from: https://digitalcommons.chapman.edu/esi_working_papers/311/ [Accessed 27 June 2021].

Bethke, F.S. and Wolff, J. (2020) 'COVID-19 and shrinking civic spaces: patterns and consequences', *Zeitschrift für Friedens und Konfliktforschung*, 9: 363–74.

Bhaduri, S.D. (2020) 'Post-COVID healthcare reform in India: what to expect?', *Journal of Family Medicine and Primary Care*, 9(11): 5427–31.

Bischof, J., Doerrenberg, P., Rostam-Afschar, D., Simons, D. and Voget, J. (2021) *The German Business Panel: Insights on Corporate Taxation and Accounting during the Covid-19 Pandemic* (TRR 266 Accounting for Transparency Working Paper Series No. 46), Mannheim: University of Mannheim.

Blackrock (2021) 'Larry Fink's letter to CEOs', New York, NY: Blackrock, Available from: www.blackrock.com/corporate/investor-relations/larry-fink-ceo-letter [Accessed 27 April 2021].

Blakeley, G. (2021) 'Financialization, real estate and COVID-19 in the UK', *Community Development Journal*, 56(1): 79–99.

Blanchard, O. (2019) 'Public debt and low interest rates', *American Economic Review* 109(4): 1197–229.

Bloem, J.R. and Salemi, C. (2021) 'COVID-19 and conflict', *World Development*, 140, online first.

Blofield, M. and Hoffmann, B. (2020) *Social Policy Responses to the COVID-19 Crisis and the Road Ahead* (GIGA Focus Latin America No. 7), Hamburg: German Institute for Global and Area Studies.

BMF (2020) 22. Sitzung des Stabilitätsrats am 18. Dezember 2020 (Pressemitteilung), Available from: www.bundesfinanzministerium.de/Content/DE/Pressemitteilungen/Finanzpolitik/2020/12/2020-12-18-pressemitteilung-stabilitaetsrat.html [Accessed 31 May 2021].

Bobzien, L. and Kalleitner, F. (2021) 'Attitudes towards European financial solidarity during the Covid-19 pandemic: evidence from a net-contributor country', *European Societies*, 23(S1): S791–S804.

Bol, D., Giani, M., Blais, A. and Loewen, P.J. (2020) 'The effect of COVID-19 lockdowns on political support: some good news for democracy?', *European Journal of Political Research*, 60: 497–505.

Bonacini, L., Gallo, G. and Scicchitano, S. (2021) 'Working from home and income inequality: risks of a "new normal" with COVID-19', *Journal of Population Economics*, 34: 303–60.

Boshoff, W.H. (2021) 'South African competition policy on excessive pricing and its relation to price gouging during the COVID-19 disaster period', *South African Journal of Economics*, 89(1): 112–40.

Bossie, A. and Mason, J.W. (2020) *The Public Role in Economic Transformation: Lessons from World War II*, New York, NY: The Roosevelt Institute.

Bottan, N., Hoffmann, B. and Vera-Crossio, D. (2020) 'The unequal impact of the coronavirus pandemic: evidence from seventeen developing countries', *PLOS ONE*, 15(10): 1–10.

Bouhia, R. (2020) *The Global Rise and Persistence in Surplus Profits: Further Evidence of Increasing Market Power?* (UNCTAD Research Paper No. 51), Geneva: United Nations Conference on Trade and Development.

Brakman, S., Garretsen, H. and van Witteloostuijn, A. (2021) 'Robots do not get the coronavirus: the COVID-19 pandemic and the international division of labor', *Journal of International Business Studies*, online first.

Branicki, L., Sullivan-Taylor, B. and Brammer, S. (2021) 'Towards crisis protection(ism)? COVID-19 and selective de-globalization', *Critical Perspectives on International Business*, online first.

Braun, B. (2020) 'Socialize Central Bank Planning, Progressive Internationale', Available from: https://progressive.international/blueprint/4a74c8a1-1f68-46bb-bc72-a7921b94a376-benjamin-braun-socialize-central-bank-planning/en [Accessed 27 May 2021].

Braun, B. and Gabor, D. (2020) 'Central banking, shadow banking and infrastructural power', in P. Mader, D. Mertens and N. van der Zwan (eds) *The Routledge International Handbook on Financialization*, London: Routledge, pp 241–52.

Bremer, B. and McDaniel, S. (2020) 'The ideational foundations of social democratic austerity in the context of the great recession', *Socio-Economic Review*, 18(2): 439–63.

Brooks, E. and Geyer, R. (2020) 'The development of EU health policy and the Covid-19 pandemic: trends and implications', *Journal of European Integration*, 42(8): 1057–76.

Bruegel (2020) 'The fiscal response to the economic fallout from the coronavirus' (Last update: 24 November), Brussels: Bruegel, Available from: www.bruegel.org/publications/datasets/covid-national-dataset/ [Accessed 27 June 2021].

Bruff, I. (2021) 'The politics of comparing capitalisms', *Environment and Planning A: Economy and Space*, online first.

Bunyavejchewin, P. and Sirichuanjun, K. (2021) 'How regime type and governance quality affect policy responses to COVID-19: a preliminary analysis', *Heliyon*, 7, online first.

Busemeyer, M.R. (2012) 'Inequality and the political economy of education: an analysis of individual preferences in OECD countries', *Journal of European Social Policy*, 22(3): 219–40.

Busumtwi-Sam, J. (2019) 'International migrations, diasporas, and remittances', in T. Shaw, L.C. Mahrenbach, R. Modi and X. Yi-chong (eds) *The Palgrave Handbook of Contemporary Political Economy*, London/New York, NY: Palgrave, pp 183–200.

Butollo, F. (2020) 'Sozialökologischer Umbau der Weltwirtschaft oder Handelskrieg mit anderen Mitteln? Covid-19 und die Transformation globaler Produktionsnetzwerke', *WSI Mitteilungen*, 73(6): 411–17.

Büthe, T. (2019) 'Competition law and policy as an emerging IPE issue', in T. Shaw, L.C. Mahrenbach, R. Modi and X. Yi-chong (eds) *The Palgrave Handbook of Contemporary Political Economy*, London/New York, NY: Palgrave, pp 447–64.

Buzan, B., de Wilde, J. and Waever, O. (1998) *Security: A New Framework for Analysis*, Boulder, CO: Lynne Rienner.

Bylund, P.L. and Packard, M.D. (2021) 'Separation of power and expertise: evidence of the tyranny of experts in Sweden's COVID-19 responses', *Southern Economic Journal*, online first.

Camous, A. and Claeys, G. (2020) 'The evolution of the European economic institutions during the COVID-19 crisis', *European Policy Analysis*, 6(2): 328–41.

Campbell-Verduyn, M., Linsi, L., Metinsoy, S. and van Rozendaal, G. (2021) 'COVID-19 and the global political economy: same as it never was?', *Global Perspectives*, 2(1), online first.

Cantillon, B., Seeleib-Kaiser, M. and van der Veen, R. (2021) 'The COVID-19 crisis and policy responses by continental European welfare states', *Social Policy & Administration*, 55: 326–38.

Capoccia, G. and Kelemen, R. (2007) 'The study of critical junctures: theory, narrative, and counterfactuals in historical institutionalism', *World Politics*, 59(3): 341–69.

Carta, F. and De Philippis, M. (2021) *The Impact of the COVID-19 Shock on Labour Income Inequality: Evidence from Italy* (Questioni di Economia e Finanza Number 606), Banca D'Italia: Rome.

Cepaluni, G., Dorsch, M.T. and Dzebo, S. (2021) 'Populism, political regimes, and COVID-19 deaths' (preprint), Available from: https://papers.ssrn.com/sol3/papers.cfm?abstract_id=3816398 [Accessed 26 June 2021].

Chang, H.-J. (2002) *Kicking Away the Ladder*, London: Anthem Press.

Cheng, J., Powell, T., Skidmore, D. and Wessel, D. (2021) 'What's the Fed doing in response to the COVID-19 crisis? What more could it do?' (Brookings Report), Available from: www.brookings.edu/research/fed-response-to-covid19/ [Accessed 26 May 2021].

Cherif, R. and Hasanov, F. (2019) *The Return of the Policy That Shall Not Be Named: Principles of Industrial Policy* (IMF Working Paper 19/74), Washington, DC: International Monetary Fund.

Chiou, L. and Tucker, C. (2020) *Social Distancing, Internet Access and Inequality* (NBER Working Paper No. 26982), Cambridge, MA: National Bureau of Economic Research.

Chowdhury, M.B. and Chakraborty, M. (2021) 'The impact of COVID-19 on the migrant workers and remittances flow to Bangladesh', *South Asian Survey*, 28(1): 38–56.

Chung, S. (2020) 'The impact of the Covid-19 pandemic on the universal basic income debate', *Technium Social Sciences Journal*, 14: 593–600.

Cicchi, L., Genschel, P., Hemerijck, A. and Nasr, M. (2020) 'EU-Solidarität in Zeiten von Covid-19', *WSI-Mitteilungen*, 73(6): 427–37.

Claar, S. and Nölke, A. (2013) 'Deep Integration in north–south relations: compatibility issues between the EU and South Africa', *Review of African Political Economy*, 40: 136, 274–89.

Clapp J. and Moseley, W.G. (2020) 'This food crisis is different: COVID-19 and the fragility of the neoliberal food security order', *The Journal of Peasant Studies*, 47(7): 1393–417.

Clark, A.E., d'Ambrosio, C. and Lepinteur, A. (2021) *The Fall in Income Inequality during COVID-19 in Four European Countries* (Paris School of Economics Working Paper 2021–31), Paris: Paris School of Economics.

Clarkson, A. (2019) 'The political economy of border regimes', in T. Shaw, L.C. Mahrenbach, R. Modi and X. Yi-chong (eds) *The Palgrave Handbook of Contemporary Political Economy*, London/New York, NY: Palgrave, pp 587–600.

Clift, B. (2013) 'Economic patriotism, the clash of capitalisms, and state aid in the European Union', *Journal of Industry, Competition and Trade*, 13(1): 101–17.

Clift, B. (2014) *Comparative Political Economy: States, Markets and Global Capitalism*, London: Red Globe Press.

Cobham, A., Garcia-Bernardo, J. and Mansour, M.B. (2020) *The Axis of Tax Avoidance: Time for the EU to Close its Own Tax Havens*, Chesham: Tax Justice Network.

Colciago, A., Samarina, A. and de Haan, J. (2019) 'Central bank policies and income and wealth inequality: a survey', *Journal of Economic Surveys*, 33(4): 1199–231.

Collier, R., Pirlot, A. and Vella, J. (2020) *Tax Policy and the COVID-19 Crisis* (Oxford University Centre for Business Taxation Working Paper 20/01), Oxford: University of Oxford.

Collins, C., Landivar, L.C., Ruppanner, L. and Scarborough, W.J. (2021) 'COVID-19 and the gender gap in work hours', *Gender, Work & Organization*, 28(S1): 101–12.

Comarcain, R. and Bar-Siman-Tov, I. (2020) 'Legislatures in the time of Covid-19', *The Theory and Practice of Legislation*, 8(1–2): 3–9.

Condon, R. (2020) 'The coronavirus crisis and the legitimation crisis of neoliberalism', *European Societies*, 23(S1): S805–S816.

Cook, R. and Grimshaw, D. (2021) 'A gendered lens on COVID-19 employment and social policies in Europe', *European Societies*, 23(supp 1): S215–S227.

Corsini, L., Dammicco, V. and Moultrie, J. (2021) 'Frugal innovation in a crisis: the digital fabrication maker response to COVID-19', *R&D Management*, 51(2): 195–210.

Coulter, S. (2020) 'All in it together? The unlikely rebirth of Covid corporatism', *The Political Quarterly*, 91(3): 534–41.

Craig, L. (2020) 'Coronavirus, domestic labour and care: gendered roles locked down', *Journal of Sociology*, 56(4): 684–92.

Craig, L. and Churchill, B. (2021) 'Dual-earner parent couples' work and care during COVID-19', *Gender, Work & Organization*, 28(S1): 66–79.

Crenshaw, K. (1991) 'Mapping the margins: intersectionality, identity politics, and violence against women of color', *Stanford Law Review*, 43(6): 1241–99.

Criscuolo, C., Martin, R., Overman, H.G. and Van Reenen, J. (2019) 'Some causal effects of an industrial policy', *American Economic Review*, 109(1): 48–85.

Croissant, A. (2020) 'Democracies with preexisting conditions and the coronavirus in the Indo-Pacific Region', The Asan Forum, Available from: https://theasanforum.org/democracies-with-preexisting-conditions-and-the-coronavirus-in-the-indo-pacific/ [Accessed 28 June 2021].

Crouch, C., Schröder, M. and Voelzkow, H. (2009) 'Regional and sectoral varieties of capitalism', *Economy and Society*, 38(4): 654–78.

Curran, L., Eckhardt, J. and Lee, J. (2021) 'The trade policy response to COVID-19 and its implications for international business', *Critical Perspectives on International Business*, online first.

Czymara, C.S., Langenkamp, A. and Cano, T. (2021) 'Cause for concerns: gender inequality in experiencing the COVID-19 lockdown in Germany', *European Societies*, 23(supp 1): S68–S81.

Dafermos, Y., Gabor, D. and Michell, J. (2021) 'The Wall Street Consensus in pandemic times: what does it mean for climate-aligned development?', *Canadian Journal of Development Studies*, online first.

Dallas, M.P., Horner, R. and Li, L. (2021) 'The mutual constraints of states and global value chains during COVID-19: the case of personal protective equipment', *World Development*, online first.

Dang, H.H. and Cuong, N.V. (2021) 'Gender inequality during the COVID-19 pandemic: income, expenditure, savings, and job loss', *World Development*, online first.

Daoudi, S. (2020) *The War on COVID-19: The 9/11 of Health Security?* (Policy Paper PP 20–06), Rabat: Policy Center for the New South.

Dartnell, L.R. and Kish, K. (2021) 'Do responses to the COVID-19 pandemic anticipate a long-lasting shift towards peer-to-peer production or degrowth?', *Sustainable Production and Consumption*, online first.

Darvas, Z. (2021) *The Unequal Inequality Impact of the COVID-19 Pandemic* (Working Paper 06/2021), Brussels: Bruegel.

Das, A. (2021) 'Predatory FDI during economic crises: insights from outbound FDI from China and host country responses', *Critical Perspectives on International Business*, online first.

Dauvergne, P. (2020) 'The political economy of the environment', in J. Ravenhill, (ed) *Global Political Economy*, Oxford: Oxford University Press, pp 384–411.

Dave, C., Cameron, P., Basmaji, J., Campbell, G., Buga, E. and Slessarev, M. (2021) 'Frugal innovation: enabling mechanical ventilation during coronavirus disease 2019 pandemic in resource-limited settings', *Critical Care Explorations*, online first.

Davydiuk, T. and Gupta, D. (2021) 'Income Inequality, Debt Burden and COVID-19', Available from: https://europepmc.org/article/ppr/ppr238 718 [Accessed 18 June 2021].

De Boer, N. and van't Klooster, J. (2020) 'The ECB, the courts and the issue of democratic legitimacy after Weiss', *Common Market Law Review*, 57(6): 1689–724.

De Pooter, H. (2020) 'The civil protection mechanism of the European Union: a solidarity test by the COVID-19 pandemic', *American Society of International Law Insights*, 24(7).

De Wilde, P., Koopmans, R., Merkel, W., Strijbis, O. and Zürn, M. (eds) (2019) *The Struggle over Borders: Cosmopolitanism and Communitarianism*, Cambridge: Cambridge University Press.

Deaton, A. (2021) *COVID-19 and Global Income Inequality* (NBER Working Paper No. 28392), Cambridge, MA: National Bureau of Economic Research.

Debre, M.J. and Dijkstra, H. (2020) *Covid-19 and Policy Responses by International Organizations: Crisis of Liberal International Order or Window of Opportunity* (NestIOr Working Paper), Maastricht: Maastricht University.

Diesendorf, M. (2020) 'COVID-19 and economic recovery in compliance with climate targets', *Global Sustainability*, online first.

Dietrich, H., Patzina, A. and Lerche, A. (2021) 'Social inequality in the homeschooling efforts of German high school students during a school closing period', *European Societies*, 23(S1): S348–S369).

Dietsch, P. (2020) 'Independent agencies, distribution, and legitimacy: the case of central banks', *American Political Science Review*, 114(2): 591–5.

Dikau, S. and Volz, U. (2021) 'Central bank mandates, sustainability objectives and the promotion of green finance', *Ecological Economics*, 184, online first.

Dimitriadi, A. (2020) *The Future of European Migration and Asylum Policy Post COVID-19* (FEPS COVID Response Papers), Brussels: Foundation for European Progressive Studies.

Ding, W., Levine, R., Lin, C. and Xie, W. (2020) 'Corporate immunity to the COVID-19 pandemic', *Journal of Financial Economics (JFE)*, online first.

Donnelly, S. (2021) 'German politics and intergovernmental negotiations on the Eurozone budget', *Politics and Governance*, 9(2): 230–40.

Dow, S. (2017) 'Central banking in the twenty-first century', *Cambridge Journal of Economics*, 41: 1539–57.

Drezner, D.W. (2020) 'The song remains the same: international relations after COVID-19', *International Organization*, 74(Supplement): E18–E35.

Dullien, S. (2021) *Nach der Corona-Krise: Die nächste Phase der (De-) Globalisierung und die Rolle der Industriepolitik* (IMK Policy Brief 100), Düsseldorf: Institut für Makroökonomie und Konjunkturforschung.

Dummer, N. and Neuhäuser, C. (2020) 'Die Zukunft des Wirtschaftssystems nach der Pandemie', in A. Brink, B. Hollstein, M.C. Hübscher and C. Neuhauser (eds) *Lehren aus Corona: Impulse aus der Wirtschafts- und Unternehmensethik* (Sonderband der Zeitschrift für Wirtschafts- und Unternehmensethik), Baden-Baden: Nomos, 67–79.

Dunford, M. and Qi, B. (2020) 'Global reset: COVID-19, systematic rivalry and the global order', *Research in Globalization*, 2(100021): 1–12.

Dünhaupt, P., Herr, H., Mehl, F. and Teipen, C. (2021) *Economic and Social Effects of the COVID-19 Pandemic and the Future of Global Value Chains* (Working Paper No. 164), Berlin: Hochschule für Wirtschaft und Recht.

Eagleton-Pierce, M. (2019) 'Neoliberalism', in T. Shaw, L.C. Mahrenbach, R. Modi and X. Yi-chong (eds) *The Palgrave Handbook of Contemporary Political Economy*, London/New York, NY: Palgrave, pp 119–34.

Eckhardt, J. and Lee, K. (2019) 'The international political economy of health', in T. Shaw, L.C. Mahrenbach, R. Modi and X. Yi-chong (eds) *The Palgrave Handbook of Contemporary Political Economy*, London/New York, NY: Palgrave, pp 667–82.

Economy, E.E. (2007) 'The great leap backward? The cost of China's environmental crisis', *Foreign Affairs*, 8(5): 38–59.

Eder, J. and Schneider, E. (2020) 'Umkämpfte Industriepolitik: Zwischen Geopolitik, grüner Wende, Digitalisierung und Corona', *Kurswechsel*, 34(4): 3–12.

Ehnts, D. and Paetz, M. (2021) 'Wie finanzieren wir die Corona-Schulden? Versuch einer "richtigen" Antwort auf eine "falsche" Frage aus der Sicht der Modern Monetary Theory', *Wirtschaftsdienst*, 101(3): 200–6.

Elia, S., Fratocchi, L., Barbieri, P., Bofelli, A. and Kalchschmidt, M. (2021) 'Post-pandemic reconfiguration from global to domestic and regional value chains: the role of industrial policies', *Transnational Corporations*, 28(2): 67–96.

Engler, S., Brunno, P., Loviat, R., Abou-Chadi, T., Leemann, L., Glaser, A. and Kübler, D. (2021) 'Democracy in times of the pandemic: explaining the variation of COVID-19 policies across European democracies', *West European Politics*, online first.

Epstein, G. (2019) 'Reforming the Federal Reserve for the 21st century', in G. Epstein (ed) *The Political Economy of Central Banking*, Cheltenham: Edward Elgar, pp 534–46.

Esping-Andersen, G. (1990) *The Three Worlds of Welfare Capitalism*, Cambridge and Princeton, NJ: Polity and Princeton University Press.

Esses, V.M. and Hamilton, L.K. (2021) 'Xenophobia and anti-immigrant attitudes in the time of COVID-19', *Group Processes & Intergroup Relations*, 24(2): 253–9.

EURODAD (2021) *Spring Meetings 2021: Yet another insufficient response to the Covid-19 crisis?* Brussels: European Network for Debt and Development.

Eurofound (2020) *COVID-19: Policy Responses Across Europe*, Luxembourg: Publications Office of the European Union.

European Commission (2020) *A New Industrial Strategy for Europe* (Communication from the Commission COM (2020) 102 final), Brussels: European Commission.

Evenett, S.J. (2020) 'Sicken thy neighbor: the initial trade policy response to COVID-19', *The World Economy*, 43: 828–39.

Everingham, P. and Chassagne, N. (2020) 'Post COVID-19 ecological and social reset: moving away from capitalist growth models towards tourism as Buen Vivir', *Tourism Geographies*, online first.

Eversberg, D. and Schmelzer, M. (2018) 'The degrowth spectrum: convergence and divergence within a diverse and conflictual alliance', *Environmental Values*, 27: 245–67.

Fang, J., Collins, A. and Yao, S. (2021) 'On the global COVID-19 pandemic and China's FDI', *Journal of Asian Economics*, online first.

Farrell, H. and Newman, A. (2019) 'Weaponized interdependence: how global economic networks shape state coercion', *International Security*, 44(1): 42–79.

FAZ (2021) 'Interesse am Klimawandel nach Umfrage rückläufig', Frankfurter Allgemeine Zeitung, 22 June, Available from: www.faz.net/aktuell/politik/inland/interesse-am-klimawandel-nach-umfrage-ruecklaeufig-17401375.html [Accessed 22 June 2021].

Felbermayr, G. and Görg, H. (2020) 'Implications of COVID-19 for globalization', in G. Felbermayr (ed) *The World Economy after the Coronavirus Shock: Restarting Globalization?*, Kiel: Institute for the World Economy, pp 3–14.

Fernández-Reino, M., Sumption, M. and Vargas-Silva, C. (2020) 'From low-skilled to key workers: the implications of emergencies for immigration policy', *Oxford Review of Economic Policy*, online first.

Fernandez, R. and Klinge, T.J. (2020) *The Financialisation of Big Pharma*, Amsterdam: SOMO.

Ferrera, M., Mirá, J. and Ronchi, S. (2021) 'Walking the road together? EU polity maintenance during the COVID-19 crisis', *West European Politics*, online first.

Fisher, A.N. and Ryan, M.K. (2021) 'Gender inequalities during COVID-19', *Group Processes & Intergroup Relations*, 24(2): 237–45.

Flinders, M. (2021) 'Democracy and the politics of coronavirus: trust, blame and understanding', *Parliamentary Affairs*, 74: 483–502.

Florio, M. (2020) *Biomed Europa: After the Coronavirus, a Public Infrastructure to Overcome the Pharmaceutical Oligopoly* (CIRIEC Working Paper No. 2020/08), Liege: International Centre of Research and Information on the Public, Social and Cooperative Economy.

Forsyth, A. (2020) 'COVID-19 and labour law: Australia', *Italian Labour Law e-Journal*, 13(1): 1–9.

Fossati, F. and Trein, P. (2020) 'Support for Surveillance, Re-nationalization and Prevention during Times of Crisis: a Cultural, Ideological, or Personal Matter?', Available from: www.researchgate.net/profile/Philipp-Trein/publication/344417930_Protection_but_no_Control_Liberal_Democracy_and_the_Politicization_of_Crisis_Response_Policies/links/5f737be4458515b7cf5860e2/Protection-but-no-Control-Liberal-Democracy-and-the-Politicization-of-Crisis-Response-Policies.pdf [Accessed 26 May 2021].

Freshfields Bruckhaus Deringer (2021) 'International arbitration: Top trends in 2021', Available from: www.lexology.com/library/detail.aspx?g=4e4fddea-01f1-489d-b415-daca0c573230 [Accessed 13 May 2021].

Frey, C.B., Chen, C. and Presidente, G. (2020) *Democracy, Culture, and Contagion: Political Regimes and Countries Responsiveness to Covid-19*, Oxford: Oxford Martin School, Available from: www.oxfordmartin.ox.ac.uk/downloads/academic/Democracy-Culture-and-Contagion_May13.pdf [Accessed 26 June 2021].

Friedman, M. (1969) 'The optimum quantity of money', in M. Friedman (ed) *The Optimum Quantity of Money and Other Essays*, Chicago, IL: Adline Publishing Company, pp 1–50.

Friis, K. (2020) *Biowar Next? Security Implications of the Coronavirus* (LSE IDEAS Strategic Update), London: London School of Economics and Political Science.

Fukuyama, F. (1992) *The End of History and the Last Man*, London: Penguin.

Gabor, D. (2021) 'The Wall Street Consensus', *Development and Change*, 52(3): 429–59.

Gallagher, K.P., Gao, H., Kring, W.N., Ocampo, J.A. and Volz, U. (2021) 'Safety first: expanding the global financial safety net in response to COVID-19', *Global Policy*, 12(1): 140–8.

Gallarotti, G. (1995) *The Anatomy of an International Monetary Regime: The Classical Gold Standard, 1880–1914*, Oxford and New York, NY: Oxford University Press.

Gauttam, P., Singh, B. and Kaur, J. (2020) 'COVID-19 and Chinese global health diplomacy: geopolitical opportunity for China's hegemony?', *Millennial Asia*, 11(3): 318–40.

Gauttam, P., Patel, N., Singh, B., Kaur, J., Kumar Chattu, V. and Jakovljevic, M. (2021) 'Public health policy of India and COVID-19: diagnosis and prognosis of the combating response', *Sustainability*, 13(3415): 1–18.

Gay, D. and Gallagher, K. (2020) *The Need to Extend the WTO TRIPS Pharmaceuticals Transition Period for LDCs in the COVID-19 Era: Evidence from Bangladesh* (CDP Policy Review No. 10), New York, NY: United Nations Committee for Development Policy.

Gelter, M. and Puaschunder, J.M. (2021) *COVID-19 and Comparative Corporate Governance* (ECGI Working Paper Series in Law No. 563), Brussels: European Corporate Governance Institute.

Genschel, P. and Jachtenfuchs, M. (2021) 'Postfunctionalism reversed: solidarity and rebordering during the COVID-19 pandemic', *Journal of European Public Policy*, 28(3): 350–69.

Gerard, F., Imbert, C. and Orkin, K. (2020) 'Social protection response to the COVID-19 crisis: options for developing countries', *Oxford Review of Economic Policy*, 36: S281–S296.

Gereffi, G. (2020) 'What does the COVID-19 pandemic teach us about global value chains? The case of medical supplies', *Journal of International Business Policy*, 3(3): 287–301.

Gertz, B. (2021) 'Investment screening before, during, and after COVID-19', *Global Perspectives*, 2(1), online first

Gidron, N. and Hall, P.A. (2017) 'The politics of social status: economic and cultural roots of the populist right', *British Journal of Sociology*, 68(S1): S57–S84.

Giommoni, L. (2020) 'Why we should all be more careful in drawing conclusions about how COVID-19 is changing drug markets', *International Journal of Drug Policy*, 83, online first.

Giraud, O., Tietze, N., Toffanin, T. and Nous, C. (2021) 'The scalar arrangements of three European public health systems facing the COVID-19 pandemic: comparing France, Germany, and Israel', *Culture, Practice & Europeanization*, 6(1): 89–111.

Gostin, L.O., Moon, S. and Meier, B.M. (2020a) 'Reimagining global health governance in the age of COVID-19', *American Journal of Public Health*, 110(11): 1615–19.

Gostin, L.O., Habibi, R. and Meier, B.M. (2020b) 'Has global health law risen to meet the COVID-19 challenge? Revising the international health regulations to prepare for future threats', *Journal of Law, Medicine & Ethics*, 48: 376–81.

Gräbner, C., Heimberger, P. and Kapeller, J. (2020) 'Pandemic pushes polarisation: the corona crisis and macroeconomic divergence in the Eurozone', *Journal of Industrial and Business Economics*, 47: 425–38.

Grancayova, M. (2021) 'Plagues of Egypt: the COVID-19 crisis and the role of securitization dilemmas in the authoritarian regime survival strategies in Egypt and Turkey', *Czech Journal of International Relations*, 56(1): 69–97.

Greer, S.L., King, E.J. and Massard da Fonseca, E. (2021a) 'Introduction: explaining pandemic response', in S.L. Greer, E.J. King, E. Massard da Fonseca and A. Peralta-Santos (eds) *Coronavirus Politics: The Comparative Politics and Policy of COVID-19*, Ann Arbor, MI: University of Michigan Press, pp 3–33.

Greer, S.L., Massard da Fonseca, E. and King, E.J. (2021b) 'Conclusion', in S.L. Greer, E.J. King, E. Massard da Fonseca and A. Peralta-Santos (eds) *Coronavirus Politics: The Comparative Politics and Policy of COVID-19*, Ann Arbor, MI: University of Michigan Press, pp 615–37.

Greitens, S.C. (2020) 'Surveillance, security, and liberal democracy in the post-COVID world', *International Organization*, 74(Supplement): E169–90.

Greve, B., Blomquist, P., Hvinden, B. and van Gerven, M. (2021) 'Nordic welfare states: still standing or changed by the COVID-19 crisis?', *Social Policy & Administration*, 55: 295–311.

Guadagno, L. (2020) *Migrants and the COVID-19 Pandemic: An Initial Analysis* (Migration Research Series 60), Geneva: International Organization for Migration.

Guasti, P. (2020) 'The impact of the COVID-19 pandemic in Central and Eastern Europe: the rise of autocracy and democratic resilience', *Democratic Theory*, 7(2): 47–60.

Guderian, C.C., Bican, P.M., Riar, F.J. and Chattopadhyay, S. (2021) 'Innovation management in crisis: patent analytics as a response to the COVID-19 pandemic', *R&D Management*, 51(2): 223–39.

Guillén, A. (2020) 'Coronavirus crisis or a new stage of the global crisis of capitalism?', *Agrarian South: Journal of Political Economy*, 9(3): 356–67.

Haffert, L. (2019) 'Tax policy as industrial policy in comparative capitalisms', *Journal of Economic Policy Research*, online first.

Haffert, L. and Mertens, D. (2019) 'Between distribution and allocation: growth models, sectoral coalitions and the politics of taxation revisited', *Socio-Economic Review*, online first.

Hall, P.A. (2013) 'The political origins of our economic discontents: contemporary adjustment problems in historical perspective', in M. Kahler and D. Lake (eds) *Politics in New Hard Times*, Ithaca, NY: Cornell University Press, pp 129–48.

Hall, P.A. and Soskice, D.W. (2001) 'An introduction to varieties of capitalism', in P.A. Hall and D.W. Soskice (eds) *Varieties of Capitalism: The Institutional Foundations of Comparative Advantage*, Oxford: Oxford University Press, pp 1–68.

Hanrieder, T. (2020) 'Priorities, partner, politics: the WHO's mandate beyond the crisis', *Global Governance*, 26: 534–43.

Hansen, J., Reinecke, A. and Schmerer, H. (2021) *Health Expenditures and the Effectiveness of Covid-19 Prevention in International Comparison* (CESifo Working Paper 9069), Munich: CESifo.

Harris, M., Bhatti, Y., Buckley, J. and Sharma, D. (2020) 'Fast and frugal innovations in response to the COVID-19 pandemic', *Nature Medicine*, 26: 814–21.

Heffron, R.J. and Sheehan, J. (2020) 'Rethinking international taxation and energy policy post COVID-19 and the financial crisis for developing countries', *Journal of Energy & Natural Resources Law*, 38(4): 465–73.

Heires, M. and Nölke, A. (2014) 'Finanzialisierung', in J. Wullweber, A. Graf and M. Behrens (eds) *Theorien der Internationalen Politischen Ökonomie*, Wiesbaden: Springer VS, pp 253–66.

Helleiner, E. (2021) 'The return of national self-sufficiency? Excavating autarkic thought in a de-globalizing era', *International Studies Review*, online first

Helm, D. (2020) 'The environmental impacts of the coronavirus', *Environmental and Resource Economics*, 76: 21–38.

Hepburn, C., O'Callaghan, B., Stern, N., Stiglitz, J. and Zenghelis, D. (2020) *Will COVID-19 Fiscal Recovery Packages Accelerate or Retard Progress on Climate Change?* (Smith School Working Paper No. 20–02), Oxford: University of Oxford.

Herndon, T., Ash, M. and Pollin, R. (2014) 'Does high public debt consistently stifle economic growth? A critique of Reinhart and Rogoff', *Cambridge Journal of Economics*, 38: 257–79.

Herstatt, C. and Tiwari, R. (2020) 'Opportunities of frugality in the post-corona-era', *International Journal of Technology Management*, 83(1/2/3): 15–33.

Heyd, T. (2021) 'Covid-19 and climate change in the times of the Anthropocene', *The Anthropocene Review*, 8(1): 21–36.

Hick, R. and Murphy, M. (2021) 'Common shock, different paths? Comparing social policy responses to COVID-19 in the UK and Ireland', *Social Policy & Administration*, 55: 312–25.

Hickel, J. (2020) 'What does degrowth mean? A few points of clarification', *Globalizations*, online first

Hilferding, R. (1910) *Das Finanzkapital. Eine Studie über die jüngste Entwicklung des Kapitalismus*, Vienna: Verlag der Wiener Volksbuchhandlung Ignaz Brand & Co.

Hobson, J.M. and Seabrooke, L. (2009) 'Everyday international political economy', in M. Blyth (ed) *Routledge Handbook of International Political Economy*, London: Routledge, pp 290–306.

Höpner, M. (2007) *Coordination and Organization. The Two Dimensions of Nonliberal Capitalism* (MPIfG Discussion Paper 07/12), Cologne: Max Planck Institut für Gesellschafts forschung.

Howarth, C., Bryant, P., Corner, A., Fankhauser, S., Gouldson, A., Whitmarsh, L. and Willis, R. (2020) 'Building a social mandate for climate action: lessons from COVID-19', *Environmental and Resource Economics*, 76: 1107–15.

Howarth, D. and Schild, J. (2021) '*Nein* to "Transfer Union": the German brake on the construction of a European Union fiscal capacity', *Journal of European Integration*, 43(2): 209–26.

Huang, Q. (2021) 'The pandemic and the transformation of liberal international order', *Journal of Chinese Political Science*, 26(1): 1–26.

Hunter, B.M. and Murray, S.F. (2019) 'Deconstructing the financialization of healthcare', *Development and Change*, 50(5): 1263–87.

Hupkau, C. and Petrongolo, B. (2020) 'Work, care and gender during the COVID-19 crisis', *Fiscal Studies*, 41(3): 623–51.

Ide, T. (2021) 'COVID-19 and armed conflict', *World Development*, 140, online first.

Ikenberry, G.J. (2020) 'The next liberal order: the age of contagion demands more internationalism, not less', *Foreign Affairs*, 99(4): 133–42.

ILO (2021) *A Global Trend Analysis on the Role of Trade Unions in Times of COVID-19*, Geneva: International Labour Organization.

IMF (2019) *World Economic Outlook April 2019*, Washington, DC: International Monetary Fund.

IMF (2020) *Global Financial Stability Report: Bride to Recovery*, Washington, DC: International Monetary Fund.

Inglehart, R. (1977) *The Silent Revolution: Changing Values and Political Styles Among Western Publics*, Princeton, NJ: Princeton University Press.

Irlacher, M. and Koch, M. (2020) *Working from Home, Wages, and Regional Inequality in the Light of COVID-19* (CESifo Working Paper No. 8232), Munich: CESifo.

Isele, E. and Dubois, S. (2020) *The COVID-19 Gender Gap: How Women's Experience and Expertise Will Drive Economic Recovery* (Strategic Action Plan), London: Chatham House.

Ivanov, D. and Dolgui, A. (2020) 'Viability of intertwined supply networks: extending the supply chain resilience angles towards survivability. A position paper motivated by COVID-19 outbreak', *International Journal of Production Research*, 58(10): 2904–15.

Iversen, T. and Soskice, D. (2019) *Democracy and Prosperity: Reinventing Capitalism through a Turbulent Century*, Princeton, NJ: Princeton University Press.

Jarass, L.J., Tokman, A.E. and Wright, M.L.J. (2017) *The Burden of Taxation in United States and Germany* (Chicago Fed Letter 382), Chicago, IL: The Federal Reserve of Chicago.

Jessen, J., Spieß, C.K. and Wrohlich, K. (2021) 'Sorgearbeit wåhrend der Corona-Pandemie: Mütter übernehmen grßeren Anteil – vor allem bei schon zuvor ungleicher Aufteilung', *DIW Wochenbericht*, 88(9): 132–8.

Johnson, A.F. and Roberto, K.J. (2020) 'The COVID-19 pandemic: time for a universal basic income?', *Public Administration and Development*, online first.

Jones, L. and Hameiri, S. (2021) 'COVID-19 and the failure of the neoliberal regulatory state', *Review of International Political Economy*, online first.

Jones, T. (2020) *Rising Debt Burdens, the Impact on Public Spending, and the Coronavirus Crisis* (CGD Policy Paper 197), Washington, DC: Center for Global Development.

Joyce, J.P. (2021) 'The International Distribution of FDI Income and Its Impact on Income Inequality', Available from: https://mpra.ub.uni-muenc hen.de/106448/ [Accessed 13 May 2021].

Joyce, R. and Xu, X. (2020) *Sector Shutdowns During the Coronavirus Crisis: Which Workers Are Most Exposed* (IFS Briefing Note BN278), London: Institute for Fiscal Studies.

Kaczmarczyk, P. (2020) *Growth Models and the Footprint of Transnational Capital* (MaxPo Discussion Paper 20/2), Paris: Maax Planck Sciences Po Center on Coping with Instability in Market Societies.

Kahn, M.E. and Kotchen, M.J. (2011) 'Business cycle effects on concern about climate change: the chilling effect of recession', *Climate Change Economics*, 2(3): 257–73.

Kalinowski, T. (2019) *Why International Cooperation is Failing: How the Clash of Capitalisms Undermines the Regulation of Finance*, Oxford: Oxford University Press.

Kalkman, J.P. (2020) 'Military crisis responses to COVID-19', *Journal of Contingencies and Crisis Management*, 29: 99–103.

Kallis, G. (2011) 'In defence of degrowth', *Ecological Economics*, 70: 873–80.

Kallis, G., Kostakis, V., Lange, S., Muraca, B. and Schmelzer, M. (2018) 'Research on degrowth', *Annual Review of Environment and Resources*, 43: 291–316.

Kasinger, J., Krahnen, J.P., Ongena, S., Pelizzon, L., Schmeling, M. and Wahrenburg, M. (2021) *Non-performing Loans: New Risks and Policies?* (Study requested by the ECON committee), Brussels: European Parliament.

Kelton, S. (2020) *The Deficit Myth: Modern Monetary Theory and the Birth of the People's Economy*, London: Hachette UK.

Khalil, L. (2020) *Digital Authoritarianism, China and COVID* (Lowy Institute Analysis), Sydney: Lowy Institute for International Policy.

Kharas, H. and Dooley, M. (2020) *COVID-19's Legacy of Debt and Debt Service in Developing Countries* (Global Working Paper No. 148), Washington, DC: Brookings Institution.

Kilic, S. (2020) 'Does COVID-19 as a long wave turning point mean the end of neo liberalism?', *Critical Sociology*, online first.

Kimura, F. (2021) 'The impact of COVID-19 and the US–China confrontation on East Asian production networks', *Seoul Journal of Economics*, 34(1): 27–41.

Kish, K., Zywert, K., Hensher, M., Davy, B.J. and Quilley, S. (2021) 'Socioecological system transformation: lessons from COVID-19', *World*, 2: 15–31.

Klatzer, E. and Rinaldi, A. (2020) *#nextGenerationEU Leaves Women Behind: Gender Impact Assessment of the European Commission Proposals for the EU Recovery Plan* (Study commissioned by The Greens/EFA Group in the European Parliament), Brussels: European Parliament.

Kleenert, D., Funke, F., Mattauch, L. and O'Callaghan, B. (2020) 'Five lessons from COVID-19 for advancing climate change mitigation', *Environmental and Resource Economics*, 76: 751–78.

Koddenbrock, K. and Sylla, N.S. (2019) *Towards a Political Economy of Monetary Dependence: The Case of the CFA Franc in Western Africa* (MaxPo Discussion Paper No. 19/2), Paris: Max Planck Sciences Po Center on Coping with Instability in Market Societies.

Kohlenberg, P.J. and Godehardt, N. (2020) 'Locating the "South" in China's connectivity politics', *Third World Quarterly*, online first.

Kohlrausch, B. and Zucco, A. (2020) *Corona trifft Frauen doppelt: Weniger Erwerbseinkommen und mehr Sorgearbeit* (WSI Policy Brief 40), Düsseldorf: Wirtschafts- und Sozialwissenschaftliches Institut.

Koos, S. and Leuffen, D. (2020) *Beds or Bonds? Conditional Solidarity in the Coronavirus Crisis* (Policy Paper No. 01), Konstanz: Cluster The Politics of Inequality.

Kose, M.A., Nagle, P., Ohnsorge, F. and Sugawara, N. (2021) *Global Waves of Debt: Causes and Consequences*, Washington: World Bank Group.

Kotz, D.M., McDonough, T. and Reich, M. (eds) (1994), *Social Structures of Accumulation: The Political Economy of Growth and Crisis*, Cambridge: Cambridge University Press.

Kowalski, P. (2020) 'Will the post-COVID world be less open to foreign direct investment?', in R. Baldwin and S.J. Evenett (eds) *COVID-19 and Trade Policy: Why Turning Inward Won't Work*, London: CEPR Press, pp 131–49.

Krampf, A. (2013) *The Life Cycles of Competing Policy Norms: Localizing European and Developmental Central Banking Ideas* (KFG Working Paper No. 49), Berlin: Freie Universität Berlin.

Krampf, A. (2015) 'Perhaps this time it's different: ideas and interests in shaping international responses to financial crisis', *Contemporary Politics*, 21(2): 179–200.

Krampf, A. (2019) 'Monetary power reconsidered: the struggle between the Bundesbank and the Fed over monetary leadership', *International Studies Quarterly*, 63(4): 938–51.

Kreuder-Sonnen, C. and Rittberger, B. (2020) *The LIOn's Share: How the Liberal International Order Contributes to its Own Legitimacy Crisis* (CES Open Forum Series 2019–2020), Cambridge, MA: Minda de Gunzburg Center for European Studies Harvard.

Kreyenfeld, M. and Zinn, S. (2021) 'Coronavirus and care: how the coronavirus crisis affected fathers' involvement in Germany', *Demographic Research*, 44(4): 99–124.

Kristal, T. and Yaish, M. (2020) 'Does the coronavirus pandemic level the gender inequality curve? (It doesn't)', *Research in Social Stratification and Mobility*, 68, online first.

Kriwoluzky, A., Pagenhardt, L. and Rieth, M. (2020) 'Fiscal rules mitigate economic setbacks during crises', *DIW-Weekly Report*, 87(52+53): 495–503.

Kuzemko, C., Bradshaw, M., Bridge, G., Goldthau, A., Jewell, J., Overland, I., Scholten, D., van de Graaf, T. and Westphal, K. (2020) 'Covid-19 and the politics of sustainable energy transitions', *Energy Research & Social Science*, online first.

Lafitte, S., Martin, J., Parenti, M., Souillard, B. and Toubal, F. (2020) *International Corporate Taxation after Covid-19: Minimum Taxation as the New Normal* (CEPII Policy Brief No. 30), Paris: Centre d'Etudes Prospectives et d'Informations Internationales.

Lake, D.A., Martin, L.L. and Risse, T. (2021) 'Challenges to the liberal order: reflections on "International Organization"', *International Organization*, 75: 225–57.

Landesmann, M.A. (2020) 'Covid-19 crisis: centrifugal vs. centripetal forces in the EU – a political-economic analysis', *Journal of Industrial and Business Economics*, 47: 439–53.

Landman, T. and Di Gennaro Splendore, L. (2020) 'Pandemic democracy: elections and COVID-19', *Journal of Risk Research*, 23(7–8): 1060–6.

Lang, K.-O. and von Ondarza, N. (2020) *Friends in Need: The Corona Pandemic Changes the Landscape and Groups and Coalitions in the EU* (SWP Comment 26/2020), Berlin: Stiftung Wissenschaft und Politik.

Lasco, G. (2020) 'Medical populism and the COVID-19 pandemic', *Global Public Health*, 15(10): 1417–29.

Laster Pirtle, W.N. (2020) 'Racial capitalism: a fundamental cause of novel coronavirus (COVID-19) pandemic inequities in the United States', *Health Education & Behavior*, 47(4): 504–8.

Lavazza, A. and Farina, M. (2020) 'The role of experts in the Covid-19 pandemic and the limits of their epistemic authority in democracy', *Frontiers in Public Health*, 8(356): 1–11.

LeBaron, G., Mügge, D., Best, J. and Hay, C. (2021) 'Blind spots in IPE: marginalized perspectives and neglected trends in contemporary capitalism', *Review of International Political Economy*, 28(2): 283–94.

Lecossier, A. and Pallot, M. (2020) 'Innovation Strategies of Mature Resilient Businesses during the Covid-19 Crisis', (2020 IEEE International Conference on Engineering, Technology and Innovation), Available from: https://iee explore.ieee.org/document/9198355 [Accessed 6 June 2021].

Legge, D.G. (2020) 'COVID-19 response exposes deep flaws in global health governance', *Global Social Policy*, 20(3): 383–7.

Legrain, P. (2020) 'The Coronavirus Is Killing Globalization as We Know It', *Foreign Affairs*, 12 March, Available from: https://foreignpolicy.com/2020/03/12/coronavirus-killing-globalization-nationalism-protectionism-trump/ [Accessed 28 March 2021].

Levy, D.L. (2021) 'COVID-19 and global governance', *Journal of Management Studies*, 58(2): 562–6.

Lidskog, R., Elander, I. and Standring, A. (2020) 'COVID-19, the climate, and transformative change: comparing the social anatomies of crisis and their regulatory responses', *Sustainability*, 12, online first.

Linsi, L. (2021) 'Speeding up "Slowballization": the political economy of global production before and after COVID-19', *Global Perspectives*, 2(1), online first.

Liu, W. (2020) *Abolish Silicon Valley: How to Liberate Technology from Capitalism*, London: Repeater.

Liu, Z., Kirkpatrick, I, Chen, Y. and Mei, J. (2021) 'Overcoming the legacy of marketization: China's response to COVID-19 and the fast-forward of healthcare reorganisation', *BMJ Leader*, 5: 42–5.

Lokot, M. and Bhatia, A. (2020) 'Unequal and invisible: a feminist political economy approach to valuing women's care labor in the COVID-19 response', *Frontiers in Sociology*, 5(588279): 1–4.

Louca, F., Abreu, A. and Pessa Costa, G. (2021) 'Disarray at the headquarters: economists and central bankers', *Industrial and Corporate Change*, online first.

Lustig, N., Martinez Pabon, V., Sanz, F. and Younger, S. (2020) *The Impact of COVID-19 Lockdowns and Expanded Social Assistance on Inequality, Poverty and Mobility in Argentina, Brazil, Colombia and Mexico* (Working Paper 556), Washington: Center for Global Development.

Mader, P., Mertens, D. and van der Zwan, N. (2020) *The Routledge International Handbook on Financialization*, London: Routledge.

Makin, A.J. and Layton, A. (2021) 'The global fiscal response to COVID-19: risks and repercussions', *Economic Analysis and Policy*, 69: 340–9.

Malm, A. (2020) *Corona, Climate, Chronic Emergency: War Communism in the Twenty-first Century*, London: Verso.

Martinez-Alier, J., Pascual, U., Vivien, F.-D. and Zaccai, E. (2010) 'Sustainable de-growth: mapping the context, criticism and future prospects of an emergent paradigm', *Ecological Economics*, 69: 1741–7.

Marx, P. (2020) 'Nationalize Amazon', *Jacobin*, 29 March, Available from: https://jacobinmag.com/2020/03/nationalize-amazon-coronavirus-delivery-usps [Accessed 28 May 2021].

Masciandaro, D. (2020) *COVID-19 Helicopter Money, Monetary Policy and Central Bank Independence* (Bocconi Working Paper No. 137), Milan: Università Bocconi.

Mason. C. (2020) *The Coronavirus Economic Crisis: Its Impact on Venture Capital and High Growth Enterprises* (Report prepared for the European Commission), Luxembourg: Publication Office of the European Union.

Mazzucato, M. (2011) *The Entrepreneurial State*, London: Demos.

Mazzucato, M. (2018) 'Mission-oriented innovation policies: challenges and opportunities', *Industrial and Corporate Change*, 27(5): 803–15.

McElwee, P. (2020) 'Ensuring a post-COVID economic agenda tackles global biodiversity loss', *One Earth*, 3, online first.

McNamara, K.R. and Newman, A.L. (2020) 'The big reveal: COVID-19 and globalization's great transformations', *International Organization*, 74(Supplement): E59–E77.

Megersa, K. (2020) *Tax Reforms After COVID-19 and Financial Crises* (K4D Helpdesk Report 809), Brighton: Institute for Development Studies.

Menezes-Filho, N., Komatsu, B.K. and Rosa, J.P. (2021) *Reducing Poverty and Inequality during the Coronavirus Outbreak: The Emergency Aid Transfer in Brazil* (Policy Paper No. 54), Sao Paulo: Insper.

Menz, G. (2017) *Comparative Political Economy: Contours of a Subfield*, Oxford: Oxford University Press.

Merkel, W. (2020) 'Wer regiert in der Krise? Demokratie in Zeiten der Pandemie', *WSI-Mitteilungen*, 73(6): 445–53.

Meunier, S. and Mickus, J. (2020) 'Sizing up the competition: explaining reform of European Union competition policy in the Covid-19 era', *Journal of European Integration*, 42(8): 1077–94.

Mizota, M. (2020) 'Coronavirus and Racial Wealth Inequality: How Will the COVID-19 Pandemic and Recession Affect the Racial Wealth Gap in the United States?', Available from: https://socialequity.duke.edu/wp-content/uploads/2020/05/Mizota.pdf [Accessed 18 June 2021].

Möhring, K., Weiland, A., Reifenscheid, M., Naumann, E., Wenz, A., Retting, A., Krieger, U., Fikel, M., Cornesse, C. and Blom, A.G. (2021) 'Inequality in Employment Trajectories and their Socio-economic Consequences during the Early Phase of the COVID-19 Pandemic in Germany', Available from: https://osf.io/preprints/socarxiv/m95df/ [Accessed 18 June 2021].

Morand, S. and Lajaunie, C. (2021) 'Outbreaks of vector-borne and zoonotic diseases are associated with changes in forest cover and oil palm expansion at global scale', *Frontiers in Veterinary Science*, 8, online first.

Moreira, A. and Hick, R. (2021) 'COVID-19, the Great Recession and social policy: is this time different?', *Social Policy & Administration*, 55: 261–79.

Moreira, A., Ljon, M., Coda Moscarola, F. and Roumpakis, A. (2020) 'In the eye of the storm … again! Social policy responses to COVID-19 in Southern Europe', *Social Policy & Administration*, 55: 339–57.

Mukherji, R. (2020) 'India's illiberal remedy', *Journal of Democracy*, 31(4): 91–105.

Muradian, R. (2019) 'Frugality as a choice vs. frugality as a social condition: is de-growth doomed to be a Eurocentric project?', *Ecological Economics*, 161: 257–60.

Naisbitt, B. (2020) *Vulnerability from Debt in the Coronavirus Crisis* (Policy Paper 020), London: National Institute of Economic and Social Research.

Narlikar, A. (2021) 'Holding up a mirror to the World Trade Organization: lessons from the COVID-19 pandemic', *Global Perspectives*, 2(1), online first.

Nassif Pires, L., Barbosa de Carvalho, L. and Lederman Rawet, E. (2021) 'Multi-dimensional inequality and COVID-19 in Brazil', *Investigación Económica*, 80(315): 33–58.

Navarro, V. (2020) 'The consequences of neoliberalism in the current pandemic', *International Journal of Health Services*, 50(3): 271–5.

Neely, M.T. and Carmichael, D. (2021) 'Profiting on crisis: how predatory financial investors have worsened inequality in the coronavirus crisis', *American Behavioral Scientist*, online first.

Nemeth, G.J. (2020) 'How did the Austrian public attitude change towards universal basic income, due to the COVID-19 virus, since the 2016 European Social Survey?', Master's thesis, Vienna: Universität Wien.

Nettle, D., Johnson, E., Johnson, M. and Saxe, R. (2021) 'Why has the COVID-19 pandemic increased support for Universal Basic Income?', *Humanities & Social Sciences Communications*, 8(79): 1–12.

New Roots Collective (2020) 'Degrowth: New Roots for the Economy', Available from: www.degrowth.info/en/open-letter/ [Accessed 26 June 2021].

Newell, P. and Taylor, O. (2018) 'Contested landscapes: the global political economy of climate-smart agriculture', *The Journal of Peasant Studies*, 45(1): 108–29.

Newland, K. (2020) *Will International Migration Governance Survive the COVID-19 Pandemic?*, Washington, DC: Migration Policy Institute.

Nikièma, H.S. and Maina, N. (2020*) The Risk of ISDS Claims Through National Investment Laws: Another 'Damocles Sword' Hanging over Governments' COVID-19 Related Measures?*, Winnipeg: International Institute for Sustainable Development.

Nölke, A. (2003a) 'The relevance of transnational policy networks: some examples from the European Commission and the World Bank', *Journal of International Relations and Development*, 6(3): 277–99.

Nölke, A. (2003b) 'Intra- und interdisziplinäre Vernetzung: die Überwindung der Regierungszentrik', in G. Hellmann, K.-D. Wolf and M. Zürn (eds) *Die Neuen Internationalen Beziehungen*, Baden-Baden: Nomos, pp 519–54.

Nölke, A. (2012) 'The rise of the B(R)IC variety of capitalism: towards a new phase of organized capitalism?', in H. Overbeek and B. van Apeldoorn (eds) *Neoliberalism in Crisis*, Houndmills: Palgrave, pp 117–33.

Nölke, A. (2014) 'Private Chinese multinationals and the long shadow of the Chinese state', in A. Nölke (ed) *Multinational Corporations from Emerging Markets: State Capitalism 3.0*, Houndmills: Palgrave, pp 77–89.

Nölke, A. (2015) 'Second image revisited: the domestic sources of China's foreign economic policies', *International Politics*, 52(6): 657–65.

Nölke, A. (2017) 'Brexit: towards a new global phase of organized capitalism?', *Competition & Change*, 21(3): 230–41.

Nölke, A. (2019a) 'Keep it straight and simple, also with respect to migration: a comment on Streeck's "Between Charity and Justice"', *Culture, Practice & Europeanization*, 4(1): 159–64.

Nölke, A. (2019b) 'Comparative capitalism', in T. Shaw, L. Mahrenbach, R. Modi and X. Yi-chong (eds) *The Palgrave Handbook of Contemporary Political Economy*, London/New York, NY: Palgrave, pp 135–51.

Nölke, A. (2021) *Exportismus: Die deutsche Droge*, Frankfurt: Westend Verlag.

Nölke, A. and Claar, S. (2013) 'Varieties of capitalism in emerging economies', *Transformation: Critical Perspectives on Southern Africa*, (81/82): 33–54.

Nölke, A. and May, C. (2019) 'Liberal versus organized capitalism: a historical-comparative perspective', in T. Gerőcs and M. Szanyi (eds) *Market Liberalism and Economic Patriotism in the Capitalist World System*, London: Palgrave, pp 21–42.

Nölke, A. and Taylor, H. (2010) 'Non-triad multinationals and global governance: still a North-South conflict?', in Morten Ougaard and Anna Leander (eds) *Business and Global Governance*, London and New York, NY: Routledge, pp 156–77.

Nölke, A. and Vliegenthart, A. (2009) 'Enlarging the varieties of capitalism: dependent market economies in East Central Europe', *World Politics*, 61(4): 670–702.

Nölke, A., ten Brink, T., May, C. and Claar, S. (2020) *State-permeated Capitalism in Large Emerging Economies*, London and New York, NY: Routledge.

Norrlöf, C. (2020a) 'Is Covid-19 a liberal economic curse? Risks for liberal economic order', *Cambridge Review of International Affairs*, 33(5): 799–813.

Norrlöf, C. (2020b) 'Is Covid-19 the end of US hegemony? Public bads, leadership failures and monetary hegemony', *International Affairs*, 96(5): 1281–1303.

Nwosu, C.O. and Oyenubi, A. (2021) 'Income-related health inequalities associated with the coronavirus pandemic in South Africa: a decomposition analysis', *International Journal for Equity in Health*, 20(21): 1–12.

Oatley, T. (2019) *International Political Economy*, New York, NY and London: Routledge.

O'Brien, R. and Williams, M. (2016) *Global Political Economy: Evolution & Dynamics* (5th edn), London and New York, NY: Palgrave.

OECD (2020a) *OECD Economic Outlook 2020–2*, Paris: Organization for Economic Cooperation and Development.

OECD (2020b) *The COVID-19 Crisis and State Ownership in the Economy: Issues and Policy Considerations*, Paris: Organization for Economic Cooperation and Development.

OECD (2020c) *VET in a Time of Crisis: Building Foundations for Resilient Vocational Education and Training Systems*, Paris: Organization for Economic Cooperation and Development.

Olivet, C. and Müller, B. (2020) 'Latin America's battle with COVID-19 hampered by investment arbitration cases', Available from: https://longre ads.tni.org/jugglingcrises [Accessed 14 May 2021].

Orbie, J. and De Ville, F. (2020) *Impact of the Corona Crisis on EU Trade Policy: Our Five Cents to the Debate*, Ghent: Centre for EU Studies Ghent University.

Oreffice, S. and Quintana-Domeque, C. (2020) *Gender Inequality in COVID-19 Times: Evidence from UK Prolific Participants* (IZA DP No. 13463), Bonn: IZA Institute of Labor Economics.

Ötsch, W. (2020) *What Type of Crisis Is This? The Coronavirus Crisis as a Crisis of the Economicised Society* (Working Paper Series No. 57), Benkastel-Kues: Cusanus Hochschule für Gesellschaftsgestaltung.

Ouimet, M.-J., Turcotte, P.-L., Rainville, L.-C., Abraham, Y.-M., Kaiser, D. and Badillo-Amberg, I. (2021) 'Public health and degrowth working synergistically: what leverage for public health?', *Visions for Sustainability*, 14: 99–116.

Pan, G. and Korolev, A. (2021) 'The struggle for certainty: ontological security, the rise of nationalism, and the Australia-China tensions after COVID-19', *Journal of Chinese Political Science*, 26: 115–38.

Parthasarathy, S. (2020) 'Innovation policy, structural inequality, and COVID-19', *Democratic Theory*, 7(2): 104–9.

Perry, B.P., Aronson, B. and Pescosolido, B.A. (2021) 'Pandemic precarity: COVID-19 is exposing and exacerbating inequalities in the American heartland', *Proceedings of the National Academy of Sciences in the USA/PNAS*, 118: 1–6.

Petersen, G. (2020) *Democracy, Authoritarianism, and COVID-19 Pandemic Management: The Case of SARS-CoV-2 Testing* (APSA Working Paper), Available from: https://preprints.apsanet.org/engage/apsa/article-details/5f105dea6283f50015cca5e7 [Accessed 14 May 2021].

Peterson, V.S. and Runyan, A.S. (1993) *Global Gender Issues*, Boulder, CO: Westview.

Phillips, N. (2020) 'The political economy of development', in J. Ravenhill (ed) *Global Political Economy*, Oxford: Oxford University Press, pp 354–383.

Pierson, P. (2000) 'Increasing returns, path dependence, and the study of politics', *American Political Science Review*, 94: 251–67.

Polanyi, K. (1944) *The Great Transformation*, New York, NY and Toronto: Farrar & Rinehart.

Powell, J. and Yurchenko, Y. (2020) 'The evolution of private provision in urban drinking water: new geographies, institutional ambiguity and the need for political economy', *New Political Economy*, 25(1): 91–106.

Purkayastha, D., Vanroelen, C., Bircan, T., Vantyghem, M.A. and Gantelet Adsera, C. (2021) *Work, Health and Covid-19: A Literature Review*, Brussels: ETUI.

Ranjan, P. (2020) 'Covid-19 and ISDS Moratorium: An Indiscreet Proposal', Available from: http://opiniojuris.org/2020/06/15/covid-19-and-isds-moratorium-an-indiscreet-proposal/ [Accessed 14 May 2021].

Ranjan, P. and Anand, P. (2020) 'Covid-19, India, and investor-state dispute settlement (ISDS): will India be able to defend its public health measures?', *Asia Pacific Law Review*, 28(1): 225–47.

Ravenhill, J. (2020) 'Regional trade agreements', in J. Ravenhill (ed) *Global Political Economy*, Oxford: Oxford University Press, pp 140–74.

Reich, S. and Dombrowski, P. (2020) 'The consequences of COVID-19: how the United States moved from security provider to security consumer', *International Affairs*, 96(5): 1253–79.

Reichelt, M., Markovi, K. and Sarsyan, A. (2021) 'The impact of COVID-19 on gender inequality in the labor market and gender-role attitudes', *European Societies*, 23(S1): S228–S245.

Reinhart, C. and Rogoff, K. (2010) 'Growth in a time of debt', *American Economic Review*, 100(2): 573–8.

Rixen, T. (2008) *The Political Economy of International Tax Governance*, Basingstoke: Palgrave Macmillan.

Rodrik, D. (2020) 'Will COVID-19 Remake the World?', *Project Syndicate*, 6 April, Available from: www.project-syndicate.org/commentary/will-covid19-remake-the-world-by-dani-rodrik-2020-04 [Accessed 24 May 2021].

Romer, C.D. and Romer, D.H. (2019) *Fiscal Space and the Aftermath of Financial Crises: How It Matters and Why* (NBER Working Paper No. 25768), Cambridge, MA: National Bureau of Economic Research.

Roos, J. (2019) *Why Not Default? The Political Economy of Sovereign Debt*, Princeton, NJ: Princeton University Press.

Roper, J., Ganesh, S. and Zorn, T.E. (2016) 'Doubt, delay, and discourse: skeptics' strategies to politicize climate change', *Science Communication*, 38(6): 776–99.

Roper, S. and Turner, J. (2020) 'R&D and innovation after COVID-19: what can we expect? A review of prior research and data trends after the great financial crisis', *International Small Business Journal*, 38(6): 504–14.

Rotarou, E.S. and Sakellariou, D. (2017) 'Neoliberal reforms in health systems and the construction of long-lasting inequalities in health care: a case study from Chile', *Health Policy*, 121: 495–503.

Rugitsky, F. (2020) 'The decline of neoliberalism: a play in three acts', *Brazilian Journal of Political Economy*, 40(4): 587–603.

Saad-Filho, A. (2020) 'From COVID-19 to the end of neoliberalism', *Critical Sociology*, 46(4–5): 477–85.

Sampat, B.N. and Shadlen, K.C. (2021) 'The COVID-19 innovation system', *Health Affairs*, 40(3): 400–9.

Samtleben, C., Lott, Y. and Müller, K. (2020) *Auswirkungen der Ort-Zeit-Flexibilisierung von Erwerbsarbeit auf informelle Sorgearbeit im Zuge der Digitalisierung* (Expertise im Rahmen des Dritten Gleichstellungsberichts der Bundesregierung), Berlin: Geschäftsstelle Dritter Gleichstellungsbericht.

Santos Rutschman, A. (2020) 'The COVID-19 vaccine race: intellectual property, collaboration(s), nationalism and misinformation', *Washington University Journal of Law and Policy*, 64, online first.

Saurugger, S. and Terpan, F. (2020) 'Integration through (case) law in the context of the Euro area and Covid-19 crises: courts and monetary answers to crises', *Journal of European Integration*, 42(8): 1161–76.

Sayed, A. and Peng, B. (2021) 'Pandemics and income inequality: a historical review', *SN Business & Economics*, 1(54): 1–17.

S2BNetwork (2020) 'Open letter to governments on ISDS and COVID-19', Seattle to Brussels Network, Available from: http://s2bnetwork.org/sign-the-pen-letter-to-governments-on-isds-and-covid-19/ [Accessed 14 May 2021].

Schedelik, M., Nölke, A, Mertens, D. and May, C. (2020) 'Comparative capitalism, growth models and emerging markets: the development of the field', in *New Political Economy*, online first.

Scheidel, W. (2017) *The Great Leveler: Violence and the History of Inequality from the Stone Age to the Twenty-first Century*, Princeton, NJ: Princeton University Press.

Scheidel, W. (2020) 'The coronavirus pandemic and the future of economic inequality', *Social Research: An International Quarterly*, 87(2): 293–5.

Schinkel, M.P. and d'Ailly, A. (2020) *Corona Crisis Cartels: Sense and Sensibility* (Amsterdam Law School Legal Studies Research Paper No. 2020–31), Amsterdam: University of Amsterdam.

Schmidt, S. (2020) 'Thoughts on the Legitimacy, Sustainability and Future of ISDS in Times of Crisis', Available from: www.mondaq.com/austria/operational-impacts-and-strategy/988580/thoughts-on-the-legitimacy-sustainability-and-future-of-isds-in-times-of-crisis [Accessed 14 May 2021].

Schmidt, V.A. (2020) 'Theorizing institutional change and governance in European responses to the Covid-19 pandemic', *Journal of European Integration* 42(8), 1177–1193.

Schoeller, M.G. and Karlsson, O. (2021) 'Championing the "German model"? Germany's consistent preferences on the integration of fiscal constraints', *Journal of European Integration*, 43(2): 191–207.

Seaman, J. (2020) 'Introduction: China as partner, competitor and rival amid Covid-19', in J. Seaman, J. (ed) *Covid-19 and Europe–China Relations: A Country-level Analysis*, Paris: European Think-tank Network on China (ETNC), pp 5–10.

Senters Piazza, K. and Stronko, K. (2020) 'Democrats, authoritarians, and the coronavirus: who is winning at policy efficacy?', *Global Policy*, online first.

Shaw, T., Mahrenbach, L.C., Modi, R. and X. Yi-chong (eds) (2019) *The Palgrave Handbook of Contemporary Political Economy*, London/New York, NY: Palgrave.

Simson, C. (2020) 'Third-Party Funders' Business Is Booming During Pandemic', Available from: www.law360.com/articles/1261213/third-party-funders-business-is-booming-during-pandemic [Accessed 14 May 2021].

Skovgaard Poulsen, L.N. and Gertz, G. (2021) *Reforming the Investment Treaty Regime: A 'Backward-looking' Approach* (Global Economy and Finance Programme Briefing Paper), London: Chatham House.

Smith, J., Davies, S.E., Feng, H., Gan, C., Grépin, K.A., Harman, S., Herten-Crabb, A., Morgan, R., Vandan, N. and Wenham, C. (2021) 'More than a public health crisis: a feminist political economic analysis of COVID-19', *Global Public Health*, online first.

Sokol, M. and Pataccini, L. (2020) 'Winners and losers in coronavirus times: financialisation, financial chains and the emerging economic geographies of the COVID-19 pandemic', *Tijdschrift voor Economische en Sociale Geografie*, 111(3): 401–15.

Sombart, W. (1932) *Die Zukunft des Kapitalismus*, Berlin: Buchholz & Weisswange.

Sondermann, E. and Ulbert, C. (2020) 'The threat of thinking in threats: reframing global health during and after COVID-19', *Zeitschrift für Friedens- und Konfliktforschung*, 9: 309–20.

Spash, C.L. (2020) '"The economy" as if people mattered: revising critiques of economic growth in a time of crisis', *Globalizations*, online first.

Spendzharova, A. (2021) 'Why ranting about the COVID-19 economy sounds different in Copenhagen and in Cincinnati', *Global Perspectives*, 2(1), online first.

Stern, N. and Zenghelis, D. (2021) *Fiscal Responsibility in Advanced Economies through Investment for Economic Recovery from the COVID-19 Pandemic* (Policy Paper), London: Grantham Research Institute on Climate Change and the Environment/Centre for Climate Change Economics and Policy, LSE.

Stevens, H. and Haines, M.B. (2020) 'TraceTogether: pandemic response, democracy, and technology', *East Asian Science, Technology and Society*, 14(3): 523–32.

Stockhammer, E. (2020) *Post-Keynesian Macroeconomic Foundations for Comparative Political Economy* (Working paper No. 2022), London: Post-Keynesian Economics Society.

Stokes, D. and Williamson, M. (2021) 'The United States, China and the WTO after Coronavirus', *The Chinese Journal of International Politics*, 14(1): 23–49.

Strange, R. (2020) 'The 2020 Covid-19 pandemic and global value chains', *Journal of Industrial and Business Economics*, 47: 455–65.

Streeck, W. (2016) *How Will Capitalism End?*, London: Verso.

Streeck, W. (2018) 'Between charity and justice: remarks on the social construction of immigration policies in rich democracies', *Culture, Practice & Europeanization*, 3(2): 3–22.

Sullivan, E. and Wolff, E.A. (2021) 'Politics, pandemics, and support: the role of political actors in Dutch state aid during COVID-19', *Brazilian Journal of Public Administration*, 55(1): 50–71.

Sumonja, M. (2020) 'Neoliberalism is not dead: on political implications of Covid-19', *Capital & Class*, online first.

Sydiq, T. (2020) 'Vom Protest- zum Quarantänejahr: Neue Arenen der Konfliktaushandlung', *Zeitschrift für Friedens- und Konfliktforschung*, 9: 351–62.

Thun, E. (2020) 'The globalization of production', in J. Ravenhill (ed) *Global Political Economy*, Oxford: Oxford University Press, pp 175–96.

Tian, W. (2020) 'How China managed the COVID-19 pandemic', *Asian Economic Papers*, 20(1): 75–101.

Tienhaara, K. (2011) 'Regulatory chill and the threat of arbitration: a view from political science', in C. Brown and K Miles (eds) *Evolution in Investment Treaty Law and Arbitration*, Cambridge: Cambridge University Press, pp 606–27.

Tokic, D. (2012) 'The economic and financial dimensions of degrowth', *Ecological Economics*, 84: 49–56.

Tsingou, E. 'Global remittances and COVID-19: locked down but not locked out', *Global Perspectives*, 2(1), online first.

Tucker, P. (2019) *Unelected Power: The Quest for Legitimacy in Central Banking and the Regulatory State*, Princeton, NJ: Princeton University Press.

UNCTAD (2020a) *Investment Policy Responses to the COVID-19 Pandemic* (Investment Policy Monitor Special Issue No. 4), Geneva: United Nations Conference on Trade and Development.

UNCTAD (2020b) *World Investment Report: International Production beyond the Pandemic*, Geneva: United Nations Conference on Trade and Development.

UNCTAD (2021) *Global FDI flows down 42% in 2020* (Investment Policy Monitor No. 38), Geneva: United Nations Conference on Trade and Development.

United Nations (2020a) *Policy Brief: The Impact of COVID-19 on Women*, New York, NY: The United Nations.

United Nations (2020b) *Policy Brief: The Impact of COVID-19 on Food Security and Nutrition*, New York, NY: The United Nations.

Usher, A.D. (2020) 'South Africa and India push for COVID-19 patents ban', *The Lancet*, 296: 1790–1

Van Apeldoorn, B. and Horn, L. (2018) *Critical Political Economy* (KFG Working Paper No. 87), Berlin: Freie Universität.

Van den Bergh, J. (2011) 'Environment versus growth: a criticism of degrowth and a plea for a-growth', *Ecological Economics*, 70: 881–90.

Van der Ploeg, J.D. (2020) 'From biomedical to politico-economic crisis: the food system in times of Covid-19', *Journal of Peasant Studies*, 47(5): 944–72.

Van der Ven, H. and Sun, Y. (2020) 'Varieties of crises: comparing the politics of COVID-19 and climate change', *Global Environmental Politics*, 21(1): 13–22.

Vermeiren, M. (2021) *Crisis and Inequality*, Cambridge: Polity.

Vesci, M., Feola, R., Parente, R. and Radjou, N. (2021) 'How to save the world during a pandemic event: a case study of frugal innovation', *R&D Management*, online first.

Vis, B., van Kerbergen, K. and Hylands, T. (2011) 'To what extent did the financial crisis intensify the pressure to reform the welfare state?', *Social Policy & Administration*, 45(4): 338–53.

Vlcek, W. (2019) 'Tax avoidance', in T. Shaw, L. Mahrenbach, R. Modi and X. Yi-chong (eds) *The Palgrave Handbook of Contemporary Political Economy*, London/New York, NY: Palgrave, pp 345–57.

Wade, R.H. (2020) 'Global growth, inequality, and poverty: power and evidence in global "best practice" economic policy', in J. Ravenhill (ed) *Global Political Economy*, Oxford: Oxford University Press, pp 313–53.

Wallace, R. (2016) *Big Farms Make Big Flu: Dispatches on Infectious Diseases, Agribusiness, and the Nature of Science*, New York, NY: Monthly Review Press.

Wallace, R. (2020) *Dead Epidemiologists: On the Origins of COVID-19*, New York, NY: Monthly Review Press.

Weghmann, V. and Hall, D. (2021) 'The unsustainable political economy of investor–state dispute settlement mechanisms', *International Review of Administrative Sciences*, online first.

Weiss, M. and Cattaneo, C. (2017) 'Degrowth: taking stock and reviewing an emerging academic paradigm', *Ecological Economics*, 137: 220–30.

WFP (2020) *WFP Global Update on COVID-19: November 2020*, Rome: World Food Programme.

Wigger, A. and Nölke, A. (2007) 'Enhanced roles of private actors in EU business regulation and the erosion of Rhenish capitalism: the case of antitrust enforcement', *Journal of Common Market Studies*, 45(2): 487–513.

Wilén, N. (2021) 'The military in the time of COVID-19', *PRISM*, 9(2): 20–33.

Wiley, L.F., McCuskey, E.Y., Lawrence, M.B. and Fuse Brown, E.C. (2021) *Health Reform Reconstruction* (Legal Studies Research Paper No. 2021–11), Atlanta, GA: Georgia State University College of Law.

Williams, O.D. (2020) 'COVID-19 and private health: market and governance failure', *Development*, 63: 181–90.

Windholz, E.L. (2020) 'Governing in a pandemic: from parliamentary sovereignty to autocratic technocracy', *The Theory and Practices of Legislation*, 8(1–2): 95–113.

Withers, M., Henderson, S. and Shivakoti, R. (2021) 'International migration, remittances and COVID-19: economic implications and policy options for South Asia', *Journal of Asian Public Policy*, online first.

Wójcik, D. and Ioannou, S. (2020) 'COVID-19 and finance: market developments so far and potential impacts on the financial sector and centres', *Tijdschrift voor Economische en Sociale Geografie*, 111(3): 387–400.

Wolff, S. and Ladi, S. (2020) 'European Union responses to the Covid-19 pandemic: adaptability in times of permanent emergency', *Journal of European Integration*, 42(8): 1025–40.

Wood, D.P. (2013) 'State aid management in the United States', *European State Aid Law Quarterly*, 12(1): 40–5.

World Bank (2020) *COVID-19 Crisis through a Migration Lens* (Migration and Development Brief No. 32), Washington, DC: World Bank.

World Bank (2021) 'COVID 19 Debt Service Suspension Initiative', Washington, DC: World Bank, Available from: www.worldbank.org/en/topic/debt/brief/covid-19-debt-service-suspension-initiative [Accessed 9 April 2021].

World Health Organization (nd) 'How WHO is funded', Geneva: WHO, Available from: www.who.int/about/funding [Accessed 16 April 2021].

Wrigley-Field, E. (2020) 'US racial inequality may be as deadly as COVID-19', *Proceedings of the National Academy of Sciences*, 117(36): 21854–6.

Wullweber, J. (2020) *The COVID-19 Financial Crisis, Global Financial Instabilities and Transformations in the Financial System*, Berlin: Finanzwende und Heinrich-Böll-Foundation.

Yildirim, U. (2020) 'Perceptions of Inequality During the Coronavirus Outbreak', Berkeley, CA: University of California, Available from: https://osf.io/preprints/socarxiv/sm9q6/ [Accessed 20 June 2021].

Zelner, J., Trangucci, R., Naraharisetti, R., Cao, A., Malosh, R., Broen, K., Masters, N. and Delamater, P. (2021) 'Racial disparities in coronavirus disease 2019 (COVID-19) mortality are driven by unequal infection risks', *Clinical Infectious Diseases*, 72: e88–e95.

Zeschky, M., Widenmayer, B. and Gassmann, O. (2011) 'Frugal innovation in emerging markets', *Research-Technology Management*, 54(4): 38–45.

Zimmermann, H. and Dür, A. (eds) (2021) *Key Controversies in European Integration*, London: Red Globe Press.

Zucco, A. and Lott, Y. (2021) *Stand der Gleichstellung: Ein Jahr mit Corona* (WSI-Report No. 64), Düsseldorf: Wirtschafts- und Sozialwissenschaftliches Institut.

Zürn, M. and de Wilde, P. (2016) 'Debating globalization: cosmopolitanism and communitarianism as political ideologies', *Journal of Political Ideologies*, 21(3): 280–301.

Index